STECK-VAUGHN

Building Strategies® MATHEMATICS

Susan D. McClanahan

Judith Andrews Green

Series Reviewers

Dr. Pamela Taylor Hakim
Curriculum Coordinator for
   Distance Learning Program
The University of Mississippi
Oxford, Mississippi

Bobby Jackson
Director of Adult Education
Roane County Schools
Kingston, Tennessee

Betty J. Kimberling
Director of Adult Basic Education
St. Joseph Adult Education Center
St. Joseph, Missouri

Faith McCaghy
Area Literacy Director
Dakota County Literacy Projects
Lakeville, Minnesota

John Ritter
Master Teacher
Oregon Women's Correctional Center
Salem, Oregon

STECK-VAUGHN
ELEMENTARY · SECONDARY · ADULT · LIBRARY

A Harcourt Company

www.steck-vaughn.com

Acknowledgments

Staff Credits

Executive Editor:	Ellen Northcutt
Supervising Editor:	Carolyn M. Hall
Design Managers:	Donna M. Brawley, Rusty Kaim
Cover Design:	D. Childress
Electronic Cover Production:	Alan Klemp
Photo Editor:	Margie Foster
Editorial Development:	McClanahan & Company, Inc.

Electronic Production

American Composition and Graphics

Photography

Cover: (calculator and paper) © Comstock; p.13 © Beringer-Dratch/The Image Works; p.29 © John Coletti/Stock Boston; pp.59, 89 Randal Alhadeff; p.117 © Eric R. Berndt/Unicorn Stock Photos; p.149 © Mike Mazzaschi/Stock Boston.

Illustration

American Composition and Graphics

ISBN 0-8114-6504-7

Building Strategies is a trademark of Steck-Vaughn Company.

Copyright © 1996 Steck-Vaughn Company

Printed in the United States of America.

11 12 DBH 06 05 04 03 02

Contents

To the Learner 5
Check What You Know 6
Skills Preview Chart 12

UNIT 1: Whole Numbers Place Value . 13
Whole Number Place Names 14
Whole Number Place Values 15
Finding Place Values for Numbers 16
Forming Numbers from Place Values 17
Renaming Whole Numbers 18
Comparing Whole Numbers. 19
Strategies for Success: Using a
 Number Line 20
Place Value to Thousands. 22
Rounding 23
Calculators 24
Unit 1 Wrap-up 25
Unit 1 Review. 26
Cumulative Review 1 28

**UNIT 2: Adding and Subtracting
 Whole Numbers** 29
Addition Facts 30
Addition Equations 31
Adding Larger Numbers 32
Adding with Renaming 34
Adding Three or More Numbers 36
Rounding and Estimation. 37
Using a Calculator to Add 38
Check-up on Addition 39
Strategies for Success: A Step-by-Step Plan . . 40
Subtraction Facts 42
Subtraction Equations. 43
Subtracting Larger Numbers 44
Subtracting with Renaming 46
Renaming Zeros 47
More Subtraction 48
Rounding and Estimation. 49
Using a Calculator to Subtract 50
Check-up on Subtraction 51
Addition and Subtraction: Two or
 More Steps 52

Unit 2 Wrap-up 54
Unit 2 Review. 55
Cumulative Review 2 57

**UNIT 3: Multiplying and Dividing
 Whole Numbers** 59
Multiplication Facts 60
Multiplication Equations 61
Multiplying by One-Digit Numbers 62
Multiplying by Two-Digit Numbers 63
Multiplying by One-Digit Numbers
 with Renaming 64
Multiplying by Two-Digit Numbers
 with Renaming 65
Multiplying by Multiples and Powers of 10 . . 66
Rounding and Estimation. 67
Using a Calculator to Multiply. 68
Check-up on Multiplication 69
Division Facts. 70
Division Equations 71
Dividing by One-Digit Numbers 72
Dividing by One-Digit Numbers
 with Remainders. 73
Zeros in Division 74
Dividing by Two-Digit Numbers 75
Strategies for Success: Problem Solving 76
Rounding and Estimation. 78
Using a Calculator to Divide 79
Check-up on Division. 80
Order of Operations 81
Calculators and Order of Operations 82
Unit 3 Wrap-up 83
Unit 3 Review. 85
Cumulative Review 3 87

UNIT 4: Decimals 89
Decimal Place Names and Values. 90
Writing Decimals 91
Zeros and Decimals 92
Comparing Decimals 93
Money Place Values 94
Writing Money Amounts 95

Rounding Decimals to the Nearest Tenth . . . 96
Rounding Decimals to the
    Nearest Hundredth 97
Rounding Money 98
Adding Decimals 99
Subtracting Decimals 100
Multiplying Decimals by Whole Numbers . 101
Multiplying Decimals by Decimals 102
Dividing Decimals by Whole Numbers . . . 103
Dividing Decimals by Whole Numbers
    with Rounding 104
Dividing Decimals by Decimals 105
Rounding and Estimation 106
Using a Calculator with Decimals 107
Strategies for Success: Problem Solving:
    Charts and Tables 108
Check-up on Decimals 110
Using Two or More Operations
    with Decimals 111
Unit 4 Wrap-up 112
Unit 4 Review 113
Cumulative Review 4 115

UNIT 5: Fractions 117
Meaning of Fractions 118
Equivalent Fractions 120
Reducing Fractions to Lowest Terms 121
Raising Fractions to Higher Terms 122
Common Denominators 123
Finding the Lowest Common
    Denominator 124
Improper Fractions and Mixed Numbers . . 125
Rounding and Estimation 126
Calculators 127
Check-up on Fractions 128
Adding Fractions and Mixed Numbers
    with Like Denominators 129
Adding Fractions and Mixed Numbers
    with Different Denominators 130
Subtracting Fractions and Mixed Numbers
    with Like Denominators 131
Subtracting Fractions and Mixed Numbers
    with Different Denominators 132

Multiplying Fractions by Fractions 133
Multiplying Mixed Numbers and
    Whole Numbers 134
Dividing Fractions by Fractions 135
Dividing Mixed Numbers and
    Whole Numbers 136
Rounding and Estimation 137
Calculators 138
Check-up on Fractions 139
Strategies for Success: Problem Solving 140
Using Two or More Steps 142
Unit 5 Wrap-up 143
Unit 5 Review 145
Cumulative Review 5 147

**UNIT 6: Ratio, Proportion,
    and Percent** 149
Ratios 150
Equal Ratios 151
Solving Proportions 152
Meaning of Percent 153
Percents as Ratios (Fractions) 154
Percents as Decimals 155
Circle Graphs 156
Finding the Part: Percent of a Number 158
Finding the Percent 159
Finding the Whole 160
Rounding and Estimation 161
Using a Calculator with Percents 162
Check-up on Ratio, Proportion,
    and Percent 163
Strategies for Success: Problem Solving 164
Using Two or More Steps 166
Percent of Increase and Decrease 167
Unit 6 Wrap-up 168
Unit 6 Review 169
Cumulative Review 6 171

Check What You've Learned 173
Skills Review Chart 179

Glossary 180
Answers and Explanations 181

To the Learner

In Steck-Vaughn's *Building Strategies*™ *Mathematics*, you will study whole numbers, decimals, and fractions. You will also solve ratios, proportions, and percent problems. This book contains the following features especially designed to help you develop your math skills and problem-solving techniques.

Skills Inventories

- Before you begin work, take the *Check What You Know* skills inventory, check your own answers, and fill out the *Skills Preview Chart*. There you will see which math skills you already know and which skills you need to practice in this book.
- After you finish the last practice page, take the *Check What You've Learned* skills inventory, check your answers, and fill out the *Skills Review Chart*. You'll see the great progress you've made. Save these inventories in a folder or portfolio.

Strategies for Success

One *Strategies for Success* section in each unit gives tips and practice for ways to develop your problem-solving skills. Review these strategies from time to time.

Calculators

Each unit includes one or more calculator pages on which you can practice using a calculator to solve various mathematical operations.

Reviews

Each unit contains three kinds of review pages:

- Wrap-up: This page gives you a chance to review the main skills in the unit. It shows models of how to solve problems plus practice problems. If you do well on it, go on the the Unit Review. If not, the handy page references tell you where to go to study the skills again.
- Unit Review: Here you can test yourself as you work the many different kinds of problems in the unit and check your own answers.
- Cumulative Review: Here you can test yourself on whether you remember the skills you learned in prior units.

Glossary

The glossary at the back of the book lists and defines the math terms in *Building Strategies*™ *Mathematics*. It also tells you the page number on which each term first appears.

Answers and Explanations

This section gives you the answers to all the problems so you can check your own work. Also, the second problem on each page is worked out for you step by step. Answers to multiple-choice problems also explain why one choice is correct and why the other possible answer choices are incorrect. Studying the explanations can help you sharpen your test-taking skills.

Place Value

Write the place value of each underlined digit.

1 4,570 _____   **2** 691 _____   **3** 211,084 _____

Write each of these numbers.

4 5 tens 4 ones _____

5 3 hundreds 1 ten 8 ones _____

6 2 thousands 7 hundreds 9 ones _____

Compare each set of numbers. Write > for _greater than_ or < for _less than_.

7 7 ☐ 5   **8** 463 ☐ 643   **9** 82 ☐ 59

Round each number to the nearest ten.

10 655 _____

11 343 _____

12 107 _____

Solve.

13 Last week, Elizabeth worked 42 hours and Barbara worked 35 hours. Who worked more hours last week?

14 A local factory hired 585 people. Rounded to the nearest ten, how many people did the factory hire?

Answer _____   Answer _____

Adding and Subtracting Whole Numbers

Solve.

15 $\boxed{} - 1 = 2$ **16** $4 + \boxed{} = 9$ **17** $13 - 8 = \boxed{}$

Write an equation to solve each problem.

18 Three and what number is equal to five? _____

19 Fifteen minus what number is equal to nine? _____

Solve.

20 $\begin{array}{r} \$53 \\ +\ 16 \\ \hline \end{array}$ **21** $\begin{array}{r} 64 \\ -\ 34 \\ \hline \end{array}$ **22** $\begin{array}{r} \$475 \\ -\ 248 \\ \hline \end{array}$ **23** $\begin{array}{r} 392 \\ +\ 116 \\ \hline \end{array}$

24 $\$36 + \$582 + \$80 =$ **25** $5{,}008 - 725 - 1{,}140 =$

Round each number to the lead digit. Then add or subtract.

26 $\begin{array}{r} 86 \\ +\ 24 \\ \hline \end{array}$ **27** $\begin{array}{r} 307 \\ -\ 188 \\ \hline \end{array}$ **28** $\begin{array}{r} 785 \\ +\ 592 \\ \hline \end{array}$

Solve.

29 During the first weekend in May, 32 men and 39 women volunteered to plant flowers in a city park. How many people volunteered all together?

30 Out of 250 people who bought tickets to a school play, 12 people did not attend the play. How many people did attend?

Answer _____   Answer _____

Multiplying and Dividing Whole Numbers

Multiply.

31 $123
     × 3

32 260 × 25 =

33 1,403
     × 46

Divide. Use multiplication to check your answers.

34 9)351

35 287 ÷ 7 =

36 6)306

Round each number to the lead digit. Then multiply or divide.

37 37 × 58 =

38 7,820 ÷ 23 =

39 396 × 51 =

Solve.

40 A charity pancake breakfast raised $3,052. If 763 tickets to the fund-raiser were sold, and each ticket cost the same amount of money, how much did each ticket cost?

41 Leon works 8 hours each day. Last month, he worked 21 days. How many hours did Leon work last month?

Answer _____

Answer _____

Decimals

Write each number as a decimal.

42 fourteen and thirty-three hundredths _____

43 sixty-eight cents _____

Write each decimal in words.

44 2.5 _____

45 $70.25 _____

Solve.

46
3.4
+ 2.5

47
9.5
× 13

48
1.9
− 0.4

49 $0.2 \overline{)4.06}$

50 $27.17 − $.74 =   **51** 9.015 ÷ 1.5 =   **52** 3.04 × 4.6 =   **53** $1.50 − $.81 + $2 =

Round both numbers and estimate each answer.

54 $0.39 \overline{)7.85}$ =   **55** $303.07 + $19.88 =   **56** 101.33 − 58.9 =   **57** 4.2 × 8.01 =

Solve.

58 Tim needs 2 boards to make a shelf for his kitchen. Each board is 39.37 inches long. How long would the 2 boards be if they were laid end-to-end?

59 Ann bought a package of 12 plastic spoons for $1.49. What is the cost of each spoon, rounded to the nearest cent?

Answer _____   Answer _____

Fractions

Compare each set of fractions. Write >, <, or =.

60 $\dfrac{1}{5}$ ☐ $\dfrac{1}{4}$ **61** $\dfrac{7}{8}$ ☐ $\dfrac{4}{5}$ **62** $\dfrac{2}{3}$ ☐ $\dfrac{3}{5}$ **63** $\dfrac{2}{9}$ ☐ $\dfrac{6}{27}$

Solve. Change improper fractions to mixed numbers. Reduce if possible.

64
$$\begin{array}{r} \frac{5}{12} \\ + \ \frac{1}{12} \\ \hline \end{array}$$

65
$$\begin{array}{r} 5\frac{3}{4} \\ - \ 2\frac{2}{7} \\ \hline \end{array}$$

66
$$\begin{array}{r} \frac{3}{5} \\ - \ \frac{1}{6} \\ \hline \end{array}$$

67
$$\begin{array}{r} 4\frac{1}{8} \\ + \ 1\frac{2}{3} \\ \hline \end{array}$$

68 $\dfrac{1}{8} \times \dfrac{2}{3} =$ **69** $7\dfrac{1}{3} \div 9 =$ **70** $4 \times 2\dfrac{3}{4} =$ **71** $15\dfrac{3}{4} \div 5\dfrac{1}{4} =$

Use the number line to round each mixed number to the nearest whole number. Then estimate each answer.

72 $6\dfrac{2}{10} \div 1\dfrac{5}{10} =$ **73** $7\dfrac{1}{10} - 1\dfrac{8}{10} =$ **74** $4\dfrac{4}{10} + 8\dfrac{9}{10} =$ **75** $3\dfrac{7}{10} \times 5\dfrac{3}{10} =$

Solve.

76 During March, $6\dfrac{1}{2}$ inches of rain fell. During April, $1\dfrac{1}{4}$ inches fell. How much rain fell during March and April?

77 Sharise walks $3\dfrac{1}{2}$ miles per day for 5 days each week. How many miles does she walk all together in a week?

Answer _____

Answer _____

Ratio, Proportion, and Percent

Solve each proportion for _n_.

78 $\frac{4}{n} = \frac{8}{14}$

79 $\frac{2}{3} = \frac{6}{n}$

80 $\frac{1}{8} = \frac{n}{40}$

81 $\frac{n}{6} = \frac{12}{24}$

Change each percent to a fraction, mixed number, or whole number.

82 45% =

83 200% =

84 8% =

85 160% =

Change each fraction or decimal to a percent.

86 $\frac{1}{4}$ =

87 2.4 =

88 $\frac{4}{5}$ =

89 0.9 =

Solve.

90 20% of 60 is what number?

91 What percent of 24 is 42?

92 550 is what percent of 220?

93 Sales tax where Jennifer lives is 5%. How much sales tax will Jennifer need to pay if she buys a pair of jeans for $24.00?

94 Charles saves 15% percent of his salary. His salary is $390 per week. How much money does Charles save each week?

Answer _____

Answer _____

When you finish _Check What You Know_, check your answers on pages 181–182. Then complete the chart on page 12.

Check What You Know

The chart will show you which mathematics skills you need to study. Reread each problem you missed. Then look at the appropriate pages of the book for help in figuring out the right answers.

Skills Preview Chart

Math Skills	Questions			Pages
The test, like this book, focuses on the skills below.	Check (√) the questions you missed.			Preview what you will learn in this book.
Whole Number Place Value	1 2 3 4	5 6 7	8 9 13	Pages 13–28
Whole Number Equations	15 16	17 18	19	Pages 31, 43, 61, 71
Addition	20 23	24	29	Pages 30–41, 52–58
Subtraction	21 22	25	30	Pages 42–58
Multiplication	31 32	33	41	Pages 60–69, 81–88
Division	34 35	36	40	Pages 70–88
Rounding and Estimation	10 11 12 14 26 27	28 37 38 39 54 55	56 57 72 73 74 75	Pages 23, 37, 49, 67, 78, 106, 126, 137
Decimals: Addition, Subtraction, Multiplication, Division	42 43 44 45 46	47 48 49 50 51	52 53 58 59	Pages 89–116
Fractions: Addition, Subtraction, Multiplication, Division, Comparing	60 61 62 63 64	65 66 67 68 69	70 71 76 77	Pages 117–148
Solving Ratios, Proportions, and Percents	78 79 80 81 82 83	84 85 86 87 88 89	90 91 92 93 94	Pages 149–172

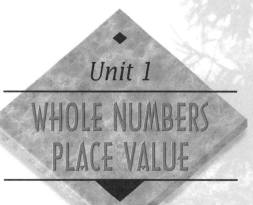

Unit 1

WHOLE NUMBERS
PLACE VALUE

When you drive, you try to stay within the speed limit. Think about speed limit signs you may have seen on streets and highways. The number shown on a speed limit sign is a whole number. Whole numbers are used for counting.

Whole numbers can be found almost everywhere in the world around you. **Where else might you find examples of whole numbers?**

In this unit you will learn about:
◆ identifying place values
◆ using a step-by-step plan
◆ regrouping and comparing whole numbers
◆ using number lines
◆ rounding and estimating
◆ using a calculator

Whole Number Place Names

When you add, subtract, multiply, or divide whole numbers, you are working with numbers that are made up of digits. A **digit** is one of the ten symbols—0, 1, 2, 3, 4, 5, 6, 7, 8, 9—used to write numbers. For example, the number 325 contains three digits—3, 2, and 5. Each digit in a number is in a different place and has a certain value. **Place value** is the value of a digit based on its position in a number.

The place value chart at the right shows the first three whole number place values.

The number 325 has been placed in the chart. The chart shows that the digit 5 is in the ones place, the digit 2 is in the tens place, and the digit 3 is in the hundreds place.

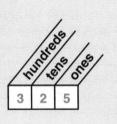

Sometimes the digit 0, or zero, appears in a number. The number 302, for example, has a 0 in the tens place. The digits 3 and 2 in the number 302 have place values of 3 hundreds and 2 ones. The number 302 has 0 tens.

Write each number in the chart. Then write each digit in the correct number group, and write the value of the digit.

1 64

   <u> 6 </u> tens = <u> 60 </u>

   <u> 4 </u> ones = <u> 4 </u>

2 739

   ___ hundreds = _____

   ___ tens = _____

   ___ ones = _____

3 87

   ___ tens = _____

   ___ ones = _____

4 406

   ___ hundreds = _____

   ___ tens = _____

   ___ ones = _____

	hundreds	tens	ones
1.		6	4
2.			
3.			
4.			

Write the place of each underlined digit.

5 5<u>4</u> = <u> tens </u>

6 <u>1</u>63 = _____

7 9<u>8</u>9 = _____

8 <u>8</u>32 = _____

9 1<u>4</u> = _____

10 <u>4</u>0 = _____

11 6<u>0</u>7 = _____

12 53<u>0</u> = _____

13 49<u>9</u> = _____

14 <u>7</u>16 = _____

15 <u>4</u> = _____

16 1<u>7</u> = _____

17 3<u>3</u> = _____

18 2<u>8</u>5 = _____

19 <u>1</u>11 = _____

20 6<u>2</u> = _____

21 <u>7</u>3 = _____

22 10<u>0</u> = _____

Check your answers on page 182.

Whole Number Place Values

Models of groups of ones, tens, and hundreds can be used to show the value of a place.

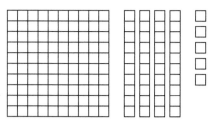

1 hundred   4 tens   5 ones

Think about the digits and the places in the number 145.

Write 223 as groups of hundreds, tens, and ones.

1. The digit 2 is in the hundreds place. Using models, the value of the hundreds place can be shown as 2 groups of hundreds, or **2 hundreds**.

2. The digit 2 is in the tens place. Using models, the value of the tens place can be shown as 2 groups of tens, or **2 tens**.

3. The digit 3 is in the ones place. Using models, the value of the ones place can be shown as 3 groups of ones, or **3 ones**.

Write the place value shown by each group of models.

1

    2 hundreds

2   _____

3 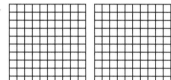   _____

Write the place value of each underlined digit.

4 6<u>2</u>4 = ___2 tens___   **5** 5<u>7</u> = _____   **6** <u>2</u>80 = _____

7 <u>9</u> = _____   **8** 9<u>9</u>3 = _____   **9** <u>4</u>0 = _____

10 3<u>0</u>4 = _____   **11** <u>1</u>88 = _____   **12** 1<u>7</u> = _____

13 <u>6</u>7 = _____   **14** 32<u>0</u> = _____   **15** <u>5</u>88 = _____

16 <u>3</u> = _____   **17** <u>4</u>7 = _____   **18** 4<u>0</u>0 = _____

19 9<u>9</u> = _____   **20** <u>7</u>13 = _____   **21** 9<u>1</u>8 = _____

Check your answers on page 182.

Finding Place Values for Numbers

Models can be used to show how the place values of a whole number can be separated, or broken apart.

Look at a model of 136.	Look at a model of 23.	Look at a model of 6.
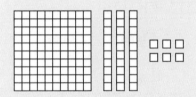		□□□□□□
The number 136 has a place value of **1 hundred 3 tens 6 ones.** 1 hundred 3 tens 6 ones = <u>136</u>	The number 23 has a place value of **2 tens 3 ones.** 2 tens 3 ones = <u>23</u>	The number 6 has a place value of **6 ones.** 6 ones = <u>6</u>

Write each of these numbers.

1 3 tens 1 one ___31___   **2** 2 hundreds 4 ones _____   **3** 9 ones _____

4 4 tens 8 ones _____   **5** 7 hundreds 7 tens 3 ones _____   **6** 5 tens _____

7 9 tens 4 ones _____   **8** 6 hundreds 8 tens 6 ones _____   **9** 7 tens _____

10 6 tens 2 ones _____   **11** 1 hundred 1 ten 1 one _____   **12** 2 tens _____

Write each digit in the correct place.

13 85 = ___8___ tens
       ___5___ ones

14 321 = _____ hundreds
          _____ tens
          _____ ones

15 803 = _____ hundreds
          _____ tens
          _____ ones

16 20 = _____ tens
        _____ ones

17 116 = _____ hundreds
          _____ tens
          _____ ones

18 200 = _____ hundreds
          _____ tens
          _____ ones

Check your answers on page 182.

Forming Numbers from Place Values

Models can be used to show how place values can be combined, or added together, to form whole numbers.

When these models are combined, the whole number 174 is formed.

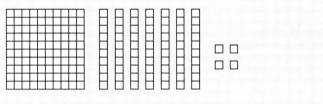

1 hundred + 7 tens + 4 ones = 100 + 70 + 4 = 174

What whole number is formed when these models are combined?

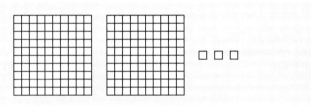

2 hundreds + 0 tens + 3 ones = 200 + 3 = 203;
There are 0 tens in the number, so write 0 in the tens place.

Write the numbers shown by these models.

1

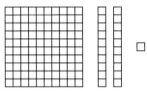

121

2

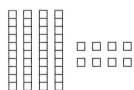

_____

3

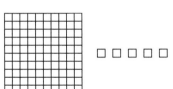

_____

4

_____

5 At the post office Cletus asked for 346 stamps. He received 3 sheets of one hundred stamps, 4 strips of ten stamps, and 6 loose stamps. Did he receive the correct number of stamps?

6 Michelle collected 7 sheets of one hundred bird stamps, 3 strips of ten deer stamps, and 5 loose stamps. How many stamps did she have in all?

Answer _____

Answer _____

Check your answers on page 182.

Renaming Whole Numbers

To add or subtract whole numbers, sometimes you have to regroup or **rename** numbers using different place values. For example, you can rename 14 ones as 1 ten and 4 ones.

Rename 10 ones.  Rename 10 ones to the next higher place. 10 ones are renamed as 1 ten. **10 ones = 1 ten**	**Rename 2 tens.**  Rename 2 tens to the next lower place. 2 tens are renamed as 20 ones. **2 tens = 20 ones**

Rename each of the following.

1 3 tens = _30_ ones

2 40 ones = ___ tens

3 1 hundred = ___ ones

4 10 tens = ___ hundred

5 100 ones = ___ hundred

6 1 hundred = ___ tens

7 2 tens 4 ones = ___ ones

8 39 ones = ___ tens ___ ones

9 1 hundred 4 tens 6 ones = ___ ones

10 2 hundreds 10 ones = ___ tens

11 30 tens = ___ ones

12 44 tens = ___ hundreds ___ ones

13 2 hundreds = ___ tens

14 1 hundred 30 ones = ___ tens

15 If you have 3 notepads of 100 sheets and 4 pads of 10 sheets, how many sheets do you have in all?

16 If you have 2 boxes of 100 paper clips and 4 chains of 10 paper clips each, how many paper clips do you have all together?

Answer _____

Answer _____

Check your answers on pages 182–183.

Comparing Whole Numbers

Place value can be used to compare any two whole numbers.

If two whole numbers have different numbers of digits, the number with more digits is greater.

317 is greater than 89   292 is greater than 89

3 digits   2 digits   3 digits   2 digits

If two whole numbers have the same number of digits, compare each digit beginning with the digits farthest to the left. Use the symbols > and < to compare. The symbol > means *greater than*. The symbol < means *less than*.

Compare 312 and 321.

1. Compare the digits farthest to the left. Both numbers have 3 hundreds. Move to the next place to the right.

3 1 2
3 2 1

2. Compare the numbers in the tens place. 321 has 2 tens, 312 has only 1 ten.

3 1 2
3 2 1

3. Use the symbols > and < to compare the numbers.

321 > 312 or 312 < 321

Compare each set of numbers. Write > for *greater than* or < for *less than*.

1. 542 > 524
2. 47 □ 463
3. 4 □ 9
4. 83 □ 80

5. 212 □ 221
6. 630 □ 603
7. 8 □ 5
8. 34 □ 43

9. 502 □ 520
10. 144 □ 195
11. 276 □ 133
12. 61 □ 580

13. 57 □ 75
14. 330 □ 334
15. 988 □ 899
16. 403 □ 304

17. 95 □ 59
18. 432 □ 423
19. 818 □ 811
20. 349 □ 344

21. 789 □ 879
22. 750 □ 705
23. 389 □ 390
24. 201 □ 210

25. 35 □ 36
26. 211 □ 311
27. 62 □ 51
28. 431 □ 74

29. 516 □ 514
30. 12 □ 21
31. 863 □ 866
32. 999 □ 998

Check your answers on page 183.

Unit 1

Strategies for SUCCESS

Using a Number Line

A number line is a line with equally spaced points that are labeled with numbers. Using a number line lets you compare numbers easily. You can see the order of numbers. You can see patterns on a number line, too.

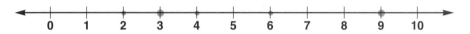

❖ STRATEGY: **Picture the numbers on a number line.**

1. To compare two numbers on a number line, look for the number that is farther left. It is the smaller number. As you look to the right, the numbers get larger. Look at the numbers 3 and 9. Since 3 is to the left of 9, 3 < 9.

2. To see patterns on a number line, find the distance between numbers. The distance tells you the rule to use to find each number in the pattern. Look at the number pattern shown by dots at the numbers 2, 4, and 6. The distance between 2 and 4 is 2. The distance between 4 and 6 is 2. Since the pattern is increasing by 2, the next number in the pattern is 8.

Exercises: **Use a number line to answer each question.**

1 Which number is greater, 34 or 43?

30 31 32 33 34 35 36 37 38 39 40 41 42 43 44 45

43 is right of 34, so 43 is greater than 34.

Answer _____ 43 > 34 _____

2 What is the next number after 10 in the pattern?

5   10   15   20   25

The distance between each pair is 5. 10 and 5 is 15.

Answer _____ 15 _____

3 Which number is greater, 131 or 129?

125 126 127 128 129 130 131 132 133 134 135

Answer _____

4 What are the next two numbers after 69 in the pattern?

54   57   60   63   66   69

Answer _____

5 Which number is less, 125 or 127?

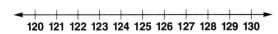

Answer _____

6 What are the next two numbers after 24 in this pattern?

3, 6, 9, 12, 15, . . .

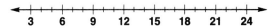

Answer _____

7 Put the following numbers in order from least to greatest.

102, 96, 95, 103, 99

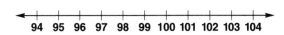

Answer _____

8 What are the next three numbers in this pattern?

4, 8, 12, 16, . . .

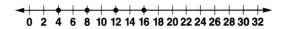

Answer _____

9 Which is greater, 200 or 210?

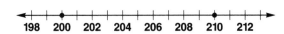

Answer _____

10 What are the next two numbers is this pattern?

30, 40, 50, 60, . . .

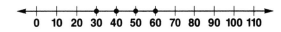

Answer _____

11 Roya worked 43 hours last week and Jack worked 47. Who worked more?

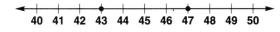

Answer _____

12 Each song on a jukebox plays 3 minutes. Use the pattern to see how many minutes it takes to play 6 songs.

3, 6, 9, . . .

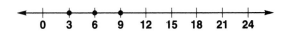

Answer _____

Check your answers on page 183.

Place Value to Thousands

A place value chart can also show thousands, ten thousands, and hundred thousands. Commas are used to separate numbers into groups of three digits. This makes numbers easier to read.

The number 674,302 has been placed in the chart. The chart shows the digit 2 is in the ones place, the digit 0 is in the tens place, the digit 3 is in the hundreds place, the digit 4 is in the thousands place, the digit 7 is in the ten-thousands place, and the digit 6 is in the hundred-thousands place.

Write each number in the chart. Then write each digit in the correct number group below, and write the value of the digit.

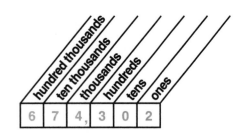

1 459,328

__4__ hundred thousands = __400,000__

___ ten thousands = _____

___ thousands = _____

___ hundreds = _____

___ tens = _____

___ ones = _____

2 206,179

___ hundred thousands = _____

___ ten thousands = _____

___ thousands = _____

___ hundreds = _____

___ tens = _____

___ ones = _____

3 47,006

___ ten thousands = _____

___ thousands = _____

___ hundreds = _____

___ tens = _____

___ ones = _____

Write the value of the underlined digit in each number.

4 3,4̲25 ____400____

5 16̲9,450 _____

6 27,9̲98 _____

7 144,30̲8 _____

8 982,0̲07 _____

9 480,3̲50 _____

Check your answers on page 183.

Rounding

Sometimes you do not need to give an exact answer to a math question. For example, if you were asked to tell how much time you spend on the telephone each day, you might answer, "About ten minutes." This answer describes *about* how much time, not *exactly* how much. When an exact answer is not necessary, you can **round** numbers. You can use a number line to round numbers.

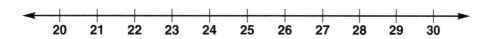

Round 22 to the nearest ten:	**Round 27 to the nearest ten:**	**Round 25 to the nearest ten:**
Find 22 on the number line. Then find the nearest tens numbers, 20 and 30. Since 22 is closer to 20, 22 rounds down to 20.	Find 27 on the number line. Then find the nearest tens numbers, 20 and 30. Since 27 is closer to 30, 27 rounds up to 30.	Find 25 on the number line. Then find the nearest tens numbers, 20 and 30. Since 25 is exactly halfway between 20 and 30, round up to 30.

Round each number to the nearest ten.

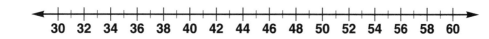

1 34 __30__   2 45 _____   3 58 _____   4 42 _____

5 33 _____   6 47 _____   7 39 _____   8 56 _____

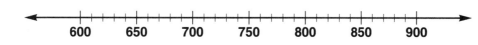

9 643 __640__   10 872 _____   11 754 _____   12 691 _____

13 776 _____   14 645 _____   15 827 _____   16 888 _____

For which of these questions would you give a rounded answer?

17 A. How many children are in your family?
    B. How many people live in the city where you live?

18 A. How many watches do you wear?
    B. How many hours do you sleep each week?

Answer _____   Answer _____

Check your answers on page 183.

Calculators

Calculators can help you solve or check your work. Although all calculators do not look exactly the same, all calculators can add, subtract, multiply, and divide numbers.

To use a calculator, find the **On/Off** key and press it once. A zero will appear on the display. This is the calculator's way of telling you it is ready to be used. Then work a problem. For example, add 8 and 7.

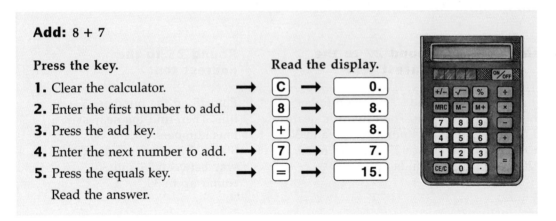

Add: 8 + 7

Press the key.   **Read the display.**

1. Clear the calculator.   ⟶ C ⟶ [0.]

2. Enter the first number to add.   ⟶ 8 ⟶ [8.]

3. Press the add key.   ⟶ + ⟶ [8.]

4. Enter the next number to add.   ⟶ 7 ⟶ [7.]

5. Press the equals key.   ⟶ = ⟶ [15.]

Read the answer.

Sometimes when you use a calculator, you may press the wrong key by mistake. When this happens, you have two choices:

- Press the **C** key once to clear the last number, then push the correct key.

- Press the **C** key twice to clear all numbers, and start again from the beginning.

The **C** key is the **Clear** key. The Clear key will erase one or more instructions you have entered.

When you finish, press the **On/Off** key to turn it off.

Use a calculator to find these answers.

1 9 + 4 = __13__   **2** 8 − 3 = _____   **3** 5 × 7 = _____   **4** 6 ÷ 2 = _____

5 18 − 8 = _____   **6** 15 × 4 = _____   **7** 27 ÷ 9 = _____   **8** 46 + 7 = _____

9 36 ÷ 18 = _____   **10** 60 + 25 = _____   **11** 79 − 37 = _____   **12** 50 × 12 = _____

13 A movie theater sold 18 tickets for the morning showing of a movie, 95 tickets for the afternoon showing, and 166 tickets for the evening showing. How many tickets were sold in all?

14 The odometer on Suzanne's car read 695 miles at the beginning of the day. At the end of the day, it read 703 miles. How many miles did Suzanne drive that day?

Answer _____

Answer _____

Unit 1 Wrap-up

Below are examples of the skills in this unit and the pages to refer to for practice. Read the examples and work the problems. Then check your answers. If you do well, go on to the unit review. If not, study the pages listed below before you do the unit review.

Read.

1. **(Refer to page 14)**

What is the place value of each digit in 68?

6 tens = 60
8 ones = 8

2. **(Refer to page 15)**

Write the place value of the underlined digit in 7̲3.

7 tens

3. **(Refer to page 16)**

274 = **2 hundreds**
     7 tens
     4 ones

4. **(Refer to pages 16–17)**

Write the whole number for 8 hundreds 3 tens 6 ones.

836

5. **(Refer to page 19)**

Compare 26 and 19.

26 > 19

6. **(Refer to page 22)**

Write the value of the underlined digit in 92̲8,347.

20,000

7. **(Refer to page 23)**

Round 59 to the nearest 10.

60

Solve.

1 What is the place value of each digit in 902?

2 Write the place value of the underlined digit in 584̲.

3 658 = ____ hundreds
       ____ tens
       ____ ones

4 Write the whole number for 5 hundreds 7 tens 2 ones.

5 Compare 37 and 73.

6 Write the value of the under-lined digit in 617̲,342.

7 Round 125 to the nearest ten.

Check your answers on page 183.

Answer these questions.

1 What is the place value of 8 in 87? _____

2 What is the place value of 3 in 4,308? _____

Write each number.

3 4 tens 1 one _____

4 9 hundreds 2 tens _____

5 7 hundreds 6 tens 5 ones _____

6 5 ones _____

Rename each of the following.

7 30 ones = _____ tens

8 1 hundred = _____ ones

9 20 tens = _____ hundreds

10 50 ones = _____ tens

Compare each set of numbers. Write > or < .

11 3 ☐ 4

12 76 ☐ 67

13 220 ☐ 202

14 53 ☐ 51

15 437 ☐ 473

16 330 ☐ 33

17 41 ☐ 40

18 78 ☐ 87

Round each number to the nearest ten.

60 62 64 66 68 70 72 74 76 78 80 82 84 86 88 90

19 84 _____

20 67 _____

21 75 _____

22 66 _____

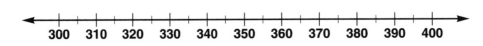

300 310 320 330 340 350 360 370 380 390 400

23 315 _____

24 362 _____

25 306 _____

26 329 _____

27 Each day Sharise and Luis deliver newspapers. Yesterday Luis delivered 32 newspapers and Sharise delivered 45. Who delivered more newspapers?

28 Mark works part-time 28 hours each week. Rounded to the nearest ten, about how many hours does Mark work each week?

Answer _____

Answer _____

What number is shown by each model? Fill in the circle for your answer.

29

Ⓐ 5

Ⓑ 6

Ⓒ 14

Ⓓ 41

30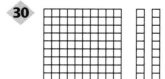

Ⓐ 102

Ⓑ 120

Ⓒ 201

Ⓓ 210

31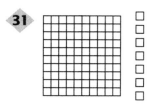

Ⓐ 107

Ⓑ 170

Ⓒ 701

Ⓓ 710

32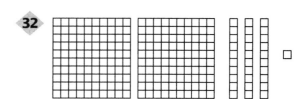

Ⓐ 132

Ⓑ 213

Ⓒ 231

Ⓓ 321

Fill in the circle for your answer.

33 What is the place value of the under-lined digit in 8<u>4</u>?

Ⓐ 4 ones

Ⓑ 4 tens

Ⓒ 8 ones

Ⓓ 8 tens

34 Which of these place values is the same as 5 tens?

Ⓐ 5 ones

Ⓑ 50 ones

Ⓒ 50 tens

Ⓓ 500 ones

35 You can rename 25 ones as ___ tens ___ ones.

Answer _____

36 Beth's change bowl has 68 dimes. To the nearest ten, how many dimes is that?

Answer _____

Check your answers on pages 183–184.

Cumulative Review 1

Write the place value of each underlined digit.

1 4̲12 _____

2 39̲0 _____

3 77,̲635 _____

Compare these numbers. Write > or < .

4 64 ☐ 67

5 850 ☐ 805

6 284 ☐ 131

Use the number line to round each number to the nearest ten.

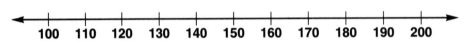

7 124 _____

8 195 _____

9 158 _____

What number is shown by each model?

10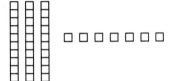

_____

11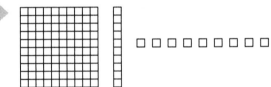

_____

Solve.

12 How many strips of ten stamps are in two sheets of one hundred stamps?

13 Rounded to the nearest ten, what is your age?

Answer _____

Answer _____

14 On Wednesday, a doctor saw 8 patients in the morning and 12 patients in the afternoon. Were more patients seen in the morning or in the afternoon?

15 Beatrice scored 860 points while playing a computer game. Mark scored 835 points playing the same game. Who scored fewer points?

Answer _____

Answer _____

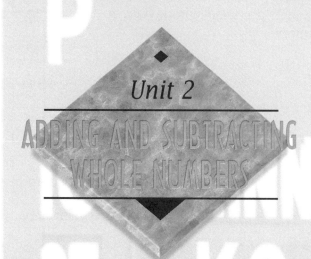

Unit 2
ADDING AND SUBTRACTING WHOLE NUMBERS

Addition and subtraction are operations you perform on numbers.

You add whole numbers when you find the total of two or more numbers. You subtract whole numbers when you take away one amount from another amount.

Describe a situation in which you add or subtract numbers.

In this unit you will learn about:

◆ adding and subtracting numbers with up to four digits

◆ renaming numbers when adding or subtracting

◆ estimating answers to addition and subtraction problems

◆ using a calculator to add or subtract numbers

◆ using addition and subtraction to solve word problems

Addition Facts

This table shows basic addition facts. Addition facts are used whenever you add numbers.

+	0	1	2	3	4	5	6	7	8	9
0	0	1	2	3	4	5				
1	1	2	3	4	5					
2	2	3	4	5						
3	3	4	5							
4	4	5								
5	5									
6										
7										
8										
9										

To find the answer to an addition fact such as 2 + 3, find the row that begins with 2 and the column that begins with 3. The answer, 5, is the number in the box where the row and the column meet.

Complete this addition facts table, looking for patterns as you work.

Complete the following addition facts.

1
  4
+ 6
‾‾
 10

2
  7
+ 2

3
  5
+ 5

4
  2
+ 3

5
  5
+ 6

6
  4
+ 9

7
  1
+ 8

8
  9
+ 7

9
  2
+ 2

10
  6
+ 8

11
  9
+ 9

12
  7
+ 5

13 8 + 9 =   **14** 7 + 6 =   **15** 9 + 3 =   **16** 5 + 9 =   **17** 2 + 9 =

18 2 + 0 =   **19** 6 + 6 =   **20** 8 + 4 =   **21** 3 + 7 =   **22** 6 + 3 =

Solve each problem.

23 Nine plus six equals what number?

<u>   9 + 6 = 15   </u>

24 Add four more to seven.

_____

25 What is six and four more?

_____

26 Add five and two.

_____

27 Add four more to three.

_____

28 What is two and eight more?

_____

Check your answers on page 184.

Addition Equations

Use the addition facts table from page 30 to fill in the boxes in these problems. Sometimes the **sum** or total is missing. Sometimes the missing number is one of the **addends**, the numbers you add in an addition problem.

1 $7 + \boxed{3} = 10$　　**2** $3 + 2 = \square$　　**3** $8 + \square = 14$　　**4** $1 + 5 = \square$

5 $8 + \square = 16$　　**6** $0 + 6 = \square$　　**7** $\square + 2 = 7$　　**8** $9 + \square = 9$

9 $5 + 3 = \square$　　**10** $1 + \square = 4$　　**11** $4 + \square = 9$　　**12** $\square + 2 = 6$

An **equation** is a number sentence in which a letter such as n or x stands for a missing number. Here are three examples of addition equations.

$$6 + n = 7 \qquad x + 4 = 12 \qquad 2 + 1 = n$$
$$n = 1 \qquad\quad\; x = 8 \qquad\quad\; n = 3$$

To solve an equation, find the missing number. In the first equation, n is equal to 1. In the second equation, x is equal to 8. In the third equation, n is equal to 3.

Solve each equation.

13 $n + 1 = 3$　　　**14** $3 + x = 9$　　　**15** $2 + 4 = n$　　　**16** $5 + n = 13$
　　　$n = 2$

17 $7 + 8 = n$　　　**18** $x + 9 = 12$　　　**19** $1 + x = 8$　　　**20** $4 + 9 = n$

21 $0 + x = 3$　　　**22** $n + 2 = 10$　　　**23** $7 + x = 14$　　　**24** $n + 8 = 17$

25 $4 + n = 12$　　　**26** $x + 3 = 9$　　　**27** $9 + 2 = x$　　　**28** $n + 7 = 8$

Write an equation to solve each problem.

29 Six and what number is eight?

　　　$6 + n = 8$
_____

30 What number equals one plus nine?

_____

31 What number plus four equals eight?

_____

32 Five plus what number equals twelve?

_____

33 Seven plus what number is seven?

_____

34 What number plus four is five?

_____

Check your answers on pages 184–185.

Adding Larger Numbers

You can use the addition facts to add larger numbers. Be sure that the digits with the same place values are lined up in the correct columns. Add only the digits that have the same place.

Add: 841
          + 3,026

1. Be sure that the digits are lined up.

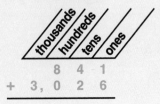

```
      8   4   1
+  3, 0   2   6
```

2. Add each column, starting with the digits in the ones place.

```
   841          841          841          841
 + 3,026      + 3,026      + 3,026      + 3,026
       7           67          867        3,867
       ↑            ↑            ↑            ↑
     ones         tens     hundreds   thousands
```

Add.

1.   13
     + 85
       98

2.   92
     + 7

3.   4
     + 62

4.   20
     + 35

5.   17
     + 40

6.   61
     + 27

7.   321
     + 48

8.   42
     + 557

9.   315
     + 663

10.   252
     + 115

11.   740
     + 126

12.   500
     + 35

13.   54
     + 702

14.   58
     + 430

15.   240
     + 603

16.   15
     + 670

17.   1,342
     +   534

18.   213
     + 4,665

19.   5,134
     + 2,632

20.   7,244
     + 1,513

21.   4,000
     +   53

22.   250
     + 5,300

23.   1,086
     + 4,002

24.   2,089
     + 6,100

25.   436
     + 122

26.   1,211
     + 388

27.   2,652
     +   21

28.   848
     + 130

Check your answers on page 185.

To add numbers that are not lined up, first put the digits in columns. Line up the digits that have the same place. Put your answers in the correct columns.

Add: 523 + 61

1. Write the digits in columns so that the digits with the same place are lined up.

```
  523
+  61
```

2. Add the digits in each column, starting with the ones place.

```
  523      523      523
+  61    +  61    +  61
           4       84      584
```

Add.

1 31 + 46 =

```
  31
+ 46
  77
```

2 24 + 55 =

3 40 + 8 =

4 12 + 72 =

5 243 + 106 =

6 68 + 521 =

7 441 + 237 =

8 305 + 80 =

9 2,314 + 625 =

10 4,100 + 700 =

11 301 + 9,036 =

12 5,881 + 1,012 =

13 4,603 + 281 =

14 722 + 165 =

15 204 + 5,462 =

16 Last week, Gwen bicycled 32 miles during the weekdays and 24 miles on the weekend. How many miles did she bicycle in all?

17 Kai bought a compact disc player for $165 and a compact disc for $21. How much did he spend all together?

Answer _____

Answer _____

Adding with Renaming

When you add the digits in a column, the sum can sometimes be 10 or more. When this happens, rename by carrying to the column to the left. You may need to rename more than once.

Add: 454
        + 276

1. Add the ones.
4 + 6 = 10 ones.
Write 0 in the ones
column. Carry 1 ten.

1 ten → 1
    454
  + 276
      0
      ↑
    ones

2. Add the tens.
1 + 5 + 7 = 13 tens.
Write 3 in the tens column.
Carry 1 hundred.

1 hundred → 11
      454
    + 276
       30
        ↑
      tens

3. Add the hundreds.
1 + 4 + 2 = 7 hundreds.
Write 7 in the hundreds
column.

        11
       454
     + 276
      730
        ↑
   hundreds

Add.

1.
 1
  57
+ 94
 151

2.
  68
+ 6

3.
   2
+ 59

4.
  44
+ 36

5.
  78
+ 49

6.
  84
+ 97

7.
  15
+ 85

8.
  19
+ 4

9.
   3
+ 77

10.
  34
+ 76

11.
  43
+ 8

12.
  55
+ 18

13.
  547
+ 67

14.
   31
+ 693

15.
  117
+ 914

16.
  454
+ 709

17.
  236
+ 481

18.
  184
+ 96

19.
  510
+ 298

20.
  532
+ 377

21.
   73
+ 848

22.
  201
+ 289

23.
 1,215
+ 883

24.
 4,070
+ 4,035

25.
 1,968
+ 2,732

26.
 5,140
+ 6,380

Check your answers on page 185.

To add numbers that are not lined up, first put the digits in columns. When you need to rename, remember to write the number you carry above the column to the left.

Add.

1 56 + 316 =

$$\begin{array}{r} 1 \\ 56 \\ + 316 \\ \hline 372 \end{array}$$

2 37 + 88 =

3 76 + 5 =

4 35 + 19 =

5 320 + 88 =

6 91 + 682 =

7 396 + 389 =

8 661 + 347 =

9 306 + 1,174 =

10 3,607 + 453 =

11 2,217 + 1,855 =

12 9,528 + 4,490 =

13 48 + 261 =

14 13 + 77 =

15 405 + 58 =

16 23 + 4,081 =

17 433 + 1,704 =

18 2,143 + 871 =

19 817 + 94 =

20 5,066 + 165 =

21 Trish spent $125 for a new winter coat, plus $28 for gloves and a scarf. How much did Trish spend in all?

22 Al and his friends held a two-day yard sale. The first day they made $135. The second day they made $68. How much money did they make all together?

Answer _____

Answer _____

Check your answers on pages 185–186.

Adding Three or More Numbers

To add three or more numbers, first write the numbers in a column.
Then, add the digits in pairs.

Add: 58 + 16 + 32

1. Line up the digits in a column.

```
  58
  16
+ 32
```

2. Add groups of digits in the ones column. Add the digits in pairs.

```
   1
  58
  16  ⟩ 8 + 6 = 14
+ 32  ⟩ 14 + 2 = 16
   6
```

3. Add groups of digits in the tens column.

```
1 + 5 = 6      1
6 + 1 = 7     58
7 + 3 = 10    16
            + 32
             106
```

Add.

1.
```
   2
  25
  19
+  6
  50
```

2.
```
   5
   2
+  6
```

3.
```
  53
  38
+ 20
```

4.
```
   64
  520
+  13
```

5.
```
   24
  279
+  50
```

6.
```
  447
  342
+  23
```

7.
```
  201
  383
   10
+ 301
```

8.
```
  212
  311
  203
+  62
```

9.
```
  340
   23
    5
+ 219
```

10.
```
  217
  224
   70
+ 321
```

11.
```
  660
   61
  382
+  17
```

12. 73 + 14 + 46 =

13. 811 + 25 + 100 =

14. 41 + 128 + 82 =

15. Harriet's home is heated with fuel oil. Her furnace used 38 gallons of fuel oil in December, 75 gallons in January, and 67 gallons in February. How many gallons did she use in all?

16. Tara writes parking tickets for the city. By last Wednesday, she had written 192 tickets. On Thursday, she wrote 67 tickets, and on Friday she wrote 59 tickets. What was her weekly total?

Answer _____

Answer _____

Rounding and Estimation

One way to estimate answers is to round each number to its greatest place. The greatest place is the place of the first digit on the left, called the **lead digit**. To round a number, look at the digit to the right of the lead digit. If the digit to the right of the lead digit is 5 or more, add 1 to the lead digit and change the other digits in the number to 0. If the digit to the right of the lead digit is less than 5, change all digits except the lead digit in the number to 0.

Estimate: 38 + 23 + 195

1. Write the digits in columns.

```
   38
   23
+ 195
```

2. Round each number to its lead digit.

```
   38  →    40
   23  →    20
+ 195  →  + 200
```

3. Add the rounded numbers.

```
   38  →    40
   23  →    20
+ 195  →  + 200
            260
```

Round each number to the lead digit. Then add.

1.
```
407 →  400
+ 53 → + 50
       450
```

2.
```
  63
+ 89
```

3.
```
  313
+ 581
```

4.
```
1,741
+  462
```

5.
```
  28
  57
+ 81
```

6.
```
  184
   37
+ 479
```

7.
```
   202
   318
+ 6,321
```

8.
```
  706
   42
   66
+ 113
```

9.
```
   27
  746
  121
+  58
```

10. 688 + 56 =

11. 65 + 16 + 173 =

12. 4,281 + 517 =

13. 46 + 5,335 + 194 =

14. A mail order catalog offers bed sheets for $19, a bedspread for $39, and a mattress for $118. Estimate the total cost of all three items.

15. Parkland Adult School held a four-day Job Fair. On the four days, 54, 82, 39, and 167 people attended. Estimate the total number of people who attended.

Answer _____

Answer _____

Using a Calculator to Add

Use a calculator to add. Always clear your calculator before you begin. Check each number after you enter it.

Add: 78 + 34

Press the key.   Read the display.

1. Clear the calculator.   ➝ [C]   ➝ [0.]
2. Enter the first number. ➝ [7][8] ➝ [78.]
3. Press the add key.   ➝ [+]   ➝ [78.]
4. Enter the next number.   ➝ [3][4] ➝ [34.]
5. Press the equals key.   ➝ [=]   ➝ [112.]
   Read the answer.

Use a calculator to solve.

1 56 + 48 = 104   **2** 237 + 66 =   **3** 4,507 + 618 =   **4** 1,534 + 6,078 =

5 49 + 8 + 64 =   **6** 85 + 243 + 491 =   **7** 748 + 36 + 4,528 =

Add.

8   51   **9**   366   **10**   702   **11**   6,016
      + 281   + 4,848   979   584
                                         + 3,364   + 1,277

12   165   **13**   801   **14**   2,433   **15**   318
        1,332   17   1,652   710
       +   17   + 159   +   428   + 5,036

16 This month Riko's water bill was $47, his telephone bill was $128, and his electric bill was $217. How much did Riko spend in all?

17 Angela bought 5,000 sheets of white paper, 1,000 sheets of yellow paper, and 500 sheets of blue paper for her office. How many sheets of paper did Angela buy all together?

Answer _____   Answer _____

Check-up on Addition

Add.

1 $\begin{array}{r} 2 \\ +\ 9 \\ \hline \end{array}$

2 $\begin{array}{r} 8 \\ +\ 1 \\ \hline \end{array}$

3 $\begin{array}{r} 26 \\ +\ 93 \\ \hline \end{array}$

4 $\begin{array}{r} 505 \\ +\ 74 \\ \hline \end{array}$

5 $\begin{array}{r} 436 \\ +\ 702 \\ \hline \end{array}$

6 $\begin{array}{r} 1{,}064 \\ +\ 615 \\ \hline \end{array}$

7 $5 + 4 =$

8 $31 + 16 =$

9 $415 + 82 =$

10 $634 + 4{,}251 =$

11 $\begin{array}{r} 25 \\ +\ 45 \\ \hline \end{array}$

12 $\begin{array}{r} 563 \\ +\ 41 \\ \hline \end{array}$

13 $\begin{array}{r} 219 \\ +\ 890 \\ \hline \end{array}$

14 $\begin{array}{r} 703 \\ +\ 1{,}461 \\ \hline \end{array}$

15 $\begin{array}{r} 9{,}421 \\ +\ 1{,}399 \\ \hline \end{array}$

16 $57 + 8 =$

17 $42 + 374 =$

18 $706 + 528 =$

19 $422 + 3{,}085 =$

20 $\begin{array}{r} 3 \\ 14 \\ +\ 5 \\ \hline \end{array}$

21 $\begin{array}{r} 21 \\ 104 \\ +\ 580 \\ \hline \end{array}$

22 $\begin{array}{r} 621 \\ 2{,}414 \\ +\ 70 \\ \hline \end{array}$

23 $\begin{array}{r} 22 \\ 115 \\ 32 \\ +\ 420 \\ \hline \end{array}$

24 $\begin{array}{r} 17 \\ 342 \\ 1{,}005 \\ +\ 620 \\ \hline \end{array}$

25 $26 + 5 + 43 =$

26 $313 + 51 + 632 =$

27 $1{,}235 + 605 + 52 + 441 =$

28 $\begin{array}{r} 693 \\ +\ 368 \\ \hline \end{array}$

29 $\begin{array}{r} 9{,}437 \\ +\ 76 \\ \hline \end{array}$

30 $\begin{array}{r} 14{,}650 \\ +\ 3{,}856 \\ \hline \end{array}$

31 $\begin{array}{r} 349 \\ +\ 48 \\ \hline \end{array}$

32 $\begin{array}{r} 17{,}043 \\ +\ 5{,}417 \\ \hline \end{array}$

33 Lee delivers packages. One day, she drove 310 miles. On the next day, she drove 250 miles. What was the total number of miles she drove?

34 Smith, Ramirez, and Hayes ran for mayor. Smith received 251 votes, 732 people voted for Ramirez, and 49 people voted for Hayes. Find the total number of votes.

Answer _____

Answer _____

Check your answers on pages 186–187.

A Step-by-Step Plan

Making a plan will help you solve word problems more easily. First, read the problem carefully. Then follow a plan to solve it.

> ❖ STRATEGY: **Make a step-by-step plan.**
>
> **1.** Write down the facts or draw a picture.
>
> **2.** Think about what you need to do.
>
> **3.** Set up a number problem. Estimate your answer.
>
> **4.** Solve the problem. Check your work.
>
> **5.** Write the answer to the problem.

Example: **Use a step-by-step plan to solve the problem.**

Cal drove 78 miles before he stopped for lunch. Then he drove 109 more miles. How far did he drive in all?

Step 1 Write down the facts or draw a picture.

78 miles
109 miles

Step 2 Decide what to do. Decide if you need to add or subtract or both. Since you need to find a total number of miles, you need to add.

Step 3 Set up a number problem. Estimate the answer.

$$
\begin{array}{ccc}
78 & \rightarrow & 80 \\
+\,109 & \rightarrow & \underline{100} \\
\end{array}
$$
about 180 miles

Step 4 Solve.

$$
\begin{array}{r}
1 \\
78 \\
+\,109 \\
\hline
187 \\
\end{array}
$$
Check your work by comparing the exact answer to your estimate.

Step 5 Write the answer.
Cal drove 187 miles in all.

Exercise: Use the step-by-step plan to solve these problems.

1 Stella takes orders over the telephone. In the morning she received 94 calls. In the afternoon she received 101 calls. How many calls did she receive in all?

Answer _____

2 During the holiday season Kara wrapped 197 large gifts and 42 small gifts. How many gifts did she wrap in all?

Answer _____

3 Eric had 1 sheet of one hundred stamps, a strip of 10 stamps, and 6 loose stamps. How many stamps did he have in all?

Answer _____

4 Glenn bought groceries for his family four times. He spent $103, $98, $89, and $111. How much did he spend all together?

Answer _____

5 A restaurant served 48 customers for breakfast, 67 customers for lunch, and 104 customers for dinner. How many customers were served in all?

Answer _____

6 Gina had $2,165 in her savings account after she withdrew $940 to pay for a college class. How much was in her account before paying for the class?

Answer _____

7 Andrea had to have her car repaired. She spent $150 on the brakes, $78 on new tires, and $30 for an oil change. How much did all the repairs cost?

Answer _____

8 The mall manager did a customer count. He counted 550 customers on Wednesday and 560 customers on Saturday. How many were counted in both days?

Answer _____

Check your answers on pages 187–188.

Subtraction Facts

Subtraction is the opposite of addition. For this reason, you can use the addition facts table to solve subtraction problems. For example, to find $14 - 8$, find the smaller number 8 in the left column of the addition table. Next, move to the right to find the larger number, 14. Finally move up to find the answer, 6.

−	0	1	2	3	4	5	6	7	8	9
0	0	1	2	3	4	5	6	7	8	9
1	1	2	3	4	5	6	7	8	9	10
2	2	3	4	5	6	7	8	9	10	11
3	3	4	5	6	7	8	9	10	11	12
4	4	5	6	7	8	9	10	11	12	13
5	5	6	7	8	9	10	11	12	13	14
6	6	7	8	9	10	11	12	13	14	15
7	7	8	9	10	11	12	13	14	15	16
8	8	9	10	11	12	13	14	15	16	17
9	9	10	11	12	13	14	15	16	17	18

Use the table to complete the following subtraction facts.

1. $\begin{array}{r} 11 \\ -\ 5 \\ \hline 6 \end{array}$
2. $\begin{array}{r} 6 \\ -\ 2 \\ \hline \end{array}$
3. $\begin{array}{r} 10 \\ -\ 7 \\ \hline \end{array}$
4. $\begin{array}{r} 11 \\ -\ 3 \\ \hline \end{array}$
5. $\begin{array}{r} 16 \\ -\ 9 \\ \hline \end{array}$
6. $\begin{array}{r} 2 \\ -\ 1 \\ \hline \end{array}$

7. $\begin{array}{r} 9 \\ -\ 4 \\ \hline \end{array}$
8. $\begin{array}{r} 13 \\ -\ 6 \\ \hline \end{array}$
9. $\begin{array}{r} 9 \\ -\ 0 \\ \hline \end{array}$
10. $\begin{array}{r} 8 \\ -\ 8 \\ \hline \end{array}$
11. $\begin{array}{r} 7 \\ -\ 5 \\ \hline \end{array}$
12. $\begin{array}{r} 8 \\ -\ 3 \\ \hline \end{array}$

13. $11 - 2 =$
14. $13 - 4 =$
15. $12 - 6 =$
16. $15 - 8 =$
17. $3 - 2 =$

18. $17 - 9 =$
19. $4 - 1 =$
20. $14 - 5 =$
21. $12 - 7 =$
22. $5 - 3 =$

Solve each problem.

23. Ten minus six equals what number?

    $\underline{\quad\ 10 - 6 = 4 \quad}$

24. What is eight less than eleven?

    _____

25. Subtract five from nine.

    _____

26. Find the difference between thirteen and six.

    _____

27. Decrease seven by two.

    _____

28. Nine is how many more than three?

    _____

Check your answers on page 188.

Subtraction Equations

Use the addition facts table from page 42 to fill in the boxes in these problems.

1 $10 - 4 = \boxed{6}$ **2** $13 - 5 = \boxed{}$ **3** $12 - \boxed{} = 3$ **4** $8 - 1 = \boxed{}$

5 $4 - \boxed{} = 2$ **6** $7 - 6 = \boxed{}$ **7** $\boxed{} - 9 = 5$ **8** $11 - \boxed{} = 4$

9 $16 - 8 = \boxed{}$ **10** $10 - \boxed{} = 9$ **11** $12 - \boxed{} = 7$ **12** $\boxed{} - 2 = 6$

Recall that an **equation** is a number sequence in which a letter such as n or x stands for a missing number. Here are three examples of subtraction equations.

$$x - 2 = 7 \qquad\qquad 12 - 4 = n \qquad\qquad 9 - x = 7$$
$$x = 9 \qquad\qquad\quad\; n = 8 \qquad\qquad\quad\; x = 2$$

To solve an equation, find the missing number. In the first equation, x is equal to 9. In the second equation, n is equal to 8. In the third equation, x is equal to 2.

Solve each equation.

13 $n - 6 = 3$ **14** $7 - x = 4$ **15** $16 - 7 = n$ **16** $6 - n = 2$
    $n = 9$

17 $13 - x = 5$ **18** $n - 5 = 5$ **19** $15 - x = 7$ **20** $n - 2 = 7$

21 $4 - 4 = n$ **22** $x - 8 = 2$ **23** $17 - x = 9$ **24** $8 - 4 = n$

Write an equation to solve each problem.

25 Fourteen minus what number is seven?

   $\underline{\qquad 14 - n = 7 \qquad}$

26 Twelve minus three equals what number?

   $\underline{\qquad\qquad\qquad\qquad}$

27 What number minus five is three?

   $\underline{\qquad\qquad\qquad\qquad}$

28 Seven equals fifteen minus what number?

   $\underline{\qquad\qquad\qquad\qquad}$

29 Six minus what number is one?

   $\underline{\qquad\qquad\qquad\qquad}$

30 What number minus two equals eight?

   $\underline{\qquad\qquad\qquad\qquad}$

Check your answers on pages 188–189.

Subtracting Larger Numbers

You can use the subtraction facts to subtract larger numbers. Be sure that the digits with the same place are lined up in the correct columns. Subtract only the digits that have the same place.

Subtract: 237
                 − 125

1. Be sure that the digits are lined up.

```
  237
− 125
```

2. Subtract each column, starting with the digits in the ones place. Check by adding the answer, 112, to the bottom number, 125. The sum should be the same as the top number, 237.

```
  237        237        237          Check:
− 125      − 125      − 125           112
─────      ─────      ─────         + 125
    2         12        112         ─────
                                     237
```

Subtract. Use addition to check your answers.

1.
```
  46     24
− 22   + 22
────   ────
  24     46
```

2.
```
  67
− 30
────
```

3.
```
  89
− 58
────
```

4.
```
  94
− 10
────
```

5.
```
  52
− 31
────
```

6.
```
  77
− 16
────
```

7.
```
  25
− 13
────
```

8.
```
  33
− 22
────
```

9.
```
  619
−   7
─────
```

10.
```
  171
−  51
─────
```

11.
```
  438
− 126
─────
```

12.
```
  794
− 503
─────
```

13.
```
  283
− 102
─────
```

14.
```
  357
−   5
─────
```

15.
```
  505
− 301
─────
```

16.
```
  867
−  54
─────
```

17.
```
  3,487
−   340
───────
```

18.
```
  1,195
−    72
───────
```

19.
```
  4,864
− 1,602
───────
```

20.
```
  7,637
− 3,214
───────
```

21.
```
  1,481
−   261
───────
```

22.
```
  5,376
− 1,261
───────
```

23.
```
  3,792
− 3,460
───────
```

24.
```
  2,654
−   410
───────
```

Check your answers on page 189.

To subtract numbers that are not lined up, first put the digits in columns. Line up the digits that have the same place. Put your answers in the correct columns.

Subtract: 267 − 53

1. Write the digits in columns so that the digits with the same place are lined up.

2. Subtract the digits in each column, starting with the ones place.

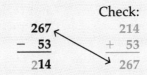

Check:

```
    267        267        267        267          214
  −  53      −  53      −  53      −  53        +  53
                  4         14        214          267
```

Subtract. Use addition to check your answers.

1 48 − 6 =

```
   48        42
 −  6      +  6
   42        48
```

2 56 − 23 =

3 65 − 14 =

4 $76 − $24 =

5 409 − 207 =

6 576 − 54 =

7 $199 − $150 =

8 632 − 410 =

9 8,527 − 315 =

10 $4,340 − $220 =

11 2,619 − 1,505 =

12 3,538 − 2,326 =

Use a step-by-step plan to solve.

13 A charity group earned $865 at a garage sale on Saturday and $520 on Sunday. How much more did they earn on Saturday than on Sunday?

14 After driving all morning, Clayton has traveled 325 miles. By the end of the day, he must drive 638 miles in all. How many miles does he have left to travel?

Answer _____

Answer _____

Check your answers on page 189.

Subtracting with Renaming

When you are subtracting, the digit you are subtracting from can sometimes be too small. When this happens, borrow from the next column to the left. Rename 1 ten as 10 ones, or 1 hundred as 10 tens.

Subtract: 256
          − 187

1. Start in ones place. Since you can't subtract 7 from 6, borrow 1 ten and rename it as 10 ones. Subtract the ones.

```
      4 16
   2 5 6
  − 1 8 7
        9
```

2. Since you can't subtract 8 from 4, borrow 1 hundred and rename it as 10 tens. Subtract the tens.

```
        14
   1 4 16
   2 5 6
  − 1 8 7
      6 9
```

3. Subtract the hundreds. 1 − 1 = 0 hundreds. Check your answer.

```
        14
   1 4 16           Check:
   2 5 6              1 1
  − 1 8 7             6 9
      6 9          + 1 8 7
                     2 5 6
```

Subtract. Use addition to check your answers.

1.
```
   2 15
   3 5        1
  − 1 7      1 8
   1 8     + 1 7
            3 5
```

2.
```
   4 6
  − 2 7
```

3.
```
   7 3
  −   6
```

4.
```
   6 1
  − 3 3
```

5.
```
   2 4
  − 1 9
```

6.
```
   8 3
  − 5 8
```

7.
```
   5 2
  − 4 6
```

8.
```
   9 4
  −   8
```

9.
```
   6 7 5
  − 2 9 0
```

10.
```
   3 4 2
  − 2 3 5
```

11.
```
   8 6 5
  −   7 4
```

12.
```
   4 1 3
  − 2 0 7
```

13.
```
   3 1 4
  − 1 6 2
```

14.
```
   9 5 6
  − 4 7 0
```

15.
```
   2 6 1
  −   6 5
```

16.
```
   1 1 7
  −   4 9
```

17.
```
   2,2 7 4
  − 1,0 9 2
```

18.
```
   5,3 8 1
  − 3,8 2 4
```

19.
```
   8,4 1 6
  − 4,0 1 8
```

20.
```
   6,1 7 2
  −   8 3 1
```

Check your answers on page 189.

Renaming Zeros

Some subtraction problems may have one or more zeros in the top number. When this happens, you need to borrow across the zero or zeros.

Subtract: 702
              − 176

1. To subtract ones, borrow 1 hundred across the zero from the hundreds column. Rename 1 hundred as 10 tens.

```
   6 10
   7 Ø 2
 − 1 7 6
```

2. Borrow 1 ten and rename as 10 ones. Now there are 6 hundreds, 9 tens, and 12 ones.

```
        9
   6 10 12
   7 Ø 2
 − 1 7 6
```

3. Subtract.
$12 − 6 = 6$ ones.
$9 − 7 = 2$ tens.
$6 − 1 = 5$ hundreds.
Check your answer.

```
        9            Check:
   6 10 12            1 1
   7 Ø 2             5 2 6
 − 1 7 6           + 1 7 6
   5 2 6             7 0 2
```

Subtract. Use addition to check your answers.

1.
```
     9
 4 10 14    1 1
 5 Ø 4     1 3 5
− 3 6 9   + 3 6 9
 1 3 5     5 0 4
```

2.   703
       − 39

3.   510
       −   7

4.   802
       − 54

5.
```
     9
 4 10 10    1 1
 5 Ø Ø     3 6 7
− 1 3 3   + 1 3 3
 3 6 7     5 0 0
```

6.   400
       − 75

7.   600
       − 18

8.   300
       − 221

9.   106
       − 64

10.   705
        − 329

11.   201
        − 103

12.   906
        − 87

13.   8,200
        − 2,771

14.   5,500
        − 4,024

15.   4,000
        −   637

16.   2,900
        −   814

17. $3,502 − 265 =$

18. $4,002 − 1,073 =$

19. $903 − 258 =$

20. $7,304 − 760 =$

Check your answers on pages 189–190.

More Subtraction

To subtract numbers that are not lined up, first put the digits in columns. The larger number goes on top. Remember to write the renaming numbers above the top number.

Subtract. Use addition to check your answers.

1 $73 - 36 =$ 　　**2** $45 - 19 =$ 　　**3** $\$72 - \$8 =$ 　　**4** $50 - 24 =$

$$
\begin{array}{r}
{}^{6}\,{}^{13} \\
\not{7}\,\not{3} \\
-\ 3\ 6 \\
\hline
3\ 7
\end{array}
\qquad
\begin{array}{r}
{}^{1} \\
3\ 7 \\
+\ \ 3\ 6 \\
\hline
7\ 3
\end{array}
$$

5 $471 - 126 =$ 　　**6** $\$817 - \$174 =$ 　　**7** $652 - 87 =$ 　　**8** $801 - 233 =$

9 $7{,}264 - 3{,}092 =$ 　**10** $5{,}161 - 583 =$ 　**11** $\$3{,}204 - \$2{,}818 =$ 　**12** $7{,}003 - 4{,}625 =$

13 sixty-five minus eight = 　　　　　**14** forty-two minus twenty-five =

15 three hundred fifteen minus sixty = 　　**16** nine hundred thirty minus eighty =

Use a step-by-step plan to solve.

17 A train takes 55 minutes to travel from Park Forest to Homewood to Chicago. It takes 7 minutes to reach Homewood from Park Forest. How long is the trip from Homewood to Chicago?

18 Maria bought a used rocking chair on sale for $35. The original price of the chair was $115. How much money did Maria save?

Answer _____　　　　Answer _____

Unit 2

48

Check your answers on page 190.

Rounding and Estimation

Recall that one way to estimate answers is to round each number to its lead digit.

Estimate: 5,513 − 827

1. Write the digits in columns.

$$\begin{array}{r} 5,513 \\ -\ 827 \\ \hline \end{array}$$

2. Round each number to its lead digit.

$$\begin{array}{rcr} 5,513 & \rightarrow & 6,000 \\ -\ 827 & \rightarrow & -\ 800 \\ \hline \end{array}$$

3. Subtract the rounded numbers.

$$\begin{array}{rcr} 5,513 & \rightarrow & 6,000 \\ -\ 827 & \rightarrow & -\ 800 \\ \hline & & 5,200 \end{array}$$

Round each number to the lead digit. Then subtract.

1
$$\begin{array}{rcr} 431 & \rightarrow & 400 \\ -\ 98 & \rightarrow & -\ 100 \\ \hline & & 300 \end{array}$$

2
$$\begin{array}{r} 73 \\ -\ 35 \\ \hline \end{array}$$

3
$$\begin{array}{r} \$412 \\ -\ 167 \\ \hline \end{array}$$

4
$$\begin{array}{r} 817 \\ -\ 356 \\ \hline \end{array}$$

5
$$\begin{array}{r} 625 \\ -\ 86 \\ \hline \end{array}$$

6
$$\begin{array}{r} \$1,053 \\ -\ 497 \\ \hline \end{array}$$

7
$$\begin{array}{r} 6,512 \\ -\ 2,077 \\ \hline \end{array}$$

8
$$\begin{array}{r} 9,427 \\ -\ 3,881 \\ \hline \end{array}$$

9
$$\begin{array}{r} 7,340 \\ -\ 4,519 \\ \hline \end{array}$$

10 76 − 39 =

11 612 − 178 =

12 $8,235 − $787 =

13 5,543 − 2,394 =

14 4,025 − 332 =

15 $92 − $59 =

16 916 − 593 =

17 3,867 − 1,984 =

Solve.

18 The computer Henry's company bought cost $1,999. The printer cost $897. About how much more did the computer cost than the printer?

19 The distance through the center (diameter) of the earth is 7,927 miles. The diameter of the moon is 2,160 miles. About how much larger is the diameter of earth than the diameter of the moon?

Answer _____

Answer _____

Check your answers on page 190.

Unit 2

Using a Calculator to Subtract

Use a calculator to subtract. Always clear your calculator before you begin. Check each number after you enter it.

Subtract: 846 − 479

Press the key.   **Read the display.**

1. Clear the calculator.   → [C] → [0.]
2. Enter the larger number.   → [8][4][6] → [846.]
3. Press the subtract key.   → [−] → [846.]
4. Enter the smaller number.   → [4][7][9] → [479.]
5. Press the equals key.   → [=] → [367.]
   Read the answer.

Use a calculator to solve.

1 84 − 39 = 45   **2** $92 − $18 =   **3** 376 − 89 =   **4** 452 − 68 =

5 385 − 166 =   **6** 820 − 157 =   **7** $303 − $264 =   **8** 631 − 490 =

9 3,602 − 764 =   **10** 7,441 − 3,095 =   **11** $1,220 − $668 =   **12** 5,358 − 2,471 =

Solve. Use a calculator to check your answers.

13   487   **14** $806   **15**   2,217   **16**   6,333   **17**   8,001
        −   58   −   293   −   818   − 3,380   − 4,129

Use a step-by-step plan to solve.

18 Rita is planning to save $225 to buy a refrigerator. She has already saved $160. How much does Rita still need to save?

19 A company survey found that 473 employees wanted to change their health care plan. The survey was filled out by 1,051 employees. How many employees did not want to change health plans?

Answer _____   Answer _____

Check your answers on page 190.

Check-up on Subtraction

Subtract. Use addition to check your answers.

1 $\begin{array}{r} 15 \\ -\ 6 \\ \hline \end{array}$ **2** $\begin{array}{r} 14 \\ -\ 8 \\ \hline \end{array}$ **3** $\begin{array}{r} 11 \\ -\ 6 \\ \hline \end{array}$ **4** $\begin{array}{r} \$38 \\ -\ 23 \\ \hline \end{array}$ **5** $\begin{array}{r} 47 \\ -\ 16 \\ \hline \end{array}$ **6** $\begin{array}{r} 64 \\ -\ 34 \\ \hline \end{array}$

7 $\$18 - \$9 =$ **8** $9 - 3 =$ **9** $25 - 2 =$ **10** $56 - 40 =$

11 $\begin{array}{r} 762 \\ -\ 311 \\ \hline \end{array}$ **12** $\begin{array}{r} 454 \\ -\ 32 \\ \hline \end{array}$ **13** $\begin{array}{r} 295 \\ -\ 102 \\ \hline \end{array}$ **14** $\begin{array}{r} \$429 \\ -\ 127 \\ \hline \end{array}$ **15** $\begin{array}{r} 3{,}609 \\ -\ 3{,}506 \\ \hline \end{array}$

16 $574 - 261 =$ **17** $874 - 52 =$ **18** $8{,}070 - 160 =$ **19** $7{,}115 - 2{,}010 =$

20 $\begin{array}{r} 37 \\ -\ 8 \\ \hline \end{array}$ **21** $\begin{array}{r} \$91 \\ -\ 25 \\ \hline \end{array}$ **22** $\begin{array}{r} 827 \\ -\ 253 \\ \hline \end{array}$ **23** $\begin{array}{r} 303 \\ -\ 164 \\ \hline \end{array}$ **24** $\begin{array}{r} 4{,}740 \\ -\ 850 \\ \hline \end{array}$

25 $34 - 16 =$ **26** $81 - 18 =$ **27** $\$604 - \$129 =$ **28** $3{,}008 - 1{,}275 =$

29 $708 - 99 =$ **30** $2{,}233 - 1{,}675 =$ **31** $6{,}300 - 1{,}582 =$ **32** $4{,}782 - 1{,}834 =$

Use a step-by-step plan to solve.

33 A painter charges $225 to paint a garage. If the paint costs $45, how much can you save if you do the work yourself?

34 A local firehouse received calls 317 days last year. On how many days were no calls received? (1 year = 365 days)

Answer _____

Answer _____

Addition and Subtraction: Two or More Steps

When a problem has more than two steps, work from left to right.

Solve: $231 - 107 + 88 - 125$

1. Start at the left. Subtract the first two numbers $231 - 107$. Line up the digits.

$$231 - 107 = \begin{array}{r} 231 \\ - 107 \\ \hline 124 \end{array}$$

2. Add 88 to the answer from Step 1.

$$\begin{array}{r} 124 \\ + 88 \\ \hline 212 \end{array}$$

3. Subtract 125 from the answer from Step 2.

$$\begin{array}{r} 212 \\ - 125 \\ \hline 87 \end{array}$$

Solve. Work from left to right.

1 $19 + 27 - 13 =$

$$\begin{array}{r} 1 \\ 19 \\ + 27 \\ \hline 46 \end{array} \qquad \begin{array}{r} 46 \\ - 13 \\ \hline 33 \end{array}$$

2 $76 - 19 + 23 =$

3 $56 + 12 - 41 =$

4 $81 - 5 - 32 =$

5 $302 - 118 + 65 =$

6 $\$58 + \$476 - \$109 =$

7 $\$689 - \$47 - \$124 =$

8 $92 - 57 + 76 - 14 =$

9 $37 + 691 - 44 - 246 =$

10 $883 - 219 - 57 + 330 =$

Use a calculator to solve. Work from left to right.

11 $\$36 + \$8 - \$16 =$

12 $90 - 35 + 26 =$

13 $13 + 53 - 28 =$

14 $586 + 442 - 703 =$

15 $\$406 - \$168 + \$635 =$

16 $335 + 921 - 274 =$

Solve.

17 For his son's birthday, Greg bought a birthday cake for $13 and balloons for $4. How much change should he get from $20?

Answer _____

18 A concert hall has 3,000 seats. One Saturday, 1,287 adults and 365 children attended. How many seats in the hall were empty?

Answer _____

Check your answers on pages 190–191.

When a problem has parentheses ( ), do the operation inside the parentheses first.

Solve: $(18 + 83) - (25 + 19)$

1. Add $18 + 83$.

2. Add 25 to 19.

3. Subtract the answers from Steps 1 and 2.

$$\begin{array}{r} 18 \\ + 83 \\ \hline 101 \end{array}$$

$$\begin{array}{r} 25 \\ + 19 \\ \hline 44 \end{array}$$

$$\begin{array}{r} 101 \\ - 44 \\ \hline 57 \end{array}$$

Solve.

1 $256 - (73 - 14) =$

$256 - 59 = 197$

2 $256 - 73 - 14 =$

3 $45 + (121 - 56) =$

4 $45 + 121 - 56 =$

5 $802 - (71 + 26) =$

6 $(802 - 71) + 26 =$

Use a calculator to solve.

7 $24 + 195 - (84 - 32) =$

8 $430 - 65 + (71 - 23) =$

9 $56 + 604 - 122 + 118 =$

10 $500 - (383 - 61) + 72 =$

11 $825 - 247 - (73 + 62) =$

12 $334 - (55 + 14) - 26 =$

Use two or more steps to solve each problem.

13 Vinnie began the day with $30. During the day, he spent $4 on lunch and $17 on books. How much money did Vinnie have left at the end of the day?

14 Alicia had a $20 bill, a $5 bill, and a $1 bill in her wallet. She used the $20 bill to buy gas that cost $7. How much money did Alicia have after she bought the gas?

Answer _____

Answer _____

Check your answers on page 191.

Unit 2 Wrap-up

Below are examples of the skills in this unit and the pages to refer to for practice. Read the examples and work the problems. Then check your answers. If you do well here, go on to the unit review. If not, study the pages listed below before you do the unit review.

Read.

1. 4,368 + 521   (Refer to pages 30–33)

4,368	4,368	4,368	4,368
+ 521	+ 521	+ 521	+ 521
9	89	889	4,889

2. 364 + 2,797   (Refer to pages 34–36)

1	11	1 11	1 11
364	364	364	364
+ 2,797	+ 2,797	+ 2,797	+ 2,797
1	61	161	3,161

3. Estimate: 943 + 89 + 1,549   (Refer to page 37)

$$943 \rightarrow 900$$
$$89 \rightarrow 90$$
$$+ 1,549 \rightarrow + 2,000$$
$$2,990$$

4. 7,384 − 1,062   (Refer to pages 42–45)

Check:

7,384	7,384	7,384	7,384	6,322
− 1,062	− 1,062	− 1,062	− 1,062	+ 1,062
2	22	322	6,322	7,384

5. 543 − 274   (Refer to pages 46–48)

Check:

3 13	13 4 ̷3 13	13 4 ̷3 13	11
5 4̷ 3̷	5̷ 4̷ 3̷	5̷ 4̷ 3̷	269
− 2 7 4	− 2 7 4	− 2 7 4	+ 274
9	6 9	2 6 9	543

6. Estimate: 3,095 − 857   (Refer to page 49)

$$3,095 \rightarrow 3,000$$
$$− 857 \rightarrow − 900$$
$$2,100$$

Solve.

1 6,012 + 23

2 3,648 + 273

3 Estimate: 3,219 + 658 + 71

4 1,306 − 702

5 5,062 − 937

6 Estimate: 759 − 128

Check your answers on page 191.

Unit 2 ◆ Review

Add.

1   64
   + 81

2   45
   + 37

3   567
  + 328

4 3,562
  +   784

5   370
   4,219
  +   47

6 73 + 4 =

7 93 + 78 =

8 395 + 462 =

9 565 + 36 + 2,101 =

Subtract.

10   76
   − 24

11   81
   − 35

12 893
  − 46

13 703
  − 249

14 5,026
  − 1,273

15 58 − 5 =

16 70 − 16 =

17 415 − 162 =

18 7,580 − 237 =

Estimate. Round each number to the lead digit.

19   85
  + 194

20 841
  − 378

21   349
  + 6,512

22 279
  525
  + 3,064

23 7,278
  −   853

24 639 − 92 =

25 94 + 557 =

26 9,137 − 4,822 =

27 87 + 315 + 61 =

Use a step-by-step plan to solve.

28 Last year Harriet's company used 456 reams of white paper and 78 reams of colored paper. How many more reams of white paper than colored paper did her company use?

29 Tino works at a restaurant. One week he earned $160 in salary and $288 in tips. How much did Tino earn in all for that week?

Answer _____

Answer _____

Check your answers on page 191.

Unit 2
55

Solve. Fill in the circle.

30 $75 + 486 =$

Ⓐ 451

Ⓑ 461

Ⓒ 551

Ⓓ 561

31 $3,451 + 2,280 =$

Ⓐ 5,631

Ⓑ 5,731

Ⓒ 6,631

Ⓓ 6,731

32 $948 - 137 =$

Ⓐ 811

Ⓑ 871

Ⓒ 1,071

Ⓓ 1,085

33 $6,081 - 346 =$

Ⓐ 2,621

Ⓑ 5,345

Ⓒ 5,745

Ⓓ 5,735

34 Estimate: $673 + 429$

Ⓐ 100

Ⓑ 1,000

Ⓒ 1,100

Ⓓ 1,200

35 Estimate: $3,512 - 797$

Ⓐ 2,000

Ⓑ 2,200

Ⓒ 3,200

Ⓓ 3,300

36 Yoshi's car odometer reads 5,862 miles. She needs to change the oil at 6,000 miles. How many more miles can Yoshi drive before she needs to change the oil?

Ⓐ 138 miles

Ⓑ 248 miles

Ⓒ 862 miles

Ⓓ 11,862 miles

37 On a weekend bicycle trip, Ellen rode 89 miles on Saturday and 146 miles on Sunday. How many miles did she ride in all?

Ⓐ 57 miles

Ⓑ 67 miles

Ⓒ 135 miles

Ⓓ 235 miles

38 Last year the recycling center processed 578 tons of glass and 243 tons of aluminum. How many more tons of glass than of aluminum were processed?

Ⓐ 235 tons

Ⓑ 335 tons

Ⓒ 811 tons

Ⓓ 821 tons

39 George bought 86 yards of striped material to recover his living room furniture. He also bought 25 yards of plain red material for pillows. How many yards of material did he buy in all?

Ⓐ 51 yards

Ⓑ 61 yards

Ⓒ 111 yards

Ⓓ 121 yards

Check your answers on pages 191–192.

Write the place of the digit 5 in each number.

1 25 **2** 50 **3** 205 **4** 5,738 **5** 14,652 **6** 500

Compare the numbers. Write > or < .

7 13 ☐ 8 **8** 6 ☐ 16 **9** 72 ☐ 27 **10** 314 ☐ 341 **11** 706 ☐ 76

Round each number to the lead digit.

12 58 **13** 23 **14** 87 **15** 286 **16** 2,753 **17** 934

Add or subtract.

18 $\begin{array}{r} 8 \\ + 41 \\ \hline \end{array}$ **19** $\begin{array}{r} 23 \\ - 6 \\ \hline \end{array}$ **20** $\begin{array}{r} 823 \\ + 145 \\ \hline \end{array}$ **21** $\begin{array}{r} 462 \\ - 37 \\ \hline \end{array}$ **22** $\begin{array}{r} 34 \\ 7 \\ + 82 \\ \hline \end{array}$

23 27 + 6 = **24** 78 − 13 = **25** 699 − 128 = **26** 675 + 391 =

27 703 − 128 = **28** 59 + 463 = **29** 3,056 − 1,728 = **30** 792 + 1,408 =

31 Alex ordered 125 square yards of carpet. Then he measured his rooms again and found he needed 140 square yards. How many more square yards of carpet does Alex need to order?

32 On a four-day car trip, the Kickert family drove 145 miles the first day, 209 miles the second day, and 653 miles in the last two days. How many miles did they drive in all?

Answer _____

Answer _____

Check your answers on page 192.

Solve. Fill in the circle.

33 Which number is less than 27?

Ⓐ 17

Ⓑ 72

Ⓒ 207

Ⓓ 702

34 Round 658 to the lead digit.

Ⓐ 600

Ⓑ 650

Ⓒ 660

Ⓓ 700

35 Which digit is in the hundreds place in the number 708?

Ⓐ 0

Ⓑ 7

Ⓒ 8

Ⓓ 100

36 Which statement shows that 403 is greater than 304?

Ⓐ $403 < 430$

Ⓑ $403 < 304$

Ⓒ $304 > 403$

Ⓓ $403 > 304$

37 $342 + 15 + 601 =$

Ⓐ 418

Ⓑ 957

Ⓒ 958

Ⓓ 1,048

38 $967 - 43 =$

Ⓐ 564

Ⓑ 924

Ⓒ 929

Ⓓ 1,010

39 $74 + 308 =$

Ⓐ 112

Ⓑ 372

Ⓒ 382

Ⓓ 1,012

40 $5,908 - 1,369 =$

Ⓐ 4,539

Ⓑ 4,549

Ⓒ 4,611

Ⓓ 7,277

41 A hardware store owner ordered 120 boxes of nails, 180 boxes of screws, and 40 boxes of nuts and bolts. How many boxes were ordered in all?

Ⓐ 310 boxes

Ⓑ 340 boxes

Ⓒ 450 boxes

Ⓓ 650 boxes

42 The regular price of an airplane ticket is $675. Hal finds he can save $123 if he buys the ticket one month in advance. How much will Hal pay if he buys the less expensive ticket?

Ⓐ $543

Ⓑ $552

Ⓒ $798

Ⓓ $807

◆

Unit 3

MULTIPLYING AND DIVIDING WHOLE NUMBERS

▼

When you are working with equal groups, multiplication and division are useful.

You can multiply whole numbers when you need to add the same number over and over. You can divide whole numbers to find how many are in each group.

Describe a situation in which you would multiply numbers.

_____

_____

In this unit you will learn about:
◆ multiplying and dividing by one- and two-digit numbers
◆ renaming numbers when multiplying or dividing
◆ rounding and estimating answers to multiplication and division problems
◆ using a calculator to multiply and divide numbers
◆ using multiplication and division to solve word problems

Multiplication Facts

To multiply larger numbers, you should first know the 100 basic multiplication facts. Complete this fact table, looking for patterns as you work. Check back to Unit 2, if you are unsure how to find the correct answer using the columns and rows.

×	0	1	2	3	4	5	6	7	8	9
0	0	0	0	0	0	0				
1	0	1	2	3	4					
2	0	2	4	6	8					
3	0	3	6	9						
4	0	4	8							
5	0	5								
6										
7										
8										
9	0	9	18	27	36	45	54	63	72	81

Complete the following multiplication facts.

1 $\begin{array}{r} 5 \\ \times\,4 \\ \hline 20 \end{array}$
2 $\begin{array}{r} 6 \\ \times\,7 \\ \hline \end{array}$
3 $\begin{array}{r} 3 \\ \times\,0 \\ \hline \end{array}$
4 $\begin{array}{r} 2 \\ \times\,6 \\ \hline \end{array}$
5 $\begin{array}{r} 7 \\ \times\,5 \\ \hline \end{array}$
6 $\begin{array}{r} 4 \\ \times\,3 \\ \hline \end{array}$

7 $\begin{array}{r} 7 \\ \times\,4 \\ \hline \end{array}$
8 $\begin{array}{r} 3 \\ \times\,7 \\ \hline \end{array}$
9 $\begin{array}{r} 4 \\ \times\,0 \\ \hline \end{array}$
10 $\begin{array}{r} 5 \\ \times\,9 \\ \hline \end{array}$
11 $\begin{array}{r} 8 \\ \times\,2 \\ \hline \end{array}$
12 $\begin{array}{r} 1 \\ \times\,1 \\ \hline \end{array}$

13 $\begin{array}{r} 6 \\ \times\,8 \\ \hline \end{array}$
14 $\begin{array}{r} 3 \\ \times\,3 \\ \hline \end{array}$
15 $\begin{array}{r} 7 \\ \times\,2 \\ \hline \end{array}$
16 $\begin{array}{r} 8 \\ \times\,8 \\ \hline \end{array}$
17 $\begin{array}{r} 3 \\ \times\,2 \\ \hline \end{array}$
18 $\begin{array}{r} 8 \\ \times\,9 \\ \hline \end{array}$

19 $\begin{array}{r} 7 \\ \times\,8 \\ \hline \end{array}$
20 $\begin{array}{r} 5 \\ \times\,0 \\ \hline \end{array}$
21 $\begin{array}{r} 4 \\ \times\,8 \\ \hline \end{array}$
22 $\begin{array}{r} 9 \\ \times\,3 \\ \hline \end{array}$
23 $\begin{array}{r} 7 \\ \times\,1 \\ \hline \end{array}$
24 $\begin{array}{r} 6 \\ \times\,3 \\ \hline \end{array}$

25 $8 \times 7 =$
26 $2 \times 1 =$
27 $9 \times 6 =$
28 $4 \times 8 =$
29 $3 \times 3 =$

30 $6 \times 8 =$
31 $5 \times 6 =$
32 $3 \times 7 =$
33 $7 \times 2 =$
34 $9 \times 4 =$

35 $3 \times 8 =$
36 $0 \times 1 =$
37 $4 \times 6 =$
38 $1 \times 5 =$
39 $6 \times 2 =$

Check your answers on page 193.

Multiplication Equations

Use the multiplication facts table from page 60 to fill in the boxes in these problems.

1 $4 \times \boxed{9} = 36$ **2** $\boxed{} \times 8 = 24$ **3** $5 \times 9 = \boxed{}$ **4** $1 \times \boxed{} = 7$

5 $9 \times 5 = \boxed{}$ **6** $3 \times \boxed{} = 9$ **7** $\boxed{} \times 8 = 72$ **8** $2 \times 4 = \boxed{}$

9 $\boxed{} \times 3 = 15$ **10** $3 \times 2 = \boxed{}$ **11** $2 \times \boxed{} = 16$ **12** $\boxed{} \times 7 = 42$

Remember: an **equation** is a number sentence in which a letter such as n or x stands for the missing number. To solve an equation, find the missing number.

Solve each equation.

13 $2 \times n = 12$
$n = 6$

14 $n \times 3 = 12$

15 $7 \times 7 = n$

16 $3 \times 6 = n$

17 $n \times 1 = 6$

18 $8 \times n = 48$

19 $1 \times n = 9$

20 $n \times 7 = 14$

21 $4 \times 4 = n$

22 $8 \times 7 = n$

23 $n \times 8 = 40$

24 $5 \times n = 0$

25 $n \times 3 = 9$

26 $5 \times n = 45$

27 $8 \times 4 = n$

28 $n \times 6 = 54$

Write an equation to solve each problem.

29 Three times what number is equal to six?

$$3 \times n = 6$$

30 Eight times four is equal to what number?

31 What number times eight is equal to zero?

32 Six times six is equal to what number?

33 What number times two is equal to two?

34 Five times what number is equal to ten?

35 Eight times nine is equal to what number?

36 What number times seven is equal to seven?

Multiplying by One-Digit Numbers

Use the multiplication facts to multiply larger
numbers. Begin by multiplying the ones digits.
Be sure to line up your answers in the correct column.

Multiply: 201 × 4

1. Line up the digits. Multiply
the ones. 4 × 1 = 4 ones.
Write 4 in the ones column.

$$\begin{array}{r} 201 \\ \times\ \ 4 \\ \hline 4 \end{array}$$
↑
4 ones

2. Multiply the tens.
4 × 0 = 0 tens. Write 0
in the tens column.

$$\begin{array}{r} 201 \\ \times\ \ 4 \\ \hline 04 \end{array}$$
↑
0 tens

3. Multiply the hundreds.
4 × 2 = 8 hundreds. Write
8 in the hundreds column.

$$\begin{array}{r} 201 \\ \times\ \ 4 \\ \hline 804 \end{array}$$
↑
8 hundreds

Multiply.

1
$$\begin{array}{r} \$32 \\ \times\ \ 3 \\ \hline \$96 \end{array}$$

2
$$\begin{array}{r} \$10 \\ \times\ \ 2 \end{array}$$

3
$$\begin{array}{r} 21 \\ \times\ \ 4 \end{array}$$

4
$$\begin{array}{r} 13 \\ \times\ \ 1 \end{array}$$

5
$$\begin{array}{r} 153 \\ \times\ \ 1 \end{array}$$

6
$$\begin{array}{r} 432 \\ \times\ \ 2 \end{array}$$

7
$$\begin{array}{r} 101 \\ \times\ \ 6 \end{array}$$

8
$$\begin{array}{r} \$312 \\ \times\ \ 3 \end{array}$$

9
$$\begin{array}{r} \$1,233 \\ \times\ \ 3 \end{array}$$

10
$$\begin{array}{r} 2,324 \\ \times\ \ 2 \end{array}$$

11
$$\begin{array}{r} 3,122 \\ \times\ \ 2 \end{array}$$

12
$$\begin{array}{r} 5,896 \\ \times\ \ 1 \end{array}$$

13 $43 × 2 =

$$\begin{array}{r} \$43 \\ \times\ \ 2 \\ \hline \$86 \end{array}$$

14 1,211 × 3 =

15 34 × $2 =

16 121 × 4 =

17 2,102 × 3 =

18 12 × 4 =

19 123 × 3 =

20 $3,133 × 2 =

21 There are 3 boxes on a shelf in a
sporting goods store. Each box contains 12 baseballs. All together, how
many baseballs are in the boxes?

22 A school bus has 32 seats. Each seat
holds 2 children. How many children
can be seated on the bus?

Answer _____

Answer _____

Check your answers on pages 193–194.

Multiplying by Two-Digit Numbers

When you multiply by a two-digit number, multiply each digit in the top number by each digit in the bottom number. You will get two partial products. A **partial product** is the total you get when you multiply a number by one digit of another number. Add the partial products to get the answer.

Multiply: 43 × 12

1. Line up the digits. Multiply by 2 ones. 2 × 3 = 6 ones. Write 6 in the ones column. 2 × 4 = 8 tens. Write 8 in the tens column.

```
   43
 × 12
   86  ← partial product
```

2. Multiply by 1 ten. 1 × 3 = 3 tens. Write 3 in the tens column under the 8. 1 × 4 = 4 hundreds. Write 4 in the hundreds column to the left of the 3.

```
   43
 × 12
   86
   43  ← partial product
```

3. Add the partial products.

```
    43
  × 12
    86
  + 43
   516
```

Multiply.

1.
```
   $32
 ×  21
    32
 +  64
  $672
```

2.
```
  $423
 ×   12
```

3.
```
    13
 ×  13
```

4.
```
   302
 ×   11
```

5.
```
    10
 ×  75
```

6.
```
   134
 ×  12
```

7.
```
   $13
 ×  23
```

8.
```
  1,202
 ×    14
```

9.
```
   $12
 ×  43
```

10.
```
  1,321
 ×    13
```

11. $12 × 11 =
```
   $12
 ×  11
    12
 +  12
  $132
```

12. 304 × 12 =

13. $11 × 83 =

14. 220 × $14 =

15. A group of 11 friends plans to attend a concert. Tickets for it cost $24 each. Find the cost of tickets for the entire group.

Answer _____

16. An average of 120 customers shop at a supermarket each hour of the day. At that rate, how many customers shop in a 24-hour day?

Answer _____

Check your answers on page 194.

Multiplying by One-Digit Numbers with Renaming

When you multiply two digits, the product is sometimes 10 or more. As in addition, when the answer is 10 or more, rename by carrying to the next column. Multiply first, and then add the carried numbers. You may need to rename several times.

Multiply: 184 × 3

1. Line up the digits. Multiply the 4 by 3 ones. 4 × 3 = 12 ones. Rename 12 as 1 ten and 2 ones. Write 2 in the ones column. Carry 1 ten to the top of the next column.

$$\begin{array}{r} 1 \\ 184 \\ \times\quad 3 \\ \hline 2 \end{array}$$

2. Multiply the 8 tens by 3 ones. 8 × 3 = 24 tens. Then add the carried 1 ten. 24 tens + 1 ten = 25 tens. Rename 25 as 2 hundreds and 5 tens. Write 5 in the tens column. Carry 2 hundreds to the top of the next column.

$$\begin{array}{r} 21 \\ 184 \\ \times\quad 3 \\ \hline 52 \end{array}$$

3. Multiply the 1 hundred by 3 ones. 1 × 3 = 3 hundreds. Then add the carried 2 hundreds. 3 hundreds + 2 hundreds = 5 hundreds. Write 5 in the hundreds column.

$$\begin{array}{r} 21 \\ 184 \\ \times\quad 3 \\ \hline 552 \end{array}$$

Multiply.

1.
$$\begin{array}{r} 11 \\ 356 \\ \times\quad 2 \\ \hline 712 \end{array}$$

2.
$$\begin{array}{r} 14 \\ \times\ 7 \\ \hline \end{array}$$

3.
$$\begin{array}{r} 2{,}140 \\ \times\quad 3 \\ \hline \end{array}$$

4.
$$\begin{array}{r} \$187 \\ \times\quad 4 \\ \hline \end{array}$$

5.
$$\begin{array}{r} 91 \\ \times\ 8 \\ \hline \end{array}$$

6.
$$\begin{array}{r} \$1{,}372 \\ \times\qquad 5 \\ \hline \end{array}$$

7.
$$\begin{array}{r} 905 \\ \times\quad 9 \\ \hline \end{array}$$

8.
$$\begin{array}{r} 83 \\ \times\ 2 \\ \hline \end{array}$$

9.
$$\begin{array}{r} 526 \\ \times\quad 7 \\ \hline \end{array}$$

10.
$$\begin{array}{r} 1{,}315 \\ \times\qquad 6 \\ \hline \end{array}$$

11. 15 × 4 =

$$\begin{array}{r} 2 \\ 15 \\ \times\ 4 \\ \hline 60 \end{array}$$

12. 6,012 × 2 =

13. 828 × $5 =

14. 2,130 × 7 =

15 Each day, the Lakeview School cafeteria needs 130 cartons of milk. The cafeteria is open 5 days a week. How many cartons of milk does the cafeteria need each week?

Answer _____

16 There are 6 people in an elevator. The average weight of each person is 145 pounds. All together, what is the weight of the people in the elevator?

Answer _____

Check your answers on page 194.

Multiplying by Two-Digit Numbers with Renaming

Multiplying by 2-digit multipliers may also require you to rename a number by carrying to the next column. You may need to carry several times.

Multiply: $1,406 \times 53$

1. Line up the digits.

$$\begin{array}{r} 1,406 \\ \times \quad 53 \end{array}$$

2. Multiply by 3 ones. Multiply by 5 tens.

$$\begin{array}{r} 1,406 \\ \times \quad 53 \\ \hline 4218 \\ 7030 \end{array}$$

3. Add the partial products.

$$\begin{array}{r} 1,406 \\ \times \quad 53 \\ \hline 4218 \\ + \ 7030 \\ \hline 74,518 \end{array}$$

Multiply.

1.
$$\begin{array}{r} 47 \\ \times \ 23 \\ \hline 141 \\ + \ 94 \\ \hline 1,081 \end{array}$$

2.
$$\begin{array}{r} 1,806 \\ \times \quad 37 \end{array}$$

3.
$$\begin{array}{r} \$421 \\ \times \quad 56 \end{array}$$

4.
$$\begin{array}{r} 2,307 \\ \times \quad 48 \end{array}$$

5.
$$\begin{array}{r} \$718 \\ \times \quad 45 \end{array}$$

6.
$$\begin{array}{r} \$24 \\ \times \ 61 \end{array}$$

7.
$$\begin{array}{r} 3,219 \\ \times \quad 72 \end{array}$$

8.
$$\begin{array}{r} \$95 \\ \times \ 38 \end{array}$$

9. $903 \times \$14 =$

$$\begin{array}{r} 903 \\ \times \ \$14 \\ \hline 3612 \\ + \ 903 \\ \hline \$12,642 \end{array}$$

10. $8,215 \times 51 =$

11. $70 \times 32 =$

12. The civic auditorium seats 1,450 people. A musical scheduled for 15 performances has completely sold out. How many tickets have been sold?

Answer _____

13. The Greenway Recycling Club estimates that it collects 2,500 cans each month. At this rate, how many cans does the club collect each year? (Hint: There are 12 months in a year.)

Answer _____

Check your answers on page 194.

Multiplying by Multiples and Powers of 10

When you multiply by 10, 100, or multiples of 10, you don't have to write a row of partial products with zeros. There is an easier way to work these problems.

Multiply: 3,425 × 100

1. Multiply by 0 ones. Write zero in the ones column.

$$\begin{array}{r} 3,425 \\ \times\ \ 100 \\ \hline 0 \end{array}$$

2. Multiply by 0 tens. Write zero in the tens column.

$$\begin{array}{r} 3,425 \\ \times\ \ 100 \\ \hline 00 \end{array}$$

3. Multiply by 1 hundred. Write the answer to the left of the zeros. The answer is the same as the top number plus two zeros.

$$\begin{array}{r} 3,425 \\ \times\ \ 100 \\ \hline 342,500 \end{array}$$

Multiply.

1.
$$\begin{array}{r} 61 \\ \times\ 40 \\ \hline 2,440 \end{array}$$

2.
$$\begin{array}{r} 4,231 \\ \times\ \ \ 100 \\ \hline \end{array}$$

3.
$$\begin{array}{r} \$131 \\ \times\ \ \ 80 \\ \hline \end{array}$$

4.
$$\begin{array}{r} \$735 \\ \times\ \ 100 \\ \hline \end{array}$$

5.
$$\begin{array}{r} 1,812 \\ \times\ \ \ \ 70 \\ \hline \end{array}$$

6.
$$\begin{array}{r} \$421 \\ \times\ \ 400 \\ \hline \end{array}$$

7.
$$\begin{array}{r} 54 \\ \times\ 10 \\ \hline \end{array}$$

8.
$$\begin{array}{r} \$213 \\ \times\ \ 300 \\ \hline \end{array}$$

9.
$$\begin{array}{r} 6,231 \\ \times\ \ \ \ 40 \\ \hline \end{array}$$

10.
$$\begin{array}{r} \$476 \\ \times\ \ 800 \\ \hline \end{array}$$

11. 311 × 50 = 15,550

$$\begin{array}{r} 311 \\ \times\ \ 50 \\ \hline 15,550 \end{array}$$

12. 161 × $700 =

13. 103 × 90 =

14. $25 × 20 =

15. 67 × 30 =

16. 420 × 600 =

17. 3,306 × 50 =

18. 833 × 200 =

19. There are 150 reams of paper in an office supply room. One ream contains 500 sheets of paper. How many sheets of paper are in the supply room?

20. There are 80 boxes stacked on a pallet. Each box contains 12 bottles of shampoo. How many bottles of shampoo are on the pallet?

Answer _____

Answer _____

Check your answers on pages 194–195.

Rounding and Estimation

When an exact answer is not necessary, rounding can be used to estimate an answer. Round each number to the lead digit, and then multiply.

Estimate: 28×92

$$92 \rightarrow 90$$
$$\times 28 \rightarrow \times 30$$
$$\overline{2,700}$$

Estimate: 29×713

$$713 \rightarrow 700$$
$$\times 29 \rightarrow \times 30$$
$$\overline{21,000}$$

Estimate: $55 \times 6,875$

$$6,875 \rightarrow 7,000$$
$$\times 55 \rightarrow \times 60$$
$$\overline{420,000}$$

Round each number to the lead digit. Then multiply.

1
$$34 \rightarrow 30$$
$$\times 16 \rightarrow \times 20$$
$$\overline{600}$$

2
$$93$$
$$\times 41$$

3
$$86$$
$$\times 27$$

4
$$72$$
$$\times 49$$

5
$$68$$
$$\times 32$$

6
$$284$$
$$\times 23$$

7
$$459$$
$$\times 36$$

8
$$764$$
$$\times 93$$

9
$$379$$
$$\times 42$$

10
$$917$$
$$\times 35$$

11
$$6,140$$
$$\times 64$$

12
$$2,492$$
$$\times 37$$

13
$$4,097$$
$$\times 58$$

14
$$3,208$$
$$\times 46$$

15 $85 \times 92 =$

16 $304 \times 34 =$

17 $7,982 \times 56 =$

18 $133 \times 66 =$

19 $368 \times 24 =$

20 $1,231 \times 17 =$

21 $852 \times 54 =$

22 $1,638 \times 78 =$

23 $221 \times 11 =$

24 Fast-Oil changed the oil for 39 cars in one day. At this rate, estimate the number of cars Fast-Oil will service in 312 days.

25 Reach Out Cards sold 8,765 greeting cards in May. Estimate the number of greeting cards the company will sell in 1 year.

Answer _____

Answer _____

Check your answers on page 195.

Using a Calculator to Multiply

You can use a calculator to multiply. Always clear your calculator before you begin. Check each number after you enter it to be sure you have not made a mistake. You can also estimate the answer to check yourself.

Multiply: 923 × 42

Press the key.   **Read the display.**

1. Clear the calculator.   → [C]   → [0.]
2. Enter the number to be multiplied. → [9][2][3] → [923.]
3. Press the multiply key.   → [×]   → [923.]
4. Enter the multiplier.   → [4][2]   → [42.]
5. Press the equals key.   → [=]   → [38766.]
   Read the answer.

Use a calculator to solve.

1 76 × 45 = 3,420   **2** 23 × 66 =   **3** 92 × 37 =   **4** 458 × 18 =

5 71 × 365 =   **6** 352 × 913 =   **7** 608 × 244 =   **8** 3,429 × 175 =

9 318 × 54 =   **10** 1,263 × 219 =   **11** 581 × 188 =   **12** 2,046 × 362 =

Solve. Then use a calculator to check your answers.

13 46	**14** 59	**15** 75	**16** 62	**17** 86
× 35	× 24	× 53	× 49	× 75

18 $497	**19** 247	**20** 509	**21** 693	**22** $753
× 82	× 58	× 66	× 19	× 25

23 Jorge earns $1,123 a month. How much does he earn in 12 months?

24 Ellen earns $773 a week. How much does she earn in 52 weeks?

Answer _____

Answer _____

Check your answers on page 195.

Check-up on Multiplication

Multiply.

1 $7 \times \boxed{} = 21$ **2** $\boxed{} \times 9 = 72$ **3** $n \times 4 = 24$ **4** $8 \times 5 = n$

5 $\begin{array}{r} 42 \\ \times\ 11 \\ \hline \end{array}$ **6** $\begin{array}{r} 124 \\ \times\ \ \ 2 \\ \hline \end{array}$ **7** $\begin{array}{r} 100 \\ \times\ \ 75 \\ \hline \end{array}$ **8** $\begin{array}{r} 341 \\ \times\ \ 12 \\ \hline \end{array}$

9 $\begin{array}{r} 63 \\ \times\ \ 4 \\ \hline \end{array}$ **10** $\begin{array}{r} 36 \\ \times\ 22 \\ \hline \end{array}$ **11** $\begin{array}{r} \$480 \\ \times\ \ \ \ 3 \\ \hline \end{array}$ **12** $\begin{array}{r} 2{,}401 \\ \times\ \ \ \ \ 52 \\ \hline \end{array}$

13 $35 \times 4 =$ **14** $601 \times 7 =$ **15** $747 \times 13 =$

16 $28 \times 10 =$ **17** $305 \times 100 =$ **18** $425 \times 100 =$

Estimate. Then multiply.

19 $57 \times 416 =$ **20** $1{,}961 \times 29 =$ **21** $833 \times 38 =$

Estimate _____   Estimate _____   Estimate _____

Answer _____   Answer _____   Answer _____

22 On a 5-day tour, a bus traveled 150 miles each day. How many miles were traveled on the tour in all?

23 A receptionist answers an average of 30 phone calls each hour. At that rate, how many calls does the receptionist answer in an 8-hour day?

Answer _____   Answer _____

69

Check your answers on page 195.

Division Facts

You can use a multiplication table to complete division facts.

$$\begin{array}{c} 5 \\ \times\, 2 \\ \hline 10 \end{array} \longrightarrow \quad 2\,\overline{)\,10} \quad \begin{array}{l} \leftarrow \textbf{quotient} \\ \leftarrow \textbf{dividend} \end{array}$$

$$\uparrow$$
$$\textbf{divisor}$$

To find the answer to a division fact such as 48 ÷ 8, first find the row that begins with the divisor, 8. Next, move to the right until you find the dividend, 48. Then, move up the column to the top of the chart to find the answer, 6.

÷	0	1	2	3	4	5	6	7	8	9
1	0	1	2	3	4	5	6	7	8	9
2	0	2	4	6	8	10	12	14	16	18
3	0	3	6	9	12	15	18	21	24	27
4	0	4	8	12	16	20	24	28	32	36
5	0	5	10	15	20	25	30	35	40	45
6	0	6	12	18	24	30	36	42	48	54
7	0	7	14	21	28	35	42	49	56	63
8	0	8	16	24	32	40	48	56	64	72
9	0	9	18	27	36	45	54	63	72	81

Complete the following division facts.

1 $5\,\overline{)\,30}$ (6) **2** $9\,\overline{)\,72}$ **3** $2\,\overline{)\,6}$ **4** $7\,\overline{)\,35}$ **5** $3\,\overline{)\,12}$ **6** $4\,\overline{)\,8}$

7 $8\,\overline{)\,16}$ **8** $1\,\overline{)\,2}$ **9** $1\,\overline{)\,8}$ **10** $4\,\overline{)\,36}$ **11** $5\,\overline{)\,35}$ **12** $2\,\overline{)\,16}$

13 $4\,\overline{)\,20}$ **14** $8\,\overline{)\,48}$ **15** $7\,\overline{)\,21}$ **16** $6\,\overline{)\,6}$ **17** $7\,\overline{)\,56}$ **18** $9\,\overline{)\,36}$

19 $9\,\overline{)\,45}$ **20** $5\,\overline{)\,15}$ **21** $8\,\overline{)\,72}$ **22** $2\,\overline{)\,12}$ **23** $3\,\overline{)\,0}$ **24** $4\,\overline{)\,4}$

25 36 ÷ 9 = 4 **26** 14 ÷ 2 = **27** 24 ÷ 6 = **28** 24 ÷ 3 = **29** 48 ÷ 8 =

30 42 ÷ 6 = **31** 45 ÷ 5 = **32** 1 ÷ 1 = **33** 10 ÷ 2 = **34** 0 ÷ 5 =

35 24 ÷ 8 = **36** 20 ÷ 4 = **37** 15 ÷ 5 = **38** 54 ÷ 9 = **39** 42 ÷ 7 =

40 28 ÷ 7 = **41** 20 ÷ 5 = **42** 32 ÷ 4 = **43** 12 ÷ 4 = **44** 40 ÷ 5 =

Check your answers on page 196.

Division Equations

Use the division facts table from page 70 to fill in the boxes in these division problems.

Solve each equation.

1 $4 \div \boxed{4} = 1$ **2** $\boxed{} \div 7 = 5$ **3** $25 \div 5 = \boxed{}$ **4** $56 \div \boxed{} = 7$

5 $18 \div 2 = \boxed{}$ **6** $63 \div \boxed{} = 9$ **7** $\boxed{} \div 8 = 9$ **8** $36 \div 6 = \boxed{}$

9 $\boxed{} \div 3 = 5$ **10** $10 \div 5 = \boxed{}$ **11** $16 \div \boxed{} = 4$ **12** $\boxed{} \div 2 = 4$

13 $27 \div \boxed{} = 3$ **14** $72 \div 8 = \boxed{}$ **15** $\boxed{} \div 2 = 7$ **16** $\boxed{} \div 7 = 6$

Solve each equation.

17 $15 \div n = 3$
$n = 5$

18 $21 \div 7 = n$

19 $n \div 3 = 2$

20 $7 \div 7 = n$

21 $n \div 8 = 2$

22 $49 \div n = 7$

23 $18 \div n = 6$

24 $n \div 1 = 6$

25 $18 \div 6 = n$

26 $n \div 2 = 6$

27 $14 \div 7 = n$

28 $21 \div n = 7$

29 $64 \div n = 8$

30 $n \div 4 = 4$

31 $n \div 9 = 5$

32 $54 \div 9 = n$

33 $n \div 7 = 3$

34 $3 \div n = 1$

35 $16 \div 8 = n$

36 $n \div 2 = 5$

Write an equation to solve each problem.

37 Three divided by what number is equal to one?

$3 \div n = 1$

38 Twenty-eight divided by four is equal to what number?

39 What number divided by four is equal to eight?

40 Twelve divided by six is equal to what number?

41 What number divided by five is equal to eight?

42 Forty divided by what number is equal to five?

Check your answers on page 196.

Dividing by One-Digit Numbers

Use the division facts when you divide. Be sure to put each answer in the correct column.

Divide: 186 ÷ 3

1. Divide. Since you can't divide 1 by 3 evenly, divide 18 by 3. 18 ÷ 3 = 6. Write the 6 above the 8.

$$\begin{array}{r} 6 \\ 3\overline{)186} \end{array}$$

2. Divide again. 6 ÷ 3 = 2. Write the 2 above the 6.

$$\begin{array}{r} 62 \\ 3\overline{)186} \end{array}$$

3. Check by multiplying the answer, 62, by the number you divided by, 3.

$$\begin{array}{r} 62 \\ 3\overline{)186} \end{array} \longleftrightarrow \begin{array}{r} 62 \\ \times\ 3 \\ \hline 186 \end{array}$$

Divide. Use multiplication to check your answers.

1 $\begin{array}{r} 74 \\ 2\overline{)148} \end{array}$ $\begin{array}{r} 74 \\ \times\ 2 \\ \hline 148 \end{array}$

2 $3\overline{)\$273}$

3 $8\overline{)88}$

4 $5\overline{)2,055}$

5 $5\overline{)555}$

6 $6\overline{)3,066}$

7 $6\overline{)486}$

8 $7\overline{)\$147}$

9 $9\overline{)\$3,699}$

10 $3\overline{)96}$

11 $2\overline{)82}$

12 $6\overline{)426}$

13 156 ÷ 3 =

14 $284 ÷ 4 =

15 1,684 ÷ 4 =

16 186 ÷ 2 =

17 A charity group has 88 presents to distribute to 8 children. Each child is to receive the same number of presents. How many presents should each child receive?

18 An apple orchard gives 2 free apples to each customer. Last weekend 128 apples were given away. How many customers went to the apple orchard last weekend?

Answer _____

Answer _____

Unit 3

72

Check your answers on page 196.

Dividing by One-Digit Numbers with Remainders

Sometimes you will have an amount left over after you have finished dividing two numbers. The amount left over is called a **remainder**. A remainder is part of the answer. Use the letter R to represent a remainder.

$$\begin{array}{r} 2\ R1 \\ 4\overline{)9} \\ -8 \\ \hline 1 \end{array}$$

Divide: 189 ÷ 4

1. Divide. Since 18 ÷ 4 is not a basic fact, use the next lower basic fact, 16 ÷ 4, instead. 16 ÷ 4 = 4, so 18 ÷ 4 = 4 with an amount left over. Write the 4 above the 8. Multiply. 4 × 4 = 16. Write the 16 under the 18 and subtract. The amount left is 2.

$$\begin{array}{r} 4 \\ 4\overline{)189} \\ -16 \\ \hline 2 \end{array}$$

2. Divide again by bringing down the next digit, 9. The 9 brought down beside the 2 makes 29. 29 ÷ 4 = 7, plus an amount left over. Multiply. 7 × 4 = 28. Write the 28 under the 29 and subtract. 29 − 28 = 1. The remainder is 1.

$$\begin{array}{r} 47\ R1 \\ 4\overline{)189} \\ -16 \\ \hline 29 \\ -28 \\ \hline 1 \end{array}$$

3. Check your answer by multiplying. Add the remainder.

$$\begin{array}{r} 47 \\ \times\ 4 \\ \hline 188 \\ +\ 1 \\ \hline 189 \end{array}$$

Divide. Use multiplication to check your answers.

1
$$\begin{array}{r} 27\ R5 \\ 6\overline{)167} \\ -12 \\ \hline 47 \\ -42 \\ \hline 5 \end{array} \qquad \begin{array}{r} 27 \\ \times\ 6 \\ \hline 162 \\ +\ 5 \\ \hline 167 \end{array}$$

2 $4\overline{)295}$

3 $7\overline{)317}$

4 $2\overline{)35}$

5 $3\overline{)71}$

6 $5\overline{)493}$

7 $9\overline{)257}$

8 $8\overline{)99}$

9 187 ÷ 4 =

10 87 ÷ 7 =

11 98 ÷ 6 =

12 228 ÷ 9 =

Check your answers on page 196.

Zeros in Division

When you divide a number with one or more zeros in the dividend
follow the steps you follow when solving other division problems.
Bring down the next digit, even if it is a zero.

Divide: 1,302 ÷ 3

1. Divide. 13 ÷ 3 = 4, plus an amount left over. Multiply, subtract, and bring down the 0.

```
      4
3) 1,302
  - 12↓
     10
```

2. Divide. 10 ÷ 3 = 3, plus an amount left over. Multiply and subtract. Bring down the 2.

```
     43
3) 1,302
  - 12
     10
    - 9↓
     12
```

3. Divide. 12 ÷ 3 = 4. Multiply and subtract. There is no remainder. Check your answer.

```
    434
3) 1,302        434
  - 12        ×   3
     10       1,302
    - 9
     12
   - 12
      0
```

Divide. Use multiplication to check your answers.

1
```
    402 R1
3) 1,207        402
  - 12        ×   3
    007       1,206
  -   6      +    1
      1       1,207
```

2 4) 2,432

3 6) 3,083

4 7) 1,449

5 1,808 ÷ 2 =

6 $2,550 ÷ 3 =

7 1,062 ÷ 9 =

8 1,608 ÷ 8 =

9 A large supermarket received a delivery of 600 tomatoes. The tomatoes will be packaged in groups of 4. How many packages will there be?

Answer _____

10 A total of 2,400 guests were served at 3 fundraising dinners. Each dinner served the same number of guests. How many guests were served at each dinner?

Answer _____

Check your answers on page 197.

Dividing by Two-Digit Numbers

When you divide a two-digit number, first estimate, then multiply.
If the answer is too large, try dividing by a smaller number.

Divide: $807 \div 25$

1. Estimate how many times 2, the first digit of 25, goes into 8, the first digit of 807. Because 2 goes into 8 exactly 4 times, try 4.

$4 \times 25 = 100$, and 100 is greater than 80, so 4 is too large.

$$\begin{array}{r} 4 \\ 25\overline{)807} \\ -100 \\ \hline \end{array}$$

2. Try the next smaller number, 3. $3 \times 25 = 75$. Subtract 75 from 80. $80 - 75 = 5$. Bring down the 7.

$$\begin{array}{r} 3 \\ 25\overline{)807} \\ -75 \\ \hline 57 \end{array}$$

3. Decide how many times the first digit of 25 goes into the first digit of 57. Because 2 goes into 5 about 2 times, try 2.

$2 \times 25 = 50$. Since 50 is less than 57, subtract. $57 - 50 = 7$. The remainder is 7. Check your answer.

$$\begin{array}{r} 32 \text{ R7} \\ 25\overline{)807} \\ -75 \\ \hline 57 \\ -50 \\ \hline 7 \end{array} \qquad \begin{array}{r} 32 \\ \times 25 \\ \hline 160 \\ +64 \\ \hline 800 \\ +7 \\ \hline 807 \end{array}$$

Divide. Use multiplication to check your answers.

1.
$$\begin{array}{r} 14 \text{ R2} \\ 39\overline{)548} \\ -39 \\ \hline 158 \\ -156 \\ \hline 2 \end{array} \qquad \begin{array}{r} 14 \\ \times 39 \\ \hline 126 \\ +42 \\ \hline 546 \\ +2 \\ \hline 548 \end{array}$$

2. $24\overline{)771}$

3. $53\overline{)639}$

4. $12\overline{)558}$

5. $912 \div 43 =$

6. $864 \div 61 =$

7. $\$962 \div 26 =$

8. $930 \div 34 =$

9. At an engineering firm, 14 employees worked a total of 490 hours last week. Each employee worked the same number of hours. How many hours did each employee work?

Answer _____

10. A textbook contains 330 pages that are divided into chapters that are each 22 pages long. How many chapters are in the textbook?

Answer _____

Check your answers on page 197.

Problem Solving

When you are solving word problems, certain words called key words act as a signal. *Key* words tell you what operation to use to solve the problem.

❖ STRATEGY: **Choose the operation.**

1. Read the problem carefully. Look for key words to help you decide what operation to use. See the list below.

2. Set up the problem and solve it. Write your answer.

3. Read the problem again to check that your answer makes sense.

Addition	**Subtraction**	**Multiplication**	**Division**
all together	decrease	in all	average
and	difference	of	cut
in all	left	product	each
more	less than	(times) as much	equally
plus	more than	total	every
sum	remain	twice	half
total		whole	split

Exercise 1: **Write the key word or words and operation you would use to solve each problem. Do not solve.**

1 A bag of pretzels contains 36 pretzels. Another bag contains twice as many. How many pretzels does that bag contain?

Key word(s) ___twice as many___

Operation ___multiplication___

2 White potatoes cost $.85 per pound. Red potatoes cost $.99 per pound. What is the difference in cost between white and red potatoes?

Key word(s) _____

Operation _____

3 A small box of cereal weighs 24 ounces. A large box weighs 48 ounces. How much do the boxes weigh in all?

Key word(s) _____

Operation _____

4 A case of 48 grapefruit will be split equally between 3 families. How many grapefruit will each family receive?

Key word(s) _____

Operation _____

Exercise 2: **For each problem, write the operation. Then solve.**

5 Tom bought 15 items at the grocery store. Martita bought 45 items. How many more items did Martita buy than Tom?

Operation _____

Answer _____

6 Angela has 3 coupons that are each worth $1 off. What is the total amount she will save if she uses all 3 of the coupons?

Operation _____

Answer _____

7 A pound of ham is on sale for $4. A pound of cheese costs $2. How much will it cost all together to buy a pound of each?

Operation _____

Answer _____

8 Eric bought a carton of 12 eggs at the store. After arriving home, he found that 3 eggs were broken. How many eggs were unbroken?

Operation _____

Answer _____

9 Kathy bought 128 ounces of laundry detergent. If she shares the detergent equally with her mother, how many ounces of detergent will each person get?

Operation _____

Answer _____

10 Richard spent $35 at the grocery store. Rochelle spent about 4 times as much. About how much did Rochelle spend?

Operation _____

Answer _____

11 A frozen dinner contains 760 calories. Of these, 60 calories are from fat. How many calories are from other ingredients?

Operation _____

Answer _____

12 A slice of apple pie contains 350 calories. If 2 people were to cut the slice in half and eat it, how many calories would each person eat?

Operation _____

Answer _____

Check your answers on page 197.

Rounding and Estimation

When an exact answer is not necessary, rounding can be used to estimate the quotient of a division problem. Round each number to the lead digit and then divide.

Estimate: $629 \div 21$

1. Round 21 to the nearest ten and 629 to the nearest hundred.

$$21\overline{)629} \rightarrow 20\overline{)600}$$

2. Then divide. 600 divided by 20 is exactly 30.

$$\begin{array}{r} 30 \\ 20\overline{)600} \\ -60 \\ \hline 00 \\ -0 \\ \hline 0 \end{array}$$

Round each number to the lead digit. Then divide.

1 $28\overline{)312} \rightarrow$ $\begin{array}{r} 10 \\ 30\overline{)300} \\ -30 \\ \hline 00 \\ -0 \\ \hline 0 \end{array}$

2 $42\overline{)\$785}$

3 $13\overline{)248}$

4 $\$606 \div 58 =$

5 $959 \div 19 =$

6 $639 \div 22 =$

7 A company paid about $825 in overtime pay to 19 different employees. Each employee earned the same amount of overtime pay. About how much overtime pay did each employee earn?

Answer _____

8 A music store has 950 music tapes displayed on 9 wall racks. Each wall rack contains about the same number of tapes. About how many tapes does each rack contain?

Answer _____

9 Jeremy has collected 192 car magazines. The magazines are displayed on 8 shelves. If each shelf displays the same number of magazines, about how many magazines are on each shelf?

Answer _____

10 A library has 575 mystery books that are organized on 28 different shelves. If each shelf displays about the same number of books, how many books are on each shelf?

Answer _____

Check your answers on page 197.

Using a Calculator to Divide

You can use a calculator to divide. Always clear your calculator before you begin. Check each number after you enter it to be sure you have not made a mistake. You can also estimate the answer to check yourself.

Divide: $378 \div 18$

Press the key.		Read the display.
1. Clear the calculator.	→ [C] →	[0.]
2. Enter the number to be divided.	→ [3][7][8] →	[378.]
3. Press the divide key.	→ [÷] →	[378.]
4. Enter the number you are dividing by.	→ [1][8] →	[18.]
5. Press the equals key.	→ [=] →	[21.]
Read the answer.		

Use a calculator to solve.

1 $28\overline{)896}$ = 32   **2** $32\overline{)\$576}$ =   **3** $19\overline{)399}$ =   **4** $38\overline{)760}$ =

5 $53\overline{)\$2,650}$ =   **6** $15\overline{)615}$ =   **7** $45\overline{)810}$ =   **8** $22\overline{)\$1,980}$ =

9 $1,458 \div 6 =$ **10** $1,614 \div 3 =$ **11** $18,942 \div 3 =$ **12** $3,225 \div 5 =$

13 $2,858 \div 2 =$ **14** $1,900 \div 20 =$ **15** $1,000 \div 50 =$ **16** $83,270 \div 10 =$

Solve. Then use a calculator to check your answers.

17 $624 \div 8 =$ **18** $\$1,840 \div 40 =$ **19** $\$1,092 \div 13 =$ **20** $480 \div 8 =$

21 A monthly allowance of $60 is split equally between 4 children. What is the allowance of each child?

22 Robin made a long distance phone call to a friend. The call cost $12. If Robin and her friend each decide to pay half of the cost, how much should each person pay?

Answer _____

Answer _____

Check your answers on page 198.

Check-up on Division

Divide. Use multiplication to check your answers.

1 $6\overline{)186}$ **2** $120 \div 4 =$ **3** $8\overline{)341}$ **4** $298 \div 14 =$

5 $51\overline{)1,430}$ **6** $3,744 \div 36 =$ **7** $\$2,706 \div 22 =$ **8** $50\overline{)3,249}$

Estimate. Then divide.

9 $21\overline{)609}$ **10** $528 \div 48 =$ **11** $32\overline{)928}$

Estimate _____ Estimate _____ Estimate _____

For each problem, write the operation. Then solve.

12 Only 65 fans attended Parkland School's first soccer match of the season. Three times as many fans attended Parkland's first playoff match at the end of the season. How many fans attended the first playoff match?

13 Reggie rides his exercise bike each morning and each evening for the same number of minutes. If Reggie rides for 60 minutes every day, how many minutes does he ride each morning and each evening?

Operation _____ Operation _____

Answer _____ Answer _____

Unit 3

80

Check your answers on page 198.

Order of Operations

When a problem asks you to use more than one operation, always follow this order of operations to solve the problem.

Step 1: Do any operations in parentheses ( ) first.

Step 2: Next, multiply and divide working from left to right.

Step 3: Finally, add and subtract working from left to right.

Solve: $8 + 6 \div 2$

1. First, do any operations shown in ( ). There are none. Move to the next step.

$8 + 6 \div 2 =$

2. Do all multiplications and divisions. There is one division. $6 \div 2 = 3$.

$8 + 6 \div 2 =$

$8 + 3 =$

3. Do all additions and subtractions. There is one addition. $8 + 3 = 11$.

$8 + 6 \div 2 =$

$8 + 3 = 11$

Solve.

1 $(4 + 5) \times 2 =$
$9 \times 2 = 18$

2 $4 + 5 \times 2 =$
$4 + 10 = 14$

3 $6 + 2 \times 1 =$

4 $7 - 4 + 2 =$

5 $10 \div (2 + 3) =$

6 $5 \times 4 - 1 =$

7 $8 + 2 \div 2 =$

8 $18 \div 6 - 3 =$

9 $(14 - 8) \times 1 =$

10 $12 + 6 \div 2 =$

11 $21 + 9 \div 3 =$

12 $15 \times 2 - 1 =$

13 $12 \div 6 - 2 =$

14 $16 \div (4 + 4) =$

15 $(7 + 0) \times 7 =$

16 $9 \times 5 - 5 =$

17 $(24 - 12) \times 2 =$

18 $30 + 6 \div 2 =$

19 $14 + 8 \div 2 =$

20 $33 + 12 \div 3 =$

21 $(75 - 30) \div 9 =$

22 $11 + 6 \times 8 =$

23 $65 - 10 \div 2 =$

24 $6 + 4 \times 3 =$

Check your answers on page 198.

Calculators and Order of Operations

Calculators can be used to solve problems that ask you to do more than one operation. Follow the order of operations.

Solve: $128 + (192 \div 24)$

Press the key.   **Read the display.**

1. Clear the calculator. → C → [0.]
2. Do division first.
3. Enter the number 192. → 1 9 2 → [192.]
4. Press the divide sign. → ÷ → [192.]
5. Enter the number 24. → 2 4 → [24.]
6. Press the equals sign. → = → [8.]

   Read the answer. Remember that the operation inside ( ) gives an answer of 8.

Complete the problem: $128 + (8)$

Press the key.   **Read the display.**

1. Clear the calculator. → C → [0.]
2. Enter the number 128. → 1 2 8 → [128.]
3. Press the plus sign. → + → [128.]
4. Enter the number 8, your answer from the first step of the problem. → 8 → [8.]
5. Press the equals sign. → = → [136.]

   Read the answer.

Solve using a calculator. Follow the order of operations.

1 $144 \div 12 - 9 =$
   $12 \quad - 9 = 3$

2 $107 + 14 \times 8 =$

3 $200 \div 25 - 5 =$

4 $318 - (17 \times 12) =$

5 $8 \times 48 \div 24 =$

6 $85 + 10 \div 5 =$

7 $765 + 113 - 52 =$

8 $16 \times 18 \div 3 =$

9 $405 \div 9 + 36 =$

10 $55 \times (84 - 29) =$

11 $(34 \times 42) \div 7 =$

12 $950 - 672 + 222 =$

Check your answers on page 198.

Unit 3 Wrap-up

Below are examples of the skills in this unit and the pages to refer to for practice. Read the examples and work the problems. Then check your answers. If you do well here, go on to the unit review. If not, study the pages listed below before you do the unit review.

Read.		Solve.

Read.

1. $6 \times n = 42$ (Refer to pages 60–61)

$n = 7$

2. 231×3 (Refer to page 62)

```
  231        231        231
×   3      ×   3      ×   3
    3         93        693
```

3. $\$14 \times 11$ (Refer to page 63)

```
  $14        $14        $14
× 11       × 11       × 11
  14         14         14
             14       + 14
                      $154
```

4. 193×4 (Refer to page 64)

```
    1         31         31
  193        193        193
×   4      ×   4      ×   4
    2         72        772
```

5. 268×100 (Refer to page 66)

```
  268        268        268
× 100      × 100      × 100
    0         00      26,800
```

Solve.

1 $4 \times n = 32$

2 201×4

3 $\$42 \times 12$

4 157×4

5 516×100

Check your answers on page 198.

Read.

6. Round and estimate: (Refer to page 67)
193 × 42. Then find the exact answer.

$$
\begin{array}{rcl}
193 & \to & 200 \\
\times\ 42 & \to & \times\ 40 \\
\hline
& & 8,000
\end{array}
$$

$$
\begin{array}{r}
193 \\
\times\ 42 \\
\hline
386 \\
+\ 772 \\
\hline
8,106
\end{array}
$$

---

7. $28 \div 4 = 7$ (Refer to page 70)

---

8. $36 \div \boxed{9} = 4$ (Refer to page 71)

---

9. $189 \div 9$ (Refer to page 72)

Use multiplication to check your answer.

$$
\begin{array}{r}
2 \\
9\overline{)189}
\end{array}
\qquad
\begin{array}{r}
21 \\
9\overline{)189}
\end{array}
\qquad
\begin{array}{r}
21 \\
\times\ 9 \\
\hline
189
\end{array}
$$

---

10. $108 \div 5$ (Refer to page 73)

Use multiplication to check your answer.

$$
\begin{array}{r}
2 \\
5\overline{)108} \\
-\ 10 \\
\hline
0
\end{array}
\qquad
\begin{array}{r}
21\ R3 \\
5\overline{)108} \\
10 \\
\hline
08 \\
-\ 05 \\
\hline
3
\end{array}
\qquad
\begin{array}{r}
21 \\
\times\ 5 \\
\hline
105 \\
+\ \ 3 \\
\hline
108
\end{array}
$$

---

11. $7 + 3 \times 2$ (Refer to pages 81–82)

$7 + \quad 6 \quad = 13$

Solve.

6 Round and estimate 323×57.
Then find the exact answer.

$$
\begin{array}{rcl}
323 & \to & \\
\times\ 57 & \to &
\end{array}
$$

---

7 $12 \div 6 =$

---

8 $21 \div \square = 7$

---

9 $217 \div 7$ Use multiplication to check your answer.

$7\overline{)217}$

---

10 $217 \div 8$ Use multiplication to check your answer.

$8\overline{)217}$

---

11 $10 \div 2 - 1 =$

Check your answers on page 198.

Solve each equation.

1 $6 \times n = 42$ **2** $n \times 5 = 35$ **3** $9 \times n = 27$ **4** $n \times 2 = 18$

5 $n \div 4 = 4$ **6** $24 \div n = 3$ **7** $32 \div n = 8$ **8** $n \div 7 = 9$

Multiply.

9 $\begin{array}{r} 48 \\ \times\ 6 \\ \hline \end{array}$ **10** $\begin{array}{r} 512 \\ \times\ \ 4 \\ \hline \end{array}$ **11** $\begin{array}{r} 26 \\ \times\ 32 \\ \hline \end{array}$ **12** $\begin{array}{r} 403 \\ \times\ \ 81 \\ \hline \end{array}$

13 $52 \times 8 =$ **14** $5 \times 911 =$ **15** $40 \times 84 =$ **16** $3,452 \times 60 =$

Divide.

17 $5\overline{)135}$ **18** $4\overline{)93}$ **19** $6\overline{)4,027}$ **20** $14\overline{)589}$

21 $96 \div 6 =$ **22** $308 \div 7 =$ **23** $1,839 \div 5 =$ **24** $7,843 \div 32 =$

25 An 8-pound block of cheddar cheese costs $16. How much is the cheese per pound?

26 During a sale, a store sold 125 clock radios for $19 each. How much money did the store receive for the clock radios?

Answer _____   Answer _____

Solve. Fill in the circle.

27 $3 \times 592 =$
- (A) 1,576
- (B) 1,766
- (C) 1,776
- (D) 1,876

28 $58 \times 91 =$
- (A) 4,578
- (B) 5,078
- (C) 5,278
- (D) 5,288

29 $30 \times 367 =$
- (A) 1,110
- (B) 10,110
- (C) 11,010
- (D) 110,010

30 $439 \div 5 =$
- (A) 85 R7
- (B) 87 R4
- (C) 89
- (D) 89 R3

31 $4,064 \div 8 =$
- (A) 508
- (B) 580
- (C) 580 R5
- (D) 585

32 $794 \div 17 =$
- (A) 40 R14
- (B) 45 R29
- (C) 46 R2
- (D) 46 R12

33 Mrs. Salazar wants to save $1,000 to buy a computer. She plans to save $25 a week. How many weeks will it take her to save the money for the computer?
- (A) 10
- (B) 20
- (C) 25
- (D) 40

34 Roberta earns $263 a week. How much will she earn all together in 16 weeks?
- (A) $279
- (B) $2,308
- (C) $4,208
- (D) $4,408

35 If a box holds 50 envelopes, how many envelopes will there be in 28 boxes?
- (A) 22
- (B) 78
- (C) 140
- (D) 1,400

36 A case holds 24 bottles of soda. How many cases will 216 bottles fill?
- (A) 9
- (B) 24
- (C) 216
- (D) 5,184

Check your answers on page 199.

Compare the numbers. Write > or < .

1 9 ☐ 21   **2** 30 ☐ 13   **3** 64 ☐ 604   **4** 112 ☐ 97   **5** 453 ☐ 543

Round each number to the nearest hundred.

6 145   **7** 98   **8** 450   **9** 729   **10** 987

Add or subtract.

11
$$\begin{array}{r} 37 \\ -\ 9 \\ \hline \end{array}$$

12
$$\begin{array}{r} 86 \\ -24 \\ \hline \end{array}$$

13
$$\begin{array}{r} \$472 \\ +\ 69 \\ \hline \end{array}$$

14
$$\begin{array}{r} 903 \\ -287 \\ \hline \end{array}$$

15
$$\begin{array}{r} 5,352 \\ +\ 881 \\ \hline \end{array}$$

16
$$\begin{array}{r} \$1,488 \\ +\ 366 \\ \hline \end{array}$$

17
$$\begin{array}{r} 2,733 \\ -\ 895 \\ \hline \end{array}$$

18
$$\begin{array}{r} 4,831 \\ -\ 965 \\ \hline \end{array}$$

19
$$\begin{array}{r} \$135 \\ +\ 76 \\ \hline \end{array}$$

20
$$\begin{array}{r} 433 \\ +765 \\ \hline \end{array}$$

21 5 + 53 =   **22** $51 − $26 =   **23** 534 + 205 =   **24** 417 + 82 + 310 =

Multiply or divide.

25 32 × $23 =   **26** 124 × 63 =

27
$$\begin{array}{r} 54 \\ \times 10 \\ \hline \end{array}$$

28
$$\begin{array}{r} \$143 \\ \times\ 21 \\ \hline \end{array}$$

29 4)‾32   **30** 15)‾405   **31** 2,835 ÷ 7 =   **32** 1,040 ÷ 12 =

33 Sid is trying to limit the calories he eats each day to 1,800. If he eats 675 calories at breakfast and 380 calories at lunch, how many calories should he eat for dinner?

34 A state park has 136 overnight camp-sites. A maximum of 4 campers can stay at each site. How many campers can stay at the park overnight?

Answer _____

Answer _____

Check your answers on page 199.

Solve. Fill in the circle.

35 Which of these numbers has the digit 4 in the tens place?

Ⓐ 4

Ⓑ 74

Ⓒ 404

Ⓓ 2,943

36 Which of these statements shows that 837 is less than 962?

Ⓐ $837 > 962$

Ⓑ $962 < 837$

Ⓒ $837 > 837$

Ⓓ $837 < 962$

37 $47 + 568 =$

Ⓐ 605

Ⓑ 615

Ⓒ 975

Ⓓ 1,038

38 $3,026 - 975 =$

Ⓐ 1,301

Ⓑ 2,051

Ⓒ 2,151

Ⓓ 4,001

39 Which of these problems has an answer of 4?

Ⓐ $(8 + 7) \div 3 =$

Ⓑ $(16 - 2) \times 2 =$

Ⓒ $1 + (9 \div 3) =$

Ⓓ $(10 - 4) \div 2 =$

40 What number divided by eight is equal to nine?

Ⓐ 56

Ⓑ 64

Ⓒ 72

Ⓓ 81

41 What number times six is equal to twenty-four?

Ⓐ 3

Ⓑ 4

Ⓒ 6

Ⓓ 8

42 Which of these basic facts has an answer of 8?

Ⓐ $4 \div 4 =$

Ⓑ $8 \times 0 =$

Ⓒ $8 \div 1 =$

Ⓓ $4 - 4 =$

43 It took Sharon 31 minutes to print her monthly report with her old printer. Her new printer can do the same job in 17 minutes. How many minutes faster is the new printer?

Ⓐ 14 minutes

Ⓑ 24 minutes

Ⓒ 46 minutes

Ⓓ 48 minutes

44 Lenny delivers packages Monday through Saturday. He usually makes about 40 different stops each day. At that rate, about how many stops does he make each week?

Ⓐ 100

Ⓑ 200

Ⓒ 240

Ⓓ 280

Check your answers on pages 199–200.

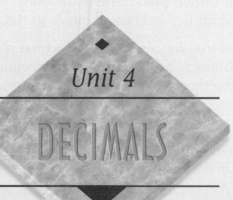

Unit 4

DECIMALS

Decimals are numbers used to show quantities less than 1 or quantities between two whole numbers. Decimals are used to show money amounts.

Describe everyday situations where decimals are used.

_____

_____

What you already know about place value and operations using whole numbers will help you learn about decimals.

In this unit you will learn about:
- identifying the place values of digits in decimals
- writing money amounts as decimals
- rounding decimals and money amounts
- adding, subtracting, multiplying, and dividing decimals
- using decimal computation to solve word problems

Decimal Place Names and Values

You have learned that whole numbers are made up of digits. Each digit is in a certain place. The places have different values, and the value of a digit depends on its place in the number.

The same is true for decimals. A **decimal** shows part of a whole number. Numbers to the right of the decimal point are used to show amounts less than 1. Read this place value chart.

The number 45.017 has been placed in the chart. The chart shows that the digit 4 is in the tens place, the digit 5 is in the ones place, the digit 0 is in the tenths place, the digit 1 is in the hundredths place, and the digit 7 is in the thousandths place.

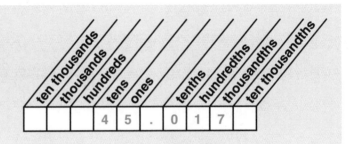

Write each number in the place value chart at the right. Then write each digit in the correct number group.

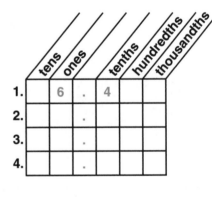

1 6.4

  <u>6</u> ones
  <u>4</u> tenths

2 1.73

  ___ ones
  ___ tenths
  ___ hundredths

3 10.28

  ___ tens
  ___ ones
  ___ tenths
  ___ hundredths

4 0.955

  ___ ones
  ___ tenths
  ___ hundredths
  ___ thousandths

In each number, write the digit in the tenths place.

5 456.71   **6** 0.9   **7** 2.071   **8** 9.3   **9** 0.18   **10** 26.428

  <u>7</u>   ___   ___   ___   ___   ___

11 76.33   **12** 4.684   **13** 0.59   **14** 1.10   **15** 21.05   **16** 119.71

  ___   ___   ___   ___   ___   ___

In each number, write the digit in the hundredths place.

17 0.306   **18** 43.68   **19** 2.71   **20** 0.254   **21** 0.042   **22** 37.329

  <u>0</u>   ___   ___   ___   ___   ___

23 418.001   **24** 4.836   **25** .01   **26** 25.703   **27** 8.06   **28** .49

  ___   ___   ___   ___   ___   ___

Check your answers on page 200.

Writing Decimals

To write a decimal in words, use the place name of the right-hand digit. Use the word *and* for the decimal point.

17.6

Write the whole number in words. Write *and* for the decimal point. The right-hand digit is in the tenths place.

17.6 =
seventeen and six tenths

17.06

The right-hand digit is in the hundredths place.

17.06 =
seventeen and six hundredths

17.60

The right-hand digit is in the hundredths place.

17.60 =
seventeen and sixty hundredths

Put each decimal in the chart to the right. Then write each decimal in words.

	hundreds	tens	ones	.	tenths	hundredths	thousandths	ten thousandths
1.	1	4		.	5			
2.				.				
3.				.				
4.				.				
5.				.				
6.				.				
7.				.				
8.				.				
9.				.				
10.				.				

1 14.5   fourteen and five tenths

2 8.225 _____

3 30.2 _____

4 7.04 _____

5 508.01 _____

6 0.63 _____

7 4.9 _____

8 40.108 _____

9 210.050 _____

10 0.0086 _____

Write each number as a decimal.

11 seventy and thirty-three hundredths

_____ 70.33 _____

12 nine and fifty-two thousandths

_____

13 twenty-six hundredths

_____

14 four hundred nine thousandths

_____

15 one and seven tenths

_____

16 ten and sixteen thousandths

_____

Check your answers on pages 200–201.

Zeros and Decimals

Zeros can be added to the right of a decimal without changing the value of a number.

$$9 = 9.0 \qquad\qquad \$20 = \$20.00 \qquad .5 = .50 = .500$$

Zeros can be dropped from the right of a decimal without changing the value of a number.

$$14.0 = 14 \qquad\qquad \$3.00 = \$3 \qquad 7.00 = 7.0 = 7$$

Zeros must *not* be dropped from the middle of a decimal. When zeros are dropped from the middle of a decimal, the value of a number changes. The symbol ≠ means *is not equal to*.

$$6.05 \neq 6.5 \qquad\qquad \$804.09 \neq \$84.9$$

Decide if these decimals are equal: 2.70 ☐ 2.7

1. If there is a zero at the end of the decimal, you can drop it off.

2.7̸ ☐ 2.7

2. The decimals are equal. Write = in the box.

2.7 ⊟ 2.7

Decide if the decimals are equal. Write = or ≠ in each box.

1 14 ≠ 104.00

14   104.0̸0̸
14 ≠ 104

2 $12 ☐ $12.00

3 55.01 ☐ 55.1

4 .230 ☐ .203

5 181.0 ☐ 181

6 30.600 ☐ 30.6

7 250.0 ☐ 2.5

8 $.04 ☐ $.40

9 502 ☐ 520

10 $8.08 ☐ $.88

11 42 ☐ 42.00

12 700 ☐ 700.00

Write *is equal to* or *is not equal to* in each blank.

13 Nineteen and zero tenths _____is equal to_____ nineteen and zero hundredths.

14 Sixty and two hundredths _____ sixty and twenty thousandths.

15 One and three tenths _____ one and thirty thousandths.

16 Forty-four dollars _____ forty-four dollars and zero cents.

Check your answers on page 201.

Comparing Decimals

To compare two decimals, line up the decimal points. Then compare the numbers starting from the left. The greater number is the number with the greater digit farthest to the left. Compare until you find two digits that are different. The symbol for *less than* is <. The symbol for *greater than* is >.

Compare 23.57 and 23.75

$$23.\boxed{5}7$$
$$23.\boxed{7}5$$

The tens and ones digits are the same. The tenths digits are different.

5 tenths < 7 tenths, so
23.57 < 23.75

Compare 0.3 and 0.071

$$0.\boxed{3}$$
$$0.\boxed{0}71$$

The ones digits are the same. The tenths digits are different.

3 tenths > 0 tenths, so
0.3 > 0.071

Compare 1.080 and 1.08

$$1.080$$
$$1.08$$

A right-hand zero does not change the value of a decimal.

80 thousandths = 8 hundredths.

1.080 = 1.08

Decide if the decimals are equal. Write = or ≠ in each box.

1 0.03 $\boxed{=}$ 0.030

$$0.\boxed{0}\boxed{3}$$
$$0.\boxed{0}\boxed{3}0$$

2 2.10 ☐ 1.20

3 41.14 ☐ 14.41

4 60.50 ☐ 60.5

5 7.0 ☐ 0.7

6 8 ☐ 8.000

Compare the decimals. Write >, <, or =.

7 0.73 $\boxed{<}$ 0.83

$$.\boxed{7}3$$
$$.\boxed{8}3$$

8 0.9 ☐ 0.91

9 0.40 ☐ 0.4

10 0.11 ☐ 1.1

11 1.362 ☐ 0.363

12 25.06 ☐ 25.6

13 9.09 ☐ 0.099

14 1.033 ☐ 1.33

Order each group of decimals from least to greatest. Write 1 in the box next to the least decimal, and write 3 in the box next to the greatest decimal. Write 2 in the box next to the decimal that is in the middle.

15 7.1 $\boxed{2}$
7.01 $\boxed{1}$
7.11 $\boxed{3}$

16 0.003 ☐
0.3 ☐
0.03 ☐

17 50.5 ☐
5.05 ☐
0.05 ☐

Check your answers on page 201.

Money Place Values

Amounts of money less than one dollar can be written in two ways. For example, 82 cents is written as 82¢ or as $.82. The number of dimes is shown in the tenths place. The number of pennies is shown in the hundredths place.

Write eight cents as a decimal.

1. Write the dollar sign and a decimal point.

$.

2. Eight cents equals 8 hundredths of a dollar. Write 0 and then 8 after the decimal point.

$.08

Write each amount as a decimal.

1 fifty-one cents

$.51

2 seven cents

_____

3 fifteen cents

_____

4 thirty cents

_____

5 sixty-three cents

_____

6 four cents

_____

Write each amount using dimes and pennies.

7 $.39 =

3 dimes + 9 pennies

8 15¢ =

_____

9 $.08 =

_____

10 $.88 =

_____

11 $.02 =

_____

12 60¢ =

_____

Write each amount in words.

13 $.06

six cents

14 73¢

_____

15 $.17

_____

16 90¢

_____

17 $.33

_____

18 2¢

_____

19 16¢

_____

20 $.49

_____

21 $.84

_____

Check your answers on page 201.

Writing Money Amounts

Amounts of money greater than 99¢ are usually written as decimals with two places after the decimal point. For example, fourteen dollars and six cents is written as $14.06.

Write four dollars and five cents as a decimal.

1. Write the dollar sign. Then write the whole dollar amount followed by a decimal point.

$4.

2. Write five cents to the right of the decimal point. Insert a zero between the decimal point and the 5 because there are no dimes, or tenths.

$4.05

Write each amount as a decimal.

1 thirty-five dollars and seventy-two cents

$35.72

2 eight dollars and two cents

_____

3 thirteen dollars and thirty cents

_____

4 seventy-five dollars and four cents

_____

5 thirty dollars and eighty-six cents

_____

6 forty-one dollars and eleven cents

_____

Write each amount using dollars, dimes and pennies.

7 $12.39 =

12 dollars + 3 dimes + 9 pennies

8 $3.95 =

_____

9 $2.07 =

_____

10 $20.50 =

_____

Write each amount in words.

11 $60.14

sixty dollars and fourteen cents

12 $3.07

_____

13 $28.18

_____

14 $66.50

_____

15 $55.23

_____

16 $7.35

_____

Check your answers on page 202.

Rounding Decimals to the Nearest Tenth

To round a decimal to the nearest tenth, look at the digit in the hundredths place. If it is less than 5, drop all the digits to the right of the tenths place.

> 0.12 rounds to 0.1
> 7.443 rounds to 7.4
> 26.008 rounds to 26.0

If the digit in the hundredths place is 5 or greater, add 1 to the number in the tenths place. Drop all digits to the right of the tenths place.

> 9.59 rounds to 9.6
> 3.761 rounds to 3.8
> 0.084 rounds to 0.1

A number line can help you understand how to round decimals.

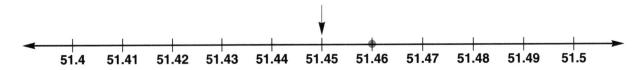

Round 51.46 to the nearest tenth.

1. 51.46 is between 51.4 and 51.5. Locate these numbers on the number line above showing the hundredths between 51.4 and 51.5.

2. Mark 51.46 on the number line.

Numbers less than 51.45 round down to 51.4.

Numbers equal to or greater than 51.45 round up to 51.5.

3. 51.46 is greater than 51.45. So, 51.46 rounds up.

51.46 → 51.5

Use the number line above to round each decimal to the nearest tenth.

1 51.45

51.5 _____

2 51.42

_____

3 51.44

_____

4 51.47

_____

5 51.41

_____

6 51.48

_____

Round each decimal to the nearest tenth.

7 0.42

0.4 _____

8 23.601

_____

9 3.152

_____

10 184.01

_____

11 17.629

_____

12 8.18

_____

13 6.96

7.0 _____

14 289.034

_____

15 19.17

_____

16 7.56

_____

17 341.67

_____

18 60.14

_____

Check your answers on page 202.

Rounding Decimals to the Nearest Hundredth

To round a decimal to the nearest hundredth, look at the digit in the thousandths place. If it is less than 5, drop all the digits to the right of the hundredths place.

3.522 rounds to 3.52
68.1406 rounds to 68.14
0.7932 rounds to 0.79

If the digit in the thousandths place is 5 or greater, add 1 to the number in the hundredths place. Drop all digits to the right of the hundredths place.

3.1589 rounds to 3.16
0.267 rounds to 0.27
4.0081 rounds to 4.01

A number line can help you understand how to round decimals.

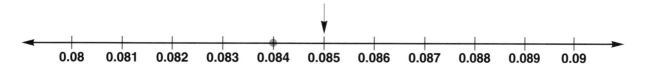

Round 0.084 to the nearest hundredth.

1. 0.084 is between 0.08 and 0.09. Locate these numbers on the number line above showing the thousandths between 0.08 and 0.09.

2. Mark 0.084 on the number line.

   Numbers less than 0.085 round down to 0.08.

   Numbers equal to or greater than 0.085 round up to 0.09.

3. 0.084 is less than 0.085. So, 0.084 rounds down.

   0.084 → 0.08

Use the number line above to round each decimal to the nearest hundredth.

1 0.089   **2** 0.087   **3** 0.082   **4** 0.085   **5** 0.083   **6** 0.086

0.09   _____   _____   _____   _____   _____

Round each decimal to the nearest hundredth.

7 1.431   **8** 0.208   **9** 16.6152   **10** 30.0078   **11** 0.402   **12** 19.426

1.43   _____   _____   _____   _____   _____

13 22.101   **14** 9.269   **15** 143.401   **16** 50.002   **17** 38.374   **18** 0.618

_____   _____   _____   _____   _____   _____

Rounding Money

Rounding amounts of money is similar to rounding decimals.

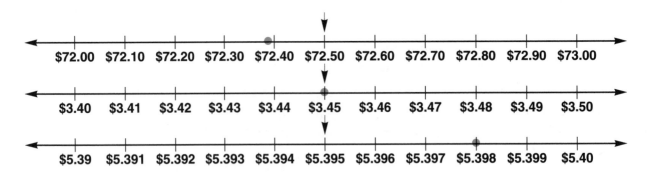

Round $72.39 to the nearest dollar.	Round $3.45 to the nearest ten cents.	Round $5.398 to the nearest cent.
The digit in the tenths place is 3. Since 3 is less than 5, round down.	The digit in the hundredths place is 5. Round up.	The digit in the thousandths place is 8. 8 is greater than 5, so round 39 up to 40.
$72.39 → $72.00	$3.45 → $3.50	$5.398 → $5.40

Round each amount to the nearest dollar.

1 $.76

　　$1.00

2 $1.09

3 $26.51

4 $9.73

5 $52.08

6 $5.56

7 $.81

8 $14.63

9 $9.734

10 $41.289

Round each amount to the nearest ten cents.

11 $6.97

　　$7.00

12 $.35

13 $.81

14 $7.03

15 $19.25

16 $8.43

17 $60.17

18 $42.96

19 $112.04

20 $.36

Round each amount to the nearest cent.

21 $.492

　　$.49

22 $12.561

23 $3.002

24 $29.194

25 $4.305

Adding Decimals

To add decimals, line up the decimal points. Add zeros on the right so that all the decimals have the same number of places after the decimal point.

Then add just as you would whole numbers. Rename if necessary. Line up the decimal point in your answer with the other decimal points in the problem.

Add: 6.72 + 3.9

1. Set up the problem by lining up the decimal points. Add a zero.

$$\begin{array}{r} 6.72 \\ + 3.90 \end{array}$$ ← **add a zero**

2. Add. Begin with the digits on the right. Rename. Put a decimal point in the answer.

$$\begin{array}{r} 1 \\ 6.72 \\ + 3.90 \\ \hline 10.62 \end{array}$$

Add. Rename if necessary.

1.
$$\begin{array}{r} 1 \\ 8.7 \\ + 4.4 \\ \hline 13.1 \end{array}$$

2.
$$\begin{array}{r} \$7.73 \\ + .98 \\ \hline \end{array}$$

3.
$$\begin{array}{r} \$2.02 \\ + 0.06 \\ \hline \end{array}$$

4.
$$\begin{array}{r} \$34.05 \\ + 9.95 \\ \hline \end{array}$$

5.
$$\begin{array}{r} 28.4 \\ + 31.6 \\ \hline \end{array}$$

6.
$$\begin{array}{r} \$0.27 \\ + 0.75 \\ \hline \end{array}$$

7.
$$\begin{array}{r} \$300.40 \\ + 51.85 \\ \hline \end{array}$$

8.
$$\begin{array}{r} 0.6 \\ 3. \\ + 1.05 \\ \hline \end{array}$$

9.
$$\begin{array}{r} 2.1 \\ 3.0 \\ + 24.8 \\ \hline \end{array}$$

10.
$$\begin{array}{r} 39.7 \\ 515.22 \\ + 3. \\ \hline \end{array}$$

11. 3.1 + 2.96 =

$$\begin{array}{r} 1 \\ 3.10 \\ + 2.96 \\ \hline 6.06 \end{array}$$ ← **add a zero**

12. $51.50 + $5 =

13. 88.4 + 21 =

14. 63.7 + 2.83 =

15. 0.04 + 7.3 + 42.1 =

16. $.90 + $1.10 + $3.85 =

17. 605 + 3.02 + 7 =

18. Clarice bought a sweater for $25. The sales tax was $1.25. How much did Clarice spend for the sweater, including tax?

Answer _____

19. Last week Tonia worked 36.75 hours. This week she worked 41.5 hours. How many hours did Tonia work all together?

Answer _____

Check your answers on page 203.

Subtracting Decimals

To subtract decimals, line up the decimal points. Add zeros on the right so that both decimals have the same number of places after the decimal point.

Then subtract just as you would whole numbers. Rename if necessary. Line up the decimal point in your answer with the other decimal points in the problem.

Subtract: 3.4 – 0.95

1. Set up the problem by lining up the decimal points. Add a zero.

```
  3.40  ← add a zero
– 0.95
```

2. Subtract. Begin with the digits on the right. Rename. Put a decimal point in the answer.

```
 2 13 10
 3.4̸ 0̸
– 0.9 5
 2.4 5
```

Subtract. Rename if necessary.

1.
```
   3 10
 6.4̸ 0̸
– 3.1 2
 3.2 8
```

2.
```
 $5.00
– 2.93
```

3.
```
 1.7
– 0.6
```

4.
```
 4.08
– 0.19
```

5.
```
 $12.15
–   3.06
```

6.
```
 4.7
– 3.52
```

7.
```
 8
– 2.75
```

8.
```
 1.4
– 1.36
```

9.
```
 2.
– 0.91
```

10.
```
 54.7
– 23.94
```

11. $5.17 – $.48 =

```
 4 10 17
 $5̸.1̸ 7̸
–   .4 8
 $4.6 9
```

12. 3 – 0.6 =

13. 7.2 – 5.52 =

14. $8 – $3.11 =

15. 4.3 – 2.02 =

16. $20 – $14.29 =

17. 75.31 – 0.8 =

18. 10 – 5.75 =

19. Rasha was running in a full marathon—26.2 miles. She pulled a muscle and dropped out after 16.75 miles. How many miles of the marathon were not completed?

20. Max bought some blank cassette tapes for $9.45, including tax. He paid for the tapes with a $20 bill. How much change should Max have received?

Answer _____

Answer _____

Check your answers on page 203.

Multiplying Decimals by Whole Numbers

To multiply decimals by whole numbers, line up the digits. The decimal point in the answer needs to show the total number of decimal places to the right of the decimal point in the problem.

Multiply: $5.47 × 9

1. Set up the problem.

$5.47
× 9

2. Multiply. Rename.

4 6
$5.47
× 9
4923

3. Put the decimal point in the answer.

4 6
$5.47 ← two decimal places
× 9 ← no decimal places
$49.23 ← two decimal places

Multiply.

1.
1
5.2
× 8
41.6

2.
$2.64
× 10

3.
$31.50
× 5

4.
40.6
× 3

5.
$0.71
× 23

6.
8.5
× 12

7.
$50.26
× 40

8.
$1.82
× 19

9. 3.5 × 5 =

2
3.5
× 5
17.5

10. 0.02 × 9 =

11. $4.75 × 31 =

12. 2.09 × 15 =

13. 3.65 × 6 =

14. $35.27 × 12 =

15. 0.06 × 8 =

16. 1.65 × 11 =

17 How much would you spend if you bought 2 pounds of dried apricots that were marked $3.69 per pound?

18 A factory shipped 20 boxes to a customer. Each box weighed 12.5 pounds. What was the total weight of the shipment?

Answer _____

Answer _____

Multiplying Decimals by Decimals

To multiply a decimal by another decimal, first multiply the way you do whole numbers. Then count the number of decimal places in the problem. Put a decimal point in the answer to show the total number of decimal places.

Multiply: 3.4×2.6

1. Set up the problem.

$$
\begin{array}{r}
3.4 \\
\times\ 2.6 \\
\end{array}
$$

2. Multiply. Rename.

$$
\begin{array}{r}
^{2} \\
3.4 \\
\times\ 2.6 \\
\hline
204 \\
+\ 68 \\
\hline
884 \\
\end{array}
$$

3. Put the decimal point in the answer.

$$
\begin{array}{r}
^{2} \\
3.4 \leftarrow \text{one decimal place} \\
\times\ 2.6 \leftarrow \text{one decimal place} \\
\hline
20\ 4 \\
+\ 68 \\
\hline
8\,8\,4 \leftarrow \text{two decimal places} \\
\end{array}
$$

Multiply. Round money amounts to the nearest cent.

1
$$
\begin{array}{r}
^{1} \\
0.19 \\
\times\ 0.02 \\
\hline
0.0038 \\
\end{array}
$$

2
$$
\begin{array}{r}
0.26 \\
\times\ \ 0.2 \\
\end{array}
$$

3
$$
\begin{array}{r}
0.5 \\
\times\ 0.7 \\
\end{array}
$$

4
$$
\begin{array}{r}
\$2.43 \\
\times\ \ 0.08 \\
\end{array}
$$

5
$$
\begin{array}{r}
4.71 \\
\times\ 0.05 \\
\end{array}
$$

6
$$
\begin{array}{r}
\$20.00 \\
\times\ \ \ \ 4.5 \\
\end{array}
$$

7
$$
\begin{array}{r}
7.5 \\
\times\ 6.3 \\
\end{array}
$$

8
$$
\begin{array}{r}
3.31 \\
\times\ \ 8.3 \\
\end{array}
$$

9 $0.2 \times 8.1 =$

$$
\begin{array}{r}
^{1} \\
0.2 \\
\times\ 8.1 \\
\hline
02 \\
+\ 16 \\
\hline
1.62 \\
\end{array}
$$

10 $0.58 \times 0.9 =$

11 $\$4.03 \times 6.1 =$

12 $1.71 \times 5.2 =$

13 Ursula earns $16.80 for each hour of overtime she works. Last week she worked 6.5 hours overtime. How much overtime pay did Ursula earn last week?

14 Hector walked at an average speed of 3.6 miles per hour for 0.75 hours. How many miles did Hector walk?

Answer _____

Answer _____

Check your answers on page 204.

Dividing Decimals by Whole Numbers

To divide decimals by whole numbers, set up the problem. Put a decimal point in the answer above the decimal point in the problem. You may need to add zeros to the number you are dividing into. Stop dividing when the remainder is zero, or when there are enough decimal places to round to a certain place.

Divide: 2.6 ÷ 4

1. Set up the problem. Put a decimal point in the answer. Since you can't divide 2 by 4, put a 0 in the quotient as a place holder.

$$\begin{array}{r} 0. \\ 4\overline{)2.6} \end{array}$$

2. Divide. Add a zero to the dividend. Keep dividing until the remainder is 0.

$$\begin{array}{r} 0.65 \\ 4\overline{)2.60} \\ -24 \\ \hline 20 \\ -20 \\ \hline 0 \end{array}$$

Divide until the remainder is zero.

1.
$$\begin{array}{r} 0.84 \\ 6\overline{)5.04} \\ -48 \\ \hline 24 \\ -24 \\ \hline 0 \end{array}$$

2. $15\overline{)2.4}$

3. $8\overline{)\$12}$

4. $4\overline{)0.25}$

5. 3.15 ÷ 5 =
$$\begin{array}{r} 0.63 \\ 5\overline{)3.15} \\ -30 \\ \hline 15 \\ -15 \\ \hline 0 \end{array}$$

6. 0.918 ÷ 3 =

7. 240.6 ÷ 2 =

8. 13.09 ÷ 7 =

9. 61.35 ÷ 15 =

10. 2.88 ÷ 36 =

11. 596.8 ÷ 80 =

12. 17.5 ÷ 25 =

13. A filmmaker used 68.46 feet of film to make 3 short movies. If the movies were of equal length, how many feet of film were used for each movie?

14. Yolanda bought 4 quarts of motor oil. The total was $6.36. If each quart was the same price, what was the price of each quart?

Answer _____

Answer _____

Check your answers on page 204.

Dividing Decimals by Whole Numbers with Rounding

If you want the answer to a division problem to have one decimal place, divide to two decimal places and then round. If you want an answer to have two places, divide to three places and then round.

Divide: 2.9 ÷ 6. Round to the nearest hundredth.

1. Set up the problem. Put a decimal point in the answer.

```
      .
6)2.9
```

2. Add zeros so you can divide to three decimal places.

```
     0.483
6)2.900
  − 2 4
     50
   − 48
      20
    − 18
       2
```

3. Round to the nearest hundredth.

0.483 rounds to 0.48

Divide. Round to the nearest tenth.

1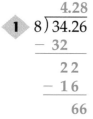
```
      4.28
8)34.26
 − 32
    22
  − 16
    66
  − 64
     2
```
4.28 rounds to 4.3

2 5)47.16

3 9.1 ÷ 4 =

4 62.64 ÷ 18 =

Divide. Round to the nearest hundredth or cent.

5
```
    0.072
7)0.509
 − 49
   19
 − 14
    5
```
0.072 rounds to 0.07

6 50)$2.60

7 2.85 ÷ 20 =

8 $4.02 ÷ 45 =

9 Jason bought 2 dozen golf balls for $47.70. What was the rounded cost of each golf ball? (1 dozen = 12)

10 A $34.25 monthly charge for cable television is shared equally between 3 roommates. What is each roommate's rounded cost per month?

Answer _____

Answer _____

Check your answers on pages 204–205.

Dividing Decimals by Decimals

To divide a decimal by another decimal, you need to move the decimal points in both numbers the same number of places to the right. You may need to add zeros to the number you are dividing into.

Divide: 29.9 ÷ 4.6

1. Set up the problem.

$$4.6\overline{)29.9}$$

2. Move both decimal points one place to the right. Put a decimal point in the answer.

$$4.6\overline{)29.9} \rightarrow 46\overline{)299.}$$

3. Divide until the remainder is zero. You need to add a zero to 299.

$$
\begin{array}{r}
6.5 \\
46\overline{)299.0} \\
-276 \\
\hline
23\,0 \\
-23\,0 \\
\hline
0
\end{array}
$$

Divide until the remainder is zero.

1
$$
\begin{array}{r}
5\,3 \\
0.2\overline{)10.6} \\
-10 \\
\hline
06 \\
-6 \\
\hline
0
\end{array}
$$

2 $0.3\overline{)\$5.40}$

3 0.232 ÷ 0.29 =

4 0.92 ÷ 2.3 =

Divide. Round to the nearest hundredth or cent.

5
$$
\begin{array}{r}
6.182 \\
0.4\overline{)2.4730} \\
-2\,4 \\
\hline
07 \\
-4 \\
\hline
33 \\
-32 \\
\hline
10 \\
-8 \\
\hline
2
\end{array}
$$
6.182 rounds to 6.18

6 $1.3\overline{)\$6.58}$

7 $6.50 ÷ 5.4 =

8 0.404 ÷ 0.25 =

9 Kirk bought 2.5 pounds of potato salad and paid $4.50. What was the cost per pound?

10 A gold chain measures 7.5 inches in length and costs $135. To the nearest cent, what is the cost of the chain per inch?

Answer _____

Answer _____

Check your answers on page 205.

Rounding and Estimation

To estimate answers to division problems, round one or both numbers until you can do the problem using a basic division fact.

Divide: $0.38\overline{)1.967}$

1. Round the number you are dividing by to a number that is easy to divide by. Round 0.38 to 0.4.

$$0.38\overline{)1.967} = 0.4\overline{)1.967}$$

2. Round the number you are dividing into to a number that is easy to divide into. Round 1.967 to 2.

$$0.4\overline{)1.967} = 0.4\overline{)2}$$

3. Add a zero. Move the decimal points and divide to complete the estimate.

$$0.4\overline{)2.0} = 4\overline{)20} \quad \begin{array}{r} 5 \\ \hline 20 \\ -20 \\ \hline 0 \end{array}$$

Round one or both numbers to estimate each answer.

1 $0.029\overline{)6.05}$

$$\begin{array}{r} 200 \\ 0.03\overline{)6.00} \\ -600 \\ \hline 0 \end{array}$$

2 $3.2\overline{)15.168}$

3 $0.88\overline{)8.27}$

4 $29\overline{)1.213}$

5 $1.6\overline{)0.48}$

6 $2.08\overline{)0.019}$

7 $12.3\overline{)3.602}$

8 $56.85\overline{)0.481}$

9 $1.923 \div 4.03 =$

$$\begin{array}{r} 0.5 \\ 4\overline{)2.00} \\ -20 \\ \hline 0 \end{array}$$

10 $0.36 \div 0.887 =$

11 $0.048 \div 2.09 =$

12 $3.1 \div 14.94 =$

13 $9.999 \div 28.17 =$

14 $2.98 \div 6.386 =$

15 $153.5 \div 0.048 =$

16 $0.398 \div 2.279 =$

17 Amy paid $8.40 for 6.7 gallons of gasoline. Estimate the cost of one gallon of gasoline.

18 In March, Rick's dog ate 32.5 pounds of dog food. Estimate the number of pounds of food Rick's dog ate each day in March. (Hint: March has 31 days.)

Answer _____

Answer _____

Check your answers on page 205.

Using a Calculator with Decimals

You can use a calculator to work problems with decimals. Always clear your calculator before you begin. Check each number after you enter it. Watch for the decimal points. Round answers to the required number of places.

Divide: $1.025 \overline{)0.5674}$. Round to the nearest hundredth.

Press the key.		Read the display.
1. Clear the calculator.	→ [C] →	[0.]
2. Enter the number you are dividing into.	→ [.][5][6][7][4] →	[0.5674]
3. Press the division key.	→ [÷] →	[0.5674]
4. Enter the number you are dividing by.	→ [1][.][0][2][5] →	[1.025]
5. Press the equals key.	→ [=] →	[0.5535609]
6. Round the answer to two decimal places.		0.55

Use a calculator to solve.

1 0.45 + 3.7 =

4.15

2 12.78 + 6.5 =

3 $2.31 + $0.58 =

4 $0.50 + $0.72 =

5 $3.80 − $0.97 =

6 $42.67 − $3.89 =

7 0.42 − 0.08 =

8 12.06 − 2.7 =

9 5.46 × 7 =

10 31 × $2.79 =

11 0.6 × 1.80 =

12 0.45 × $2.39 =

Use a calculator to solve. Round to the nearest hundredth or cent.

13 0.247 ÷ 5 =

0.05

14 $589.67 ÷ 12 =

15 $0.95 ÷ 3.2 =

16 2.6 ÷ 0.41 =

17 Find the average speed of a bicyclist who completes a 48.125-mile race in 1.75 hours.

18 A car rents for $19.95 per day. What does it cost to rent the car for 7 days?

Answer _____

Answer _____

Check your answers on pages 205–206.

Strategies for

SUCCESS

Problem Solving: Charts and Tables

Charts and tables contain information that is arranged in rows and columns.

❖ STRATEGY: **Get familiar with how a table is organized.**

Population Figures for Five U.S. Cities

City	1980	1990
Washington, DC	638,432	606,900
Tucson, Arizona	330,537	405,390
Atlanta, Georgia	425,022	394,017
Buffalo, New York	357,870	328,123
Minneapolis, Minnesota	370,951	368,383

1. Study the table above. What is the title of the table? What kind of information does it show?

   The table is titled Population Figures for Five U.S. Cities. The table shows the 1980 and 1990 population of five U.S. cities.

2. Look at the information the table shows. Rows are shown from left to right. Columns are shown up and down. Read the labels above the columns.

3. To use a table, first decide what information you need. Then move across rows and columns to find the information you need.

Exercise: Use the information in the table to solve the problems.

1 Write the name of the city that had the largest population in 1980.

1980 is in column: _____2_____

The largest number in
column 2 is: _____638,432_____

Answer _____

2 Write the name of the city that had the smallest population in 1980.

Answer _____

3 Write the name of the city that had the largest population in 1990.

Answer _____

4 Write the name of the city that had the smallest population in 1990.

Answer _____

5 Which cities had more people in 1980 than 1990?

Answer _____

_____

_____

6 Which cities had fewer people in 1980 than 1990?

Answer _____

_____

_____

7 On the lines below, order the 1980 population of the cities from greatest to least. The first line showing the city with the greatest population has been completed for you.

Washington, DC   638,432

_____

_____

_____

_____

8 On the lines below, order the 1990 population of the cities from least to greatest. The last line showing the city with the greatest population has been completed for you.

_____

_____

_____

Washington, DC   606,900

9 Which city had an increase in population between 1980 and 1990?

Answer _____

10 Which city had the greatest loss in population between 1980 and 1990?

Answer _____

Check your answers on page 206.

Check-up on Decimals

Add or subtract. Rename if necessary.

1
$$\begin{array}{r} 1.8 \\ -\ 0.27 \\ \hline \end{array}$$

2
$$\begin{array}{r} \$\ \ .32 \\ +\ 12.80 \\ \hline \end{array}$$

3
$$\begin{array}{r} 12.14 \\ -\ \ 1.5 \\ \hline \end{array}$$

4
$$\begin{array}{r} 0.06 \\ 11.2 \\ +\ \ 4.13 \\ \hline \end{array}$$

5
$$\begin{array}{r} 12.3 \\ 4.16 \\ +\ \ 0.7 \\ \hline \end{array}$$

6 $\$16.20 - \$2.49 =$ **7** $0.45 - 0.3 =$ **8** $8.1 - 3.52 =$ **9** $11.09 - 3.4 =$

Multiply.

10
$$\begin{array}{r} 5.1 \\ \times\ \ 30 \\ \hline \end{array}$$

11
$$\begin{array}{r} \$.62 \\ \times\ \ \ \ 7 \\ \hline \end{array}$$

12
$$\begin{array}{r} 0.45 \\ \times\ \ 0.8 \\ \hline \end{array}$$

13
$$\begin{array}{r} 1.08 \\ \times\ \ 1.9 \\ \hline \end{array}$$

14 $3.8 \times 5 =$ **15** $6.1 \times 20.2 =$ **16** $\$.75 \times 30.8 =$ **17** $4.02 \times 6.1 =$

Divide. Round to the nearest hundredth or cent.

18 $6\overline{)\$47.02}$ **19** $51\overline{)0.937}$ **20** $4.08 \div 0.3 =$ **21** $0.675 \div 2.02 =$

22 $12\overline{)27.1}$ **23** $7.1\overline{)50}$ **24** $48 \div .07 =$ **25** $4.5 \div 8.9 =$

Check your answers on page 206.

Using Two or More Operations with Decimals

Addition, subtraction, multiplication, and division are mathematical operations. When a problem has more than one operation, follow these steps:

Step 1: First, do any operations in parentheses ( ).

Step 2: Next, do the multiplication and division in order. Work from left to right.

Step 3: Last, do the addition and subtraction in order. Work from left to right.

Solve: $0.7 \times (3.04 - 0.8) + 2.15 \div 0.5$

1. Do the operations in the parentheses.

$0.7 \times (3.04 - 0.8) + 2.15 \div 0.5 =$

$0.7 \times \quad 2.24 \quad + 2.15 \div 0.5$

2. Do the multiplication and division.

$0.7 \times 2.24 + 2.15 \div 0.5 =$

$1.568 \quad + 2.15 \div 0.5 =$

$1.568 \quad + \quad 4.3$

3. Do the addition.

$1.568 + 4.3 = 5.868$

Solve using a calculator. Round division answers to the nearest hundredth.

1 $25.6 - 4.06 \div 0.2 =$

$25.6 - \quad 20.3 \quad =$

$\quad \quad 5.3$

2 $4.3 \times 0.6 + 7.4 =$

3 $0.78 \div 2.5 - 0.08 =$

4 $6.04 + 0.12 \times 4.1 =$

5 $8.7 - 7.43 \div 1.5 =$

6 $2.6 \times 0.61 - 0.35 =$

7 $30.5 - 3.2 \times 0.7 + 4.8 =$

8 $30.5 - 3.2 \times (0.7 + 4.8) =$

9 $7.3 + 0.6 \div 2 - 0.95 \times 3.4 + 6.03 =$

10 $7.3 + 0.6 \div (2 - 0.95) \times 3.4 + 6.03 =$

Use two or more steps to solve each problem.

11 Barb bought 3 bunches of daisies for $2.19 each. The tax was $0.53. How much change did she get from $10?

12 While loading a truck, Dirk lifted 65.5 pounds of flour 12 different times and 90.5 pounds of salt 8 different times. How many pounds of goods did he load all together?

Answer _____

Answer _____

Check your answers on page 206.

Below are examples of the skills in this unit and the pages to refer to for practice. Read the examples and work the problems. Then check your answers. If you do well here, go on to the unit review. If not, study the pages listed below before you do the unit review.

Read.

1. Compare 2.4 and 2.089   **(Refer to page 93)**

    2 . 4   Line up the decimal points. Start at
    2 . 0 8 9   the left. The ones digits are the same.
             4 tenths > 0 tenths, so
                 2.4 > 2.089

2. Round 3.485 to the   **(Refer to page 96)**
nearest tenth.

Look at the digit in the hundredths place.
It is 8, so you round up.
    3.485 → 3.5

3. 7.9 + 8.27   **(Refer to page 99)**

                    1
    7.90 ← add a zero   7.90
  + 8.27   **+ 8.27**
                   16.17

4. 7.3 − 1.06   **(Refer to page 100)**

                  2 10
    7.30 ← add a zero   7.3̸0̸
  − 1.06   **− 1.06**
                 6.24

5. 32.4 × 0.05   **(Refer to pages 101–102)**

        1 2   1 2
  3 2.4   **3 2.4**   3 2.4 ← one decimal place
× 0.0 5   **× 0.0 5** **× 0.0 5** ← two decimal places
      1620   **1.620** ← three decimal places

6. 0.112 ÷ 1.4   **(Refer to pages 103–106)**

            0.0   0.08
 1.4)0.112   **14)01.12**   **14)01.12**
                      − 1 12
                        0

Solve.

1 Compare 0.071 and 0.17

2 Round 2.08 to the nearest tenth.

3 0.6 + 1.2 + 0.45

4 15.13 − 3.7

5 1.7 × 0.32

6 4.284 ÷ 0.7

Check your answers on page 206.

Unit 4 ◆ Review

Compare the decimals. Write > , < , or =.

1 1.3 ☐ 3.1   **2** 2.10 ☐ 2.1   **3** 0.6 ☐ 0.06   **4** 1.91 ☐ 1.19

Round each decimal to the nearest hundredth or cent.

5 2.345   **6** 0.069   **7** 12.008   **8** $1.595   **9** $.403   **10** $8.097

Add, subtract, multiply, or divide. Round division answers to the nearest hundredth.

11 0.61 + 1.8 =   **12** 3.2 + 0.5 + 1.09 =   **13** 0.2 − 0.08 =   **14** 3.45 − 1.9 =

15 7 × 2.06 =   **16** 0.72 × 30 =   **17** 1.2 × 0.05 =   **18** 7.1 × 11.4 =

19 4)9.106   **20** 0.6)0.2485   **21** 0.315 ÷ 17 =   **22** 0.1 ÷ 0.32 =

23 After dieting for a month, Tim found he had lost 6.5 pounds. His current weight is 167.2 pounds. How much did Tim weigh at the start of his diet?

Answer _____

24 It is 143.5 miles from Angela's home to her sister's house. Angela has already traveled 97.2 miles. How much farther does she have to go?

Answer _____

25 In the table at the right, how much longer is song A than song C?

Answer _____

Song	Length (min)
A	2.75
B	2.43
C	2.38

Check your answers on pages 206–207.

Solve. Fill in the circle.

26 Which digit is in the hundredths place in decimal 42.156?

ⓐ 1

ⓑ 2

ⓒ 5

ⓓ 6

27 Which statement shows that 0.3 is greater than 0.081?

ⓐ $0.3 > 0.081$

ⓑ $0.3 > 0.81$

ⓒ $0.03 < 0.081$

ⓓ $0.3 < 0.081$

28 $2.03 =$

ⓐ two and three tenths

ⓑ two and three hundredths

ⓒ two and three thousandths

ⓓ twenty and three hundredths

29 seventy-eight dollars and six cents =

ⓐ $7.86

ⓑ $78.06

ⓒ $78.60

ⓓ $78.66

30 $4.1 + 0.7 + 3.012 =$

ⓐ 4.122

ⓑ 7.182

ⓒ 7.712

ⓓ 7.812

31 $2.4 - 1.16 =$

ⓐ 0.79

ⓑ 0.88

ⓒ 1.24

ⓓ 1.34

32 $0.04 \times 3.7 =$

ⓐ 0.128

ⓑ 0.148

ⓒ 1.48

ⓓ 14.8

33 $5.04 \div 0.12 =$

ⓐ 0.042

ⓑ 0.42

ⓒ 4.2

ⓓ 42

34 Maggie bought a pair of jeans for $23.69. The tax was $1.42. How much change did Maggie get from $30?

ⓐ $4.89

ⓑ $6.31

ⓒ $25.11

ⓓ $28.58

35 On a cross-country trip, George has traveled 1,391.4 miles. He still has 1,158.6 miles to travel. How far is George traveling all together?

ⓐ 232.8 miles

ⓑ 2,449 miles

ⓒ 2,550 miles

ⓓ 3,550 miles

Check your answers on page 207.

Cumulative Review 4

Write the place of the digit 4 in each number.

1 348 _____ **2** 6,401 _____ **3** 2.045 _____ **4** 14.6 _____ **5** 0.824 _____

Compare the numbers. Write >, <, or =.

6 56 ☐ 506   **7** 76 ☐ 67   **8** 2.9 ☐ 2.90

Add or subtract.

9
$$\begin{array}{r} 85 \\ + 39 \\ \hline \end{array}$$

10
$$\begin{array}{r} 704 \\ - 67 \\ \hline \end{array}$$

11
$$\begin{array}{r} 3.21 \\ + 0.8 \\ \hline \end{array}$$

12
$$\begin{array}{r} 12.4 \\ - 7.19 \\ \hline \end{array}$$

13
$$\begin{array}{r} 62.45 \\ + 13.9 \\ \hline \end{array}$$

14 $8{,}032 - 760 =$ **15** $43 + 201 + 5 =$ **16** $6.24 + 1.07 =$ **17** $10.08 - 2.5 =$

Multiply or divide. Round division answers to the nearest hundredth.

18
$$\begin{array}{r} 17 \\ \times\ 8 \\ \hline \end{array}$$

19
$$\begin{array}{r} 43 \\ \times\ 15 \\ \hline \end{array}$$

20
$$\begin{array}{r} 8.26 \\ \times\ 0.4 \\ \hline \end{array}$$

21 $7\overline{)59}$

22 $61\overline{)780}$

23 $721 \times 8 =$ **24** $16 \times 2.13 =$ **25** $63 \div 2.2 =$ **26** $5.04 \div 0.11 =$

27 Sue and her roommate share living expenses equally. One month the electric bill was $45.74, the water bill was $32.10, and the rent was $745. How much was each roommate's share?

Answer _____

28 Manuel had 16.25 feet of heavy weight canvas. He used 4.5 feet to cover a chair. How much canvas did Manuel have left?

Answer _____

Check your answers on page 207.

Solve. Fill in the circle.

29 Which digit is in the thousandths place in the number 73.1062?
- Ⓐ 0
- Ⓑ 1
- Ⓒ 3
- Ⓓ 6

30 What is 685.73 rounded to the nearest ten?
- Ⓐ 680
- Ⓑ 686
- Ⓒ 690
- Ⓓ 700

31 Which statement is false?
- Ⓐ $13 + 5 + 102 = 120$
- Ⓑ $6,108 + 493 = 6,601$
- Ⓒ $821 - 107 = 714$
- Ⓓ $7,645 - 1,902 = 5,343$

32 Which statement is false?
- Ⓐ $4 \times 68 = 242$
- Ⓑ $93 \times 51 = 4,743$
- Ⓒ $3,246 \div 8 = 405 \text{ R } 6$
- Ⓓ $825 \div 34 = 24 \text{ R } 9$

33 $82.41 + 5.6 + 0.33 =$
- Ⓐ 17.141
- Ⓑ 87.34
- Ⓒ 88.34
- Ⓓ 91.31

34 $7.06 - 2.8 =$
- Ⓐ 4.26
- Ⓑ 4.8
- Ⓒ 4.98
- Ⓓ 9.86

35 $3.7 \times 0.6 =$
- Ⓐ 1.82
- Ⓑ 2.22
- Ⓒ 18.2
- Ⓓ 22.2

36 $0.0792 \div 3.3 =$
- Ⓐ 0.024
- Ⓑ 0.0243
- Ⓒ 0.24
- Ⓓ 2.43

37 Alicia's March Earnings

Wk 1	$367.50
2	284.30
3	251.75
4	340.80

How much did Alicia earn during March?
- Ⓐ $992.60
- Ⓑ $1,144.35
- Ⓒ $1,234.35
- Ⓓ $1,244.35

38 How much would you pay for 0.91 pounds of fruit salad if the salad costs $1.80 per pound?
- Ⓐ $1.63
- Ⓑ $1.64
- Ⓒ $1.80
- Ⓓ $16.38

Check your answers on pages 207–208.

Unit 5

FRACTIONS

We use fractions to name a part of something. You may need fractions for following a recipe, measuring fabric, or finding the total number of hours you worked.

Where have you seen fractions used?

_____

_____

_____

In this unit you will learn about:
- the meaning of fractions
- equivalent fractions
- improper fractions and mixed numbers
- rounding and estimating with fractions
- adding, subtracting, multiplying, and dividing fractions

Meaning of Fractions

A fraction names part of a whole or of a group, and is written as one number over another number. The top number, or **numerator**, tells how many parts of the whole or group are being considered. The bottom number, or **denominator**, tells how many equal parts are in the whole. The line that separates the numerator and denominator is called a **fraction bar**.

numerator ⟶ 3 ⟵ number of parts being considered
fraction bar ⟶ — ⟵ separates the numerator and denominator
denominator ⟶ 4 ⟵ number of equal parts in the whole

Write a fraction for the parts that are shaded.

1. Count the number of equal parts in the whole. This number is the denominator. The square is divided into 4 equal parts. Write 4 as the denominator.

$\frac{}{4}$

2. Count the number of shaded parts. This number is the numerator. The square has 3 shaded parts. Write 3 as the numerator.

$\frac{3}{4}$

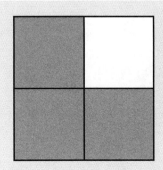

Write a fraction for each shaded part.

1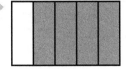

$\frac{4}{5}$

_____

2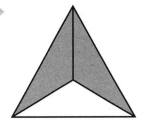

_____

3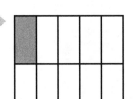

_____

4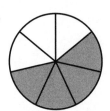

_____

Shade each figure to show the fraction.

5 $\frac{3}{8}$

6 $\frac{5}{6}$

7 $\frac{1}{2}$

8 $\frac{3}{10}$

Measuring with a ruler often includes fractions. The ruler below shows 6 inches. Each inch is divided into fourths. Line A below is $\frac{1}{4}$ of an inch long. Line B is $\frac{3}{4}$ of an inch long.

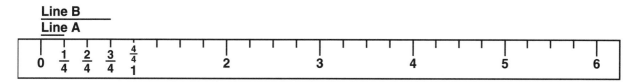

Number lines can also be used to show fractions. On the number line below, there are 10 equal units between 0 and 1. Point A is located at $\frac{1}{10}$ and Point B is located at $\frac{7}{10}$.

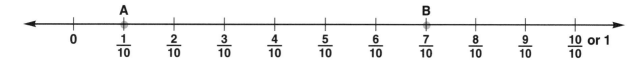

Find the length of each line using the number line below.

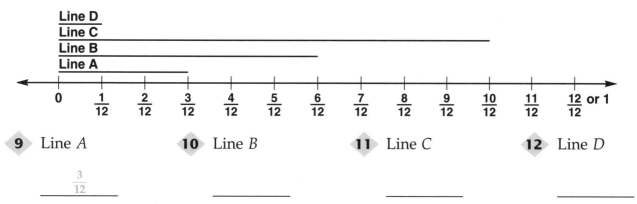

9 Line A	**10** Line B	**11** Line C	**12** Line D
$\frac{3}{12}$	_____	_____	_____

Write the location of each point.

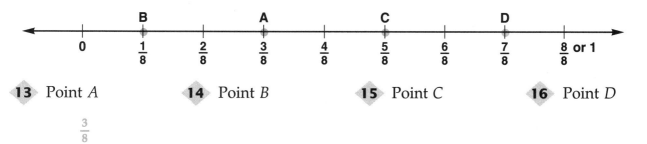

13 Point A	**14** Point B	**15** Point C	**16** Point D
$\frac{3}{8}$	_____	_____	_____

Equivalent Fractions

Equivalent fractions are different fractions that represent the same amount.

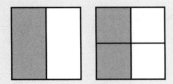 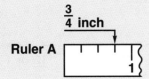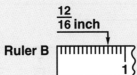
Write equivalent fractions for each figure.

 1   **2**   **3**    **4**

$$\frac{3}{4} = \frac{6}{8}$$

_____   _____   _____   _____

Write equivalent fractions for each pair of rulers.

5 ▸ Line A and Line B **6** ▸ Line C and Line D **7** ▸ Line E and Line F

Line A   Line B 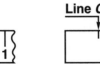   Line C   Line D 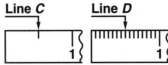   Line E   Line F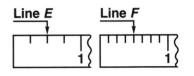

$$\frac{1}{4} = \frac{2}{8}$$

_____   _____

Unit 5

120

Check your answers on page 208.

Reducing Fractions to Lowest Terms

Fractions are reduced to lowest terms to make them easier to read and understand. **Reducing** a fraction to lowest terms means dividing both the numerator and denominator by the same number. Sometimes you may have to reduce more than once to get the fraction to lowest terms. A fraction is reduced to lowest terms when you can only divide both the numerator and denominator by 1.

Reduce $\frac{12}{30}$ to lowest terms.

1. Find a number that divides into 12 and 30 evenly.

2. If any number other than 1 goes into 6 and 15 evenly, the number is not in lowest terms. Reduce again.

3. See if you can divide both the numerator and the denominator by a number other than 1.

$$\frac{12}{30} = \frac{12 \div 2}{30 \div 2} = \frac{6}{15}$$

$$\frac{6}{15} = \frac{6 \div 3}{15 \div 3} = \frac{2}{5}$$

$\frac{2}{5}$ is in lowest terms.

Reduce each fraction to lowest terms.

1 $\frac{9}{21} =$

$$\frac{9}{21} = \frac{9 \div 3}{21 \div 3} = \frac{3}{7}$$

2 $\frac{8}{12} =$

3 $\frac{10}{18} =$

4 $\frac{10}{25} =$

5 $\frac{15}{20} =$

6 $\frac{7}{21} =$

7 $\frac{8}{10} =$

8 $\frac{20}{28} =$

Write the number used to reduce each fraction to lowest terms.

9 $\frac{9}{12} = \frac{9 \div \boxed{3}}{12 \div \boxed{3}} = \frac{3}{4}$

10 $\frac{7}{14} = \frac{7 \div \boxed{}}{14 \div \boxed{}} = \frac{1}{2}$

11 $\frac{6}{15} = \frac{6 \div \boxed{}}{15 \div \boxed{}} = \frac{2}{5}$

12 $\frac{12}{18} = \frac{12 \div \boxed{}}{18 \div \boxed{}} = \frac{2}{3}$

13 $\frac{20}{24} = \frac{20 \div \boxed{}}{24 \div \boxed{}} = \frac{5}{6}$

14 $\frac{9}{27} = \frac{9 \div \boxed{}}{27 \div \boxed{}} = \frac{1}{3}$

15 $\frac{4}{16} = \frac{4 \div \boxed{}}{16 \div \boxed{}} = \frac{1}{4}$

16 $\frac{15}{35} = \frac{15 \div \boxed{}}{35 \div \boxed{}} = \frac{3}{7}$

17 $\frac{14}{28} = \frac{14 \div \boxed{}}{28 \div \boxed{}} = \frac{1}{2}$

Check your answers on page 208.

Raising Fractions to Higher Terms

When you change a fraction to an equivalent fraction with a larger denominator, it is called raising a fraction to higher terms. To raise a fraction to higher terms, multiply both the numerator and the denominator by the same number.

Raise $\frac{3}{4}$ to higher terms by multiplying the numerator and denominator by 5.

1. Multiply the numerator by 5.

$$\frac{3}{4} = \frac{3 \times 5}{\underline{\hspace{1cm}}} = \frac{15}{\underline{\hspace{0.5cm}}}$$

2. Multiply the denominator by 5.

$$\frac{3}{4} = \frac{3 \times 5}{4 \times 5} = \frac{15}{20}$$

Multiply the numerator and denominator by 2 to raise each fraction to higher terms.

1 $\quad \frac{2}{3} = \frac{2 \times 2}{3 \times 2} = \frac{4}{6}$

2 $\quad \frac{3}{5} =$

3 $\quad \frac{4}{7} =$

4 $\quad \frac{5}{8} =$

5 $\quad \frac{4}{5} =$

6 $\quad \frac{1}{3} =$

7 $\quad \frac{5}{12} =$

8 $\quad \frac{1}{5} =$

Write the number used to raise each fraction to higher terms.

9 $\quad \frac{6}{7} = \frac{12}{14} \quad \underline{2}$

$\frac{6 \times 2}{7 \times 2} = \frac{12}{14}$

10 $\quad \frac{4}{5} = \frac{16}{20} \quad \underline{\hspace{1cm}}$

11 $\quad \frac{2}{9} = \frac{6}{27} \quad \underline{\hspace{1cm}}$

12 $\quad \frac{2}{3} = \frac{10}{15} \quad \underline{\hspace{1cm}}$

Raise each fraction to higher terms using the given numerator or denominator.

13 $\quad \frac{1}{4} = \frac{\boxed{6}}{24}$

$\frac{1}{4} = \frac{1 \times 6}{4 \times 6} = \frac{6}{24}$

14 $\quad \frac{3}{8} = \frac{\boxed{}}{16}$

15 $\quad \frac{1}{2} = \frac{\boxed{}}{20}$

16 $\quad \frac{7}{9} = \frac{\boxed{}}{27}$

17 $\quad \frac{3}{4} = \frac{6}{\boxed{}}$

18 $\quad \frac{5}{9} = \frac{15}{\boxed{}}$

19 $\quad \frac{2}{3} = \frac{10}{\boxed{}}$

20 $\quad \frac{1}{10} = \frac{10}{\boxed{}}$

Check your answers on pages 208–209.

Common Denominators

To compare some fractions, you may need to change the denominators. This is called finding a common denominator. A **common denominator** is a number that both denominators divide into evenly.

Compare $\frac{2}{3}$ and $\frac{4}{5}$.

1. Multiply the two denominators to find a common denominator. $3 \times 5 = 15$. A common denominator for both fractions is 15.

$$\frac{2}{3} = \frac{}{3 \times 5} = \frac{}{15}$$

$$\frac{4}{5} = \frac{}{5 \times 3} = \frac{}{15}$$

2. Write each fraction in higher terms with 15 as the denominator.

$$\frac{2}{3} = \frac{2 \times 5}{3 \times 5} = \frac{10}{15}$$

$$\frac{4}{5} = \frac{4 \times 3}{5 \times 3} = \frac{12}{15}$$

3. Compare the numerators of the two new fractions. 12 is greater than 10.

$$\frac{12}{15} > \frac{10}{15} \text{ so } \frac{4}{5} > \frac{2}{3}$$

Compare each set of fractions. Write $>$, $<$, or $=$.

1 $\frac{2}{7} \boxed{>} \frac{1}{4}$

$$\frac{2}{7} = \frac{2 \times 4}{7 \times 4} = \frac{8}{28}$$

$$\frac{1}{4} = \frac{1 \times 7}{4 \times 7} = \frac{7}{28}$$

2 $\frac{4}{7} \boxed{} \frac{2}{3}$

3 $\frac{8}{16} \boxed{} \frac{4}{8}$

4 $\frac{2}{3} \boxed{} \frac{3}{5}$

5 $\frac{4}{9} \boxed{} \frac{1}{2}$

6 $\frac{2}{5} \boxed{} \frac{3}{8}$

7 $\frac{3}{4} \boxed{} \frac{6}{9}$

8 $\frac{4}{5} \boxed{} \frac{5}{6}$

9 $\frac{1}{3} \boxed{} \frac{3}{9}$

10 $\frac{4}{7} \boxed{} \frac{5}{8}$

11 $\frac{2}{11} \boxed{} \frac{1}{6}$

12 $\frac{1}{2} \boxed{} \frac{3}{5}$

13 During summer vacation, Diana grew $\frac{1}{2}$ inch and Enrique grew $\frac{2}{3}$ inch. Who grew more?

14 A recipe uses $\frac{3}{8}$ cup of chopped onion and $\frac{1}{3}$ cup of chopped celery. Does the recipe use more onion or more celery?

Answer _____

Answer _____

Check your answers on page 209.

Finding the Lowest Common Denominator

Another way to find a common denominator is by making a list of multiples of each denominator. A multiple of a number is the number multiplied by 1, 2, 3, and so on. For example, some multiples of 2 are 2, 4, 6, 8, and 10.

After listing multiples for each denominator, find the smallest number that appears on both lists. This number is the **lowest common denominator** (LCD) for the fractions.

Compare $\frac{5}{6}$ and $\frac{4}{10}$.

1. List the multiples of each denominator. The smallest number on both lists is 30. 30 is the LCD.

$\frac{5}{6}$ 6 12 18 24 $\boxed{30}$ 36 42 48

$\frac{4}{10}$ 10 20 $\boxed{30}$ 40 50

2. Raise each fraction to higher terms with 30 as the LCD.

$\frac{5}{6} = \frac{25}{30}$

$\frac{4}{10} = \frac{12}{30}$

3. Compare the numerators of the new fractions. 25 is greater than 12.

$\frac{25}{30} > \frac{12}{30}$ so $\frac{5}{6} > \frac{4}{10}$

List the multiples of each denominator to find the LCD. Change the fractions. Then compare.

1 $\frac{1}{12}$ $<$ $\frac{11}{18}$

$\frac{1}{12}$ 12 24 $\boxed{36}$ 48 60

$\frac{11}{18}$ 18 $\boxed{36}$ 54

$\frac{1}{12} = \frac{3}{36}$

$\frac{11}{18} = \frac{22}{36}$

2 $\frac{8}{15}$ ☐ $\frac{2}{5}$

3 $\frac{2}{3}$ ☐ $\frac{4}{9}$

4 $\frac{2}{5}$ ☐ $\frac{7}{12}$

5 $\frac{7}{10}$ ☐ $\frac{3}{4}$

6 $\frac{5}{7}$ ☐ $\frac{3}{14}$

7 $\frac{1}{5}$ ☐ $\frac{1}{6}$

8 $\frac{7}{24}$ ☐ $\frac{5}{16}$

Improper Fractions and Mixed Numbers

A **proper fraction** is a fraction with a numerator that is smaller than the denominator ($\frac{3}{4}$). An **improper fraction** is a fraction with a numerator that is equal to or larger than the denominator ($\frac{4}{4}$, $\frac{17}{3}$).

A **mixed number** has a whole number and a fraction part ($4\frac{1}{3}$). You may need to change an improper fraction to a whole or mixed number. Sometimes you may need to change a mixed number or whole number to an improper fraction.

Change $\frac{9}{4}$ to a mixed number.

1. Set up a division problem. Divide the numerator, 9, by the denominator, 4.

$4\overline{)9}$

2. Divide.

$\begin{array}{r} 2\ R1 \\ 4\overline{)9} \\ -8 \\ \hline 1 \end{array}$

3. Write the remainder, 1, over the divisor, 4.

$2\frac{1}{4}$

Change $3\frac{2}{7}$ to an improper fraction.

1. Write a fraction with the same denominator, 7.

$3\frac{2}{7} = \frac{}{7}$

2. Multiply the denominator, 7, by the whole number, 3.

$7 \times 3 = 21$

3. Add the numerator, 2, to 21. Write the sum over 7.

$21 + 2$

$\frac{23}{7}$

Write *P* (proper fraction), *I* (improper fraction), *W* (whole number), or *M* (mixed number) on the line next to each problem.

1 $4\frac{1}{5} = $ _M_

2 $\frac{1}{8} = $ ____

3 $\frac{14}{3} = $ ____

4 $2 = $ ____

5 $\frac{7}{7} = $ ____

Change each improper fraction to a whole number or mixed number.

6 $\frac{11}{4} = 2\frac{3}{4}$

$\begin{array}{r} 2\ R3 = 2\frac{3}{4} \\ 4\overline{)11} \\ -8 \\ \hline 3 \end{array}$

7 $\frac{30}{10} = $

8 $\frac{8}{3} = $

9 $\frac{21}{5} = $

10 $\frac{16}{7} = $

Change each mixed or whole number to an improper fraction.

11 $5\frac{1}{2} = \frac{11}{2}$

$5 \times 2 = 10$
$10 + 1 = 11$

12 $8\frac{2}{3} = $

13 $6 = $

14 $12\frac{3}{4} = $

15 $1\frac{5}{8} = $

16 $3\frac{3}{5} = $

17 $7\frac{1}{2} = $

18 $9\frac{1}{7} = $

19 $10\frac{2}{3} = $

20 $5\frac{5}{6} = $

Check your answers on page 209.

Rounding and Estimation

When an exact answer is not necessary, rounding can be used to estimate the answer.

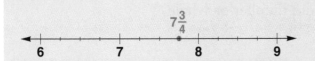

Round $7\frac{3}{4}$ to the nearest whole number.

1. The mixed number $7\frac{3}{4}$ lies between the whole numbers 7 and 8 on the number line.

2. Locate $7\frac{3}{4}$. It is closer to 8 than it is to 7.

3. Round $7\frac{3}{4}$ to 8, the nearest whole number.

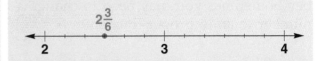

Round $2\frac{3}{6}$ to the nearest whole number.

1. The mixed number $2\frac{3}{6}$ lies between 2 and 3.

2. Locate $2\frac{3}{6}$. It is halfway between 2 and 3.

3. Round $2\frac{3}{6}$ up to 3.

Use the number line to round each mixed number to the nearest whole number.

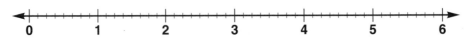

1. $2\frac{6}{8} = \underline{\quad 3 \quad}$

2. $4\frac{2}{8} = \underline{\quad\quad}$

3. $5\frac{7}{8} = \underline{\quad\quad}$

4. $3\frac{4}{8} = \underline{\quad\quad}$

5. $4\frac{5}{8} = \underline{\quad\quad}$

Use the ruler to round each mixed number to the nearest whole number.

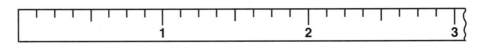

6. $1\frac{3}{8} = \underline{\quad 1 \quad}$

7. $2\frac{1}{2} = \underline{\quad\quad}$

8. $1\frac{7}{8} = \underline{\quad\quad}$

9. $2\frac{1}{8} = \underline{\quad\quad}$

10. $1\frac{1}{2} = \underline{\quad\quad}$

11. Each time Eli bakes bread, he uses $2\frac{1}{8}$ cups of flour. To the nearest whole cup, how many cups does he use each time he bakes bread?

12. On a map, two cities are $4\frac{3}{8}$ inches apart. To the nearest whole inch, how many inches apart are the two cities?

Answer _____

Answer _____

Check your answers on pages 209–210.

Calculators

A fraction bar means divide. The fraction $\frac{1}{4}$ can be read "one fourth" or "one divided by four."

If you divide the numerator of a fraction by the denominator, you can change a fraction into a decimal.

Change the fraction $\frac{1}{4}$ into a decimal.

Press the key.		Read the display.
1. Clear the calculator.	➡ C ➡	0.
2. Enter the numerator.	➡ 1 ➡	1.
3. Press the divide key.	➡ ÷ ➡	1.
4. Enter the denominator.	➡ 4 ➡	4.
5. Press the equals key.	➡ = ➡	0.25
Read the answer.		

Use a calculator to change each fraction to a decimal.

1 $\frac{1}{2} = 0.5$ **2** $\frac{3}{8} =$ **3** $\frac{1}{5} =$ **4** $\frac{3}{4} =$

5 $\frac{3}{2} = 1.5$ **6** $\frac{4}{5} =$ **7** $\frac{7}{8} =$ **8** $\frac{9}{4} =$

9 $\frac{5}{8} =$ **10** $\frac{10}{4} =$ **11** $\frac{12}{10} =$ **12** $\frac{3}{5} =$

13 $\frac{8}{5} =$ **14** $\frac{15}{20} =$ **15** $\frac{6}{10} =$ **16** $\frac{8}{50} =$

17 $\frac{18}{5} =$ **18** $\frac{6}{16} =$ **19** $\frac{24}{30} =$ **20** $\frac{21}{6} =$

21 $\frac{13}{4} =$ **22** $\frac{20}{40} =$ **23** $\frac{32}{8} =$ **24** $\frac{10}{25} =$

25 One penny is $\frac{1}{100}$ of a dollar. What is the decimal number for 1 penny?

26 Donald's son's allowance is $2\frac{1}{2}$ dollars a week. Write the amount as a decimal.

Answer _____

Answer _____

Check your answers on page 210.

Check-up on Fractions

Write a fraction for the parts that are shaded.

1

2

3

4

_____   _____   _____   _____

Shade each figure to show the fraction.

5 $\frac{3}{4}$

6 $\frac{1}{8}$

7 $\frac{2}{3}$

8 $\frac{5}{7}$

Reduce each fraction to lowest terms.

9 $\frac{6}{24} =$

10 $\frac{9}{15} =$

11 $\frac{6}{12} =$

12 $\frac{16}{28} =$

Compare each set of fractions. Write >, <, or = .

13 $\frac{5}{6}$ ☐ $\frac{7}{8}$

14 $\frac{2}{7}$ ☐ $\frac{1}{4}$

15 $\frac{4}{9}$ ☐ $\frac{12}{27}$

16 $\frac{2}{5}$ ☐ $\frac{1}{2}$

Change each improper fraction to a whole number or mixed number. Reduce the answer if possible.

17 $\frac{7}{4} =$

18 $\frac{34}{10} =$

19 $\frac{16}{8} =$

20 $\frac{9}{2} =$

21 $\frac{15}{5} =$

22 $\frac{7}{2} =$

23 $\frac{46}{7} =$

24 $\frac{35}{4} =$

Check your answers on page 210.

Adding Fractions and Mixed Numbers with Like Denominators

To add fractions or mixed numbers with the same denominator, add only the numerators. Keep the same denominator. Then add any whole numbers. Always reduce the answer to lowest terms.

Add: $\frac{2}{8} + \frac{4}{8}$

1. The denominators are the same. Write the denominator under the fraction bar.

$$\frac{2}{8} + \frac{4}{8} = \frac{}{8}$$

2. Add only the numerators. $2 + 4 = 6$. Write the sum over the denominator.

$$\frac{2}{8} + \frac{4}{8} = \frac{6}{8}$$

3. If the answer is not in lowest terms, reduce it.

$$\frac{6}{8} = \frac{6 \div 2}{8 \div 2} = \frac{3}{4}$$

Add. Change improper fraction answers to mixed numbers. Reduce the answer if possible.

1
$$\frac{4}{5}$$
$$+ \frac{3}{5}$$
$$\frac{7}{5} = 1\frac{2}{5}$$

2
$$\frac{6}{10}$$
$$+ \frac{5}{10}$$

3
$$\frac{2}{9}$$
$$+ \frac{4}{9}$$

4
$$\frac{9}{5}$$
$$+ \frac{4}{5}$$

5
$$\frac{7}{3}$$
$$+ \frac{4}{3}$$

6 $\frac{3}{6} + \frac{2}{6} =$

7 $\frac{4}{12} + \frac{7}{12} =$

8 $\frac{8}{24} + \frac{12}{24} =$

9 $\frac{6}{4} + \frac{8}{4} =$

10
$$6\frac{6}{10}$$
$$+ 3\frac{5}{10}$$
$$9\frac{11}{10} = 9 + 1\frac{1}{10}$$
$$= 10\frac{1}{10}$$

11
$$3\frac{2}{9}$$
$$+ 2\frac{1}{9}$$

12
$$9\frac{9}{10}$$
$$+ 15\frac{5}{10}$$

13
$$3\frac{3}{5}$$
$$+ 4\frac{4}{5}$$

14
$$2\frac{7}{12}$$
$$+ 7\frac{5}{12}$$

15 It is $\frac{2}{10}$ mile from the stop sign to the gas station. It is $\frac{6}{10}$ mile from the gas station to the traffic signal. How far is it from the stop sign to the traffic signal?

16 Lenore needs $3\frac{1}{8}$ yards of material for a jacket, 4 yards for a dress, and $\frac{5}{8}$ yard for a scarf. How many yards of material does she need in all?

Answer _____

Answer _____

Check your answers on pages 210–211.

dd fractions or mixed numbers with different denominators, st find the LCD. Change one or more of the fractions to higher rms. Then add the fractions and the whole numbers if there are any. Always reduce the answer to lowest terms.

Add: $2\frac{3}{4} + 1\frac{1}{3}$

1. Find the LCD. A common denominator for both fractions is 12.

$$2\frac{3}{4} = 2\frac{}{12}$$
$$+ 1\frac{1}{3} = 1\frac{}{12}$$

2. Raise each fraction to higher terms with 12 as the denominator. Add the fractions. Add the whole numbers.

$$2\frac{3}{4} = 2\frac{9}{12}$$
$$+ 1\frac{1}{3} = 1\frac{4}{12}$$
$$3\frac{13}{12}$$

3. Change the improper fraction in the answer to a mixed number. Add the new mixed number to the whole number. Reduce the answer if possible.

$$3\frac{13}{12} = 3 + 1\frac{1}{12} = 4\frac{1}{12}$$

Add. Reduce the answer if possible.

1
$$\frac{2}{9} = \frac{4}{18}$$
$$+ \frac{5}{18} = \frac{5}{18}$$
$$\frac{9}{18} = \frac{9 \div 9}{18 \div 9} = \frac{1}{2}$$

2
$$\frac{1}{3}$$
$$+ \frac{6}{12}$$

3
$$\frac{3}{8}$$
$$+ \frac{15}{16}$$

4
$$\frac{1}{4}$$
$$+ \frac{2}{7}$$

5
$$4\frac{4}{5} = 4\frac{16}{20}$$
$$+ 3\frac{3}{4} = 3\frac{15}{20}$$
$$7\frac{31}{20} = 8\frac{11}{20}$$

6
$$9\frac{2}{3}$$
$$+ 7\frac{1}{5}$$

7
$$1\frac{5}{8}$$
$$+ 8\frac{3}{10}$$

8
$$5\frac{7}{9}$$
$$+ 5\frac{1}{4}$$

9
$$2\frac{9}{16}$$
$$+ 4\frac{2}{3}$$

10 Rory jogged $2\frac{1}{2}$ miles on Saturday morning and $1\frac{3}{10}$ miles Sunday evening. How many miles did Rory jog in all?

11 Pat mailed a package that weighed $6\frac{1}{4}$ pounds and another that weighed $3\frac{1}{2}$ pounds. How much did the packages weigh all together?

Answer _____

Answer _____

Check your answers on page 211.

Subtracting Fractions and Mixed Numbers with Like Denominators

To subtract fractions with the same denominator, subtract only the numerators. Keep the same denominator. Then subtract the whole numbers if there are any. Always reduce the answer to lowest terms.

Subtract: $\frac{7}{10} - \frac{1}{10}$

1. The denominators are the same. Write the denominator under the fraction bar.

$$\frac{7}{10} - \frac{1}{10} = \frac{}{10}$$

2. Subtract only the numerators. $7 - 1 = 6$. Write the difference over the denominator.

$$\frac{7}{10} - \frac{1}{10} = \frac{6}{10}$$

3. If the answer is not in lowest terms, reduce it.

$$\frac{6}{10} = \frac{6 \div 2}{10 \div 2} = \frac{3}{5}$$

Subtract. Reduce answers if possible.

1. $\frac{3}{4}$
$-\frac{1}{4}$
$\frac{2}{4} = \frac{2 \div 2}{4 \div 2} = \frac{1}{2}$

2. $\frac{5}{6}$
$-\frac{1}{6}$

3. $\frac{7}{8}$
$-\frac{3}{8}$

4. $\frac{9}{10}$
$-\frac{3}{10}$

5. $\frac{2}{3}$
$-\frac{1}{3}$

6. $\frac{6}{7} - \frac{3}{7} =$

7. $\frac{11}{18} - \frac{7}{18} =$

8. $\frac{4}{5} - \frac{2}{5} =$

9. $\frac{7}{12} - \frac{1}{12} =$

10. $6\frac{7}{20}$
$-5\frac{3}{20}$
$1\frac{4}{20} = 1\frac{1}{5}$

11. $3\frac{6}{7}$
$-1\frac{4}{7}$

12. $12\frac{11}{15}$
$-7\frac{2}{15}$

13. $8\frac{7}{16}$
$-8\frac{1}{16}$

14. $9\frac{5}{6}$
$-\frac{1}{6}$

15 A canister contains $3\frac{3}{4}$ cups of flour. How much flour will be left in the canister if $2\frac{1}{4}$ cups is used for baking?

16 A board measures $25\frac{7}{8}$ inches in length. If an $8\frac{5}{8}$-inch piece is cut from the board, how long will the board be?

Answer _____

Answer _____

Check your answers on page 211.

Subtracting Fractions and Mixed Numbers with Different Denominators

To subtract fractions with different denominators, first find the LCD. Change one or more of the fractions to higher terms. Then subtract the fractions and the whole numbers if there are any. Always reduce the answer to lowest terms.

Subtract: $\frac{3}{5} - \frac{1}{4}$

1. Find a common denominator. A common denominator for both fractions is 20.

$$\frac{3}{5} = \frac{}{20}$$
$$-\frac{1}{4} = \frac{}{20}$$

2. Raise each fraction to higher terms with 20 as the denominator.

$$\frac{3}{5} = \frac{12}{20}$$
$$-\frac{1}{4} = \frac{5}{20}$$

3. Subtract. The answer is in lowest terms.

$$\frac{3}{5} = \frac{12}{20}$$
$$-\frac{1}{4} = \frac{5}{20}$$
$$\frac{7}{20}$$

Subtract. Reduce answers if possible.

1.
$$\frac{1}{3} = \frac{4}{12}$$
$$-\frac{1}{4} = \frac{3}{12}$$
$$\frac{1}{12}$$

2.
$$\frac{6}{6}$$
$$-\frac{1}{5}$$

3.
$$\frac{4}{7}$$
$$-\frac{1}{2}$$

4.
$$\frac{5}{8}$$
$$-\frac{1}{3}$$

5.
$$\frac{11}{12}$$
$$-\frac{5}{9}$$

6.
$$4\frac{4}{5} = 4\frac{32}{40}$$
$$-2\frac{5}{8} = 2\frac{25}{40}$$
$$2\frac{7}{40}$$

7.
$$8\frac{7}{9}$$
$$-3\frac{1}{3}$$

8.
$$12\frac{9}{10}$$
$$-10\frac{7}{8}$$

9.
$$5\frac{9}{16}$$
$$-1\frac{1}{2}$$

10.
$$7\frac{5}{12}$$
$$-6\frac{1}{10}$$

11 Chee bought a can of mixed nuts weighing $\frac{1}{2}$ pound. He used $\frac{1}{8}$ pound to bake cookies. How much of the mixed nuts was left over?

12 A roll of landscaping plastic is $32\frac{5}{8}$ yards long. Rachel used $12\frac{1}{4}$ yards in her garden. How much plastic was left on the roll?

Answer _____

Answer _____

Check your answers on pages 211–212.

Multiplying Fractions by Fractions

Multiplying fractions is one way to find a part of an amount. For example, to find $\frac{1}{2}$ of something, multiply by $\frac{1}{2}$. When working with fractions, *of* means "to multiply". To multiply fractions, set up the problem horizontally.

$\frac{2}{3}$ $\frac{1}{2}$ of $\frac{2}{3}$ is $\frac{2}{6}$ or $\frac{1}{3}$

Multiply: $\frac{1}{2} \times \frac{2}{3}$

1. Multiply the numerators.

$$\frac{1}{2} \times \frac{2}{3} = \frac{2}{}$$

2. Multiply the denominators.

$$\frac{1}{2} \times \frac{2}{3} = \frac{2}{6}$$

3. Reduce to lowest terms.

$$\frac{2}{6} = \frac{1}{3}$$

Multiply. Reduce answers if possible.

1 $\frac{1}{3} \times \frac{3}{4} =$

$$\frac{1 \times 3}{3 \times 4} = \frac{3}{12} = \frac{1}{4}$$

2 $\frac{5}{8} \times \frac{1}{3} =$

3 $\frac{1}{2} \times \frac{3}{4} =$

4 $\frac{2}{5} \times \frac{7}{12} =$

5 $\frac{3}{16} \times \frac{1}{5} =$

6 $\frac{7}{10} \times \frac{5}{6} =$

7 $\frac{1}{8} \times \frac{2}{3} =$

8 $\frac{4}{7} \times \frac{5}{12} =$

9 $\frac{3}{20} \times \frac{3}{5} =$

10 $\frac{5}{6} \times \frac{1}{4} =$

11 $\frac{3}{4} \times \frac{2}{9} =$

12 $\frac{1}{2} \times \frac{3}{8} =$

13 $\frac{5}{6} \times \frac{12}{13} =$

14 $\frac{3}{50} \times \frac{1}{2} =$

15 $\frac{2}{9} \times \frac{4}{8} =$

16 Robin prepared $\frac{1}{2}$ pound of fresh vegetables. At lunch, $\frac{1}{3}$ of the vegetables were eaten. How much of the vegetables was eaten?

17 In Mr. Roma's class, $\frac{3}{8}$ of the students are women, and $\frac{1}{2}$ of those women are married. What fraction of the class is married women?

Answer _____

Answer _____

Check your answers on page 212.

Multiplying Mixed Numbers and Whole Numbers

When multiplying mixed and whole numbers, change both numbers to improper fractions. To multiply a whole number by a fraction, write the whole number over 1. Change answers that are improper fractions to a whole or mixed number.

Multiply: $4\frac{1}{2} \times 6$

1. Write $4\frac{1}{2}$ as an improper fraction.

2. Write 6 as $\frac{6}{1}$.

3. Multiply. Change the improper fraction to a whole number. The answer is in lowest terms.

$4\frac{1}{2} = \frac{4 \times 2 + 1}{2} = \frac{9}{2}$

$6 = \frac{6}{1}$

$\frac{9}{2} \times \frac{6}{1} = \frac{54}{2} = 27$

Multiply. Change improper fraction answers to mixed numbers. Reduce answers if possible.

1 $3\frac{1}{4} \times 2 =$

$\frac{13}{4} \times \frac{2}{1} = \frac{13 \times 2}{4 \times 1} = \frac{26}{4}$

$\frac{26}{4} = 6\frac{2}{4} = 6\frac{1}{2}$

2 $2\frac{1}{2} \times 3 =$

3 $1\frac{2}{5} \times 4 =$

4 $3 \times 1\frac{2}{5} =$

5 $4\frac{1}{4} \times 3\frac{1}{2} =$

6 $2\frac{1}{3} \times 1\frac{2}{5} =$

7 $3\frac{1}{2} \times 2\frac{2}{7} =$

8 $1\frac{5}{12} \times 7 =$

9 $7 \times 9\frac{1}{3} =$

10 $5\frac{1}{2} \times 8 =$

11 $1\frac{5}{8} \times 2\frac{2}{3} =$

12 $2\frac{3}{8} \times 2\frac{4}{5} =$

13 Rita exercises regularly. Each morning, she swims $\frac{1}{2}$ mile. How many miles does Rita swim each week? (1 week = 7 days)

14 On Monday, 6 plants were in bloom at the nursery. On Friday morning, $3\frac{1}{2}$ times as many plants were blooming. How many plants were blooming on Friday morning?

Answer _____

Answer _____

134

Dividing Fractions by Fractions

To find out how many equal parts are in a fraction, you may need to divide a fraction by a fraction. To divide fractions, always **invert**, or turn upside down, the fraction to the right of the division sign. Change the division sign to a multiplication sign and multiply.

Divide: $\frac{2}{3} \div \frac{1}{5}$

1. Invert (turn upside down) the fraction to the right of the division sign.

$$\frac{1}{5} \diagup\!\!\!\!\diagdown \frac{5}{1}$$

2. Multiply by the new fraction.

$$\frac{2}{3} \times \frac{5}{1} = \frac{10}{3}$$

3. If the answer is not in lowest terms, change it to a mixed number.

$$\frac{10}{3} = 3\frac{1}{3}$$

Divide. Change improper fraction answers to mixed numbers. Reduce answers if possible.

1 $\frac{1}{2} \div \frac{7}{8} =$

$$\frac{1}{2} \times \frac{8}{7} = \frac{1 \times 8}{2 \times 7} = \frac{8}{14}$$

$$\frac{8}{14} = \frac{4}{7}$$

2 $\frac{2}{3} \div \frac{3}{4} =$

3 $\frac{3}{8} \div \frac{1}{6} =$

4 $\frac{7}{12} \div \frac{2}{3} =$

5 $\frac{1}{3} \div \frac{5}{8} =$

6 $\frac{5}{6} \div \frac{2}{5} =$

7 $\frac{1}{7} \div \frac{1}{4} =$

8 $\frac{8}{15} \div \frac{1}{2} =$

9 $\frac{3}{5} \div \frac{13}{20} =$

10 $\frac{3}{8} \div \frac{1}{4} =$

11 $\frac{4}{5} \div \frac{9}{10} =$

12 $\frac{2}{7} \div \frac{3}{13} =$

13 $\frac{1}{8} \div \frac{3}{7} =$

14 $\frac{7}{10} \div \frac{5}{12} =$

15 $\frac{5}{8} \div \frac{2}{3} =$

16 $\frac{4}{9} \div \frac{1}{2} =$

17 For a sewing project, Lara may need to divide $\frac{3}{4}$ yard of material into $\frac{1}{4}$-yard pieces. If she does, how many pieces will she get?

18 If Lara divides $\frac{3}{4}$ yard of material into $\frac{1}{8}$-yard pieces, how many pieces will she get?

Answer _____

Answer _____

Check your answers on page 213.

Unit 5

135

Dividing Mixed Numbers and Whole Numbers

To divide fractions by whole numbers, change the whole numbers to improper fractions with a denominator of 1. To divide mixed numbers by fractions, change the mixed number to an improper fraction. Invert the fraction to the right of the division sign and multiply.

Divide: $7\frac{1}{2} \div 2$

1. Change both numbers to improper fractions.

$$7\frac{1}{2} = \frac{7 \times 2 + 1}{2} = \frac{15}{2}$$

$$2 = \frac{2}{1}$$

$$7\frac{1}{2} \div 2 = \frac{15}{2} \div \frac{2}{1}$$

2. Invert the fraction to the right of the division sign.

$$\frac{15}{2} \times \frac{1}{2}$$

3. Multiply the new fractions. Change the improper fraction to a mixed number.

$$\frac{15}{2} \times \frac{1}{2} = \frac{15}{4} = 3\frac{3}{4}$$

Divide. Reduce the answer if possible.

1 $4\frac{1}{2} \div 2\frac{1}{4} =$

$$\frac{9}{2} \times \frac{4}{9} = \frac{9 \times 4}{2 \times 9} = \frac{36}{18}$$

$$\frac{36}{18} = 2$$

2 $2\frac{2}{3} \div 1\frac{1}{3} =$

3 $9\frac{3}{8} \div 3 =$

4 $12\frac{4}{5} \div 3\frac{1}{5} =$

5 $4 \div 3\frac{1}{2} =$

6 $10\frac{2}{5} \div 1\frac{1}{5} =$

7 $4 \div 2\frac{3}{4} =$

8 $8\frac{1}{3} \div 1\frac{1}{4} =$

9 $10 \div 2\frac{1}{3} =$

10 $4\frac{2}{5} \div 1\frac{2}{3} =$

11 $6\frac{1}{9} \div 3 =$

12 $5\frac{2}{3} \div \frac{1}{3} =$

13 A produce clerk must divide $2\frac{1}{2}$ pounds of chives into packages that each contain $\frac{1}{8}$ pound. How many packages can be made?

14 A 25-pound block of cheese is to be cut into pieces that each weigh $\frac{1}{2}$ pound. How many pieces of cheese can be cut from the block?

Answer _____

Answer _____

Check your answers on page 213.

Rounding and Estimation

When an exact answer is not necessary, rounding can be used to estimate.

Estimate: $5\frac{7}{10} \div 2\frac{3}{10}$

1. Use the number line below. $5\frac{7}{10}$ is closer to the whole number 6 than it is to 5. Round $5\frac{7}{10}$ to 6.

$$5\frac{7}{10} \rightarrow 6$$

2. $2\frac{3}{10}$ is closer to the whole number 2 than it is to 3. Round $2\frac{3}{10}$ to 2.

$$2\frac{3}{10} \rightarrow 2$$

3. Divide to complete the estimate.

$$6 \div 2 = 3$$

Use the number line to round each mixed number. Then estimate each answer.

1 $8\frac{5}{10} \div 3\frac{2}{10} =$

$9 \div 3 = 3$

2 $6\frac{3}{10} \div 2\frac{9}{10} =$

3 $9\frac{6}{10} \times 5\frac{2}{10} =$

4 $1\frac{8}{10} + 4\frac{1}{10} =$

5 $7\frac{5}{10} \times 3\frac{3}{10} =$

6 $8\frac{1}{10} - 1\frac{9}{10} =$

7 $5\frac{5}{10} \times 6\frac{2}{10} =$

8 $9\frac{5}{10} - 2\frac{2}{10} =$

9 $4\frac{8}{10} + 7\frac{6}{10} =$

10 Maria has $8\frac{7}{10}$ yards of fabric that will be used to make baby blankets. Each blanket requires $2\frac{9}{10}$ yards of fabric. About how many blankets can be made from the fabric?

Answer _____

11 A hiking trail is $2\frac{2}{10}$ miles long. Chantee hiked $\frac{9}{10}$ of the trail. About how many miles did Chantee hike?

Answer _____

Check your answers on page 213.

Calculators

A calculator can be used to multiply and divide fractions and whole numbers. Remember that a fraction bar means divide.

Multiply: $\frac{1}{2} \times 53$

Press the key.   **Read the display.**

1. Clear the calculator.	→	C →	0.
2. Enter the numerator of the fraction.	→	1 →	1.
3. Press the divide key.	→	÷ →	1.
4. Enter the denominator of the fraction.	→	2 →	2.
5. Press the equals key.	→	= →	0.5
6. Press the multiply key.	→	× →	0.5
7. Enter the whole number.	→	5 3 →	53.
8. Press the equals key.	→	= →	26.5

Read the answer.

Use a calculator to solve.

1 $\frac{1}{4} \times 6 =$ **2** $\frac{2}{5} \times 5 =$ **3** $\frac{5}{8} \div 2 =$ **4** $\frac{9}{10} \div 3 =$

$0.25 \times 6 = 1.5$

5 $\frac{3}{8} \times 4 =$ **6** $\frac{3}{4} \div 2 =$ **7** $\frac{3}{10} \times 20 =$ **8** $\frac{7}{8} \times 5 =$

9 $\frac{1}{5} \div 10 =$ **10** $\frac{4}{5} \times 45 =$ **11** $\frac{7}{20} \times 16 =$ **12** $\frac{12}{25} \div 4 =$

13 $\frac{3}{4} \times 13 =$ **14** $\frac{1}{4} \div 5 =$ **15** $\frac{4}{8} \times 2 =$ **16** $\frac{5}{20} \times 33 =$

17 At Lakeland High School, $\frac{7}{8}$ of the class of 1992 attended the class reunion. If there were 240 students in the class, how many went to the class reunion?

18 At a wedding, $\frac{1}{4}$ of the people present were children. If 60 people attended the wedding, how many were children?

Answer _____

Answer _____

Check your answers on page 214.

Check-up on Fractions

Add or subtract. Reduce the answer if possible.

1
$$\frac{9}{14}$$
$$+\frac{5}{14}$$

2
$$\frac{4}{7}$$
$$-\frac{2}{7}$$

3
$$6\frac{7}{8}$$
$$-1\frac{3}{8}$$

4
$$2\frac{1}{6}$$
$$+9\frac{3}{4}$$

5
$$\frac{1}{6}$$
$$+\frac{5}{18}$$

6 $8\frac{4}{9} - 3\frac{1}{3} =$

7 $\frac{9}{10} + \frac{7}{10} =$

8 $\frac{11}{12} - \frac{7}{8} =$

9 $11\frac{2}{5} + 4\frac{4}{5} =$

Multiply or divide. Reduce the answer if possible.

10 $\frac{3}{8} \times \frac{1}{3} =$

11 $2\frac{1}{4} \div 1\frac{1}{8} =$

12 $3\frac{2}{5} \times 5 =$

13 $4\frac{1}{2} \div 2 =$

14 $9 \div 2\frac{1}{4} =$

15 $6 \times 1\frac{5}{8} =$

16 $4\frac{7}{8} \div 2\frac{1}{2} =$

17 $8 \times 1\frac{3}{4} =$

18 $3\frac{1}{10} \times 7\frac{1}{3} =$

19 $\frac{4}{5} \times 20 =$

20 $7 \div \frac{1}{2} =$

21 $\frac{1}{3} \div 12 =$

22 Anthony had 3 yards of concrete delivered to replace a cracked sidewalk. Only $2\frac{5}{8}$ yards of concrete were used. How much was left over?

23 In Rachel's house, $\frac{2}{3}$ of the rooms have wallpaper. If there are 6 rooms in Rachel's house, how many rooms have wallpaper?

Answer _____

Answer _____

Check your answers on page 214.

Problem Solving

Most rulers are divided into inches and fractions of an inch—halves, fourths, eighths, and sixteenths. These fractions of an inch and whole inches are the units most often used when measuring with a ruler. The ruler below shows sixteenths.

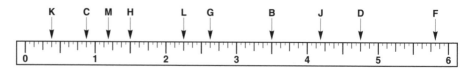

❖ STRATEGY: **Find the distance between two points on a ruler.**

1. To find the distance between two points such as point *B* and point *D*, first find the location of each point on the ruler.

2. The nearest whole inch mark to the left of point *B* on the ruler is 3. The mark at the arrow at point B is $\frac{1}{2}$ inch from 3. The location of point *B* is $3\frac{1}{2}$ inches.

The nearest whole inch mark to the left of point *D* on the ruler is 4. The mark at the arrow at point D is $\frac{3}{4}$ inch from 4. The location of point D is $4\frac{3}{4}$ inches.

3. To find the distance between points *B* and *D*, subtract. Check by adding.

$$
\begin{array}{ccc}
4\frac{3}{4} & = & 4\frac{3}{4} \\
-3\frac{1}{2} & = & -3\frac{2}{4} \\
\hline
& & 1\frac{1}{4}
\end{array}
\qquad
\begin{array}{c}
1\frac{1}{4} \\
+3\frac{2}{4} \\
\hline
4\frac{3}{4}
\end{array}
$$

4. Label the answer in inches. Point *B* and point *D* are $1\frac{1}{4}$ inches apart.

Exercise 1: Write the location of these points using the ruler above. Reduce answers if possible.

1 ▶ Point *C* $\frac{14}{16} = \frac{7}{8}$

2 ◆ Point *F* _____

3 ◆ Point *G* _____

4 ◆ Point *H* _____

5 ▶ Point *J* _____

6 ◆ Point *K* _____

7 ◆ Point *L* _____

8 ◆ Point *M* _____

Exercise 2: **Use the ruler on page 140 to answer these questions. Reduce the answer if possible.**

9 Find the distance between point *M* and point *F*.

Answer _____

10 Find the distance between point *C* and point *K*.

Answer _____

11 Find the distance between point *G* and point *H*.

Answer _____

12 Find the distance between point *L* and point *B*.

Answer _____

13 If a line is drawn from point *D* to point *J* on the ruler, how long is the line?

Answer _____

14 If a line is drawn from point *M* to point *G* on the ruler, how long is the line?

Answer _____

15 If a line is drawn from point *H* to point *F* on the ruler, how long is the line?

Answer _____

16 If a line is drawn from point *L* to point *G* on the ruler, how long is the line?

Answer _____

Check your answers on page 214.

Using Two or More Steps

Sometimes you need to use more than one operation. Remember to multiply and divide <u>before</u> you add or subtract.

Solve: $\frac{3}{4} \times \frac{1}{3} - \frac{1}{12}$

1. Multiply $\frac{3}{4}$ by $\frac{1}{3}$.

$$\frac{3}{4} \times \frac{1}{3} = \frac{3}{12}$$

2. Subtract $\frac{1}{12}$ from $\frac{3}{12}$. Reduce.

$$\frac{3}{12} - \frac{1}{12} = \frac{2}{12} = \frac{1}{6}$$

Solve: $\frac{1}{4} + \frac{2}{3} \div \frac{1}{2}$

1. Divide $\frac{2}{3}$ by $\frac{1}{2}$. Invert the fraction $\frac{1}{2}$ and multiply.

$$\frac{2}{3} \div \frac{1}{2} =$$
$$\frac{2}{3} \times \frac{2}{1} = \frac{4}{3}$$

2. Add $\frac{4}{3}$ to $\frac{1}{4}$. Use the common denominator 12. Change to a mixed number.

$$\frac{4}{3} + \frac{1}{4} =$$
$$\frac{16}{12} + \frac{3}{12} = \frac{19}{12} = 1\frac{7}{12}$$

Solve. Change improper fraction answers to mixed numbers. Reduce answers if possible.

1 $\frac{3}{4} + \frac{1}{5} + \frac{3}{20} =$

$$\frac{3}{4} + \frac{1}{5} = \frac{15}{20} + \frac{4}{20} = \frac{19}{20}$$

$$\frac{19}{20} + \frac{3}{20} = \frac{22}{20}$$

$$\frac{22}{20} = 1\frac{2}{20} = 1\frac{1}{10}$$

2 $\frac{1}{3} \times \frac{3}{4} + \frac{5}{12} =$

3 $\frac{4}{5} - \frac{1}{2} + \frac{1}{10} =$

4 $\frac{7}{8} - \frac{1}{3} + \frac{11}{24} =$

5 $\frac{2}{5} + \frac{1}{6} + \frac{7}{30} =$

6 $\frac{4}{5} \times \frac{3}{4} - \frac{1}{20} =$

7 $\frac{3}{8} \div \frac{1}{2} + \frac{1}{4} =$

8 $\frac{1}{3} \times \frac{4}{5} + \frac{2}{5} =$

9 $\frac{5}{3} \div \frac{1}{2} - \frac{2}{3} =$

10 $\frac{1}{2} + \frac{1}{4} \div \frac{2}{3} =$

11 $\frac{11}{12} - \frac{5}{2} \times \frac{1}{3} =$

12 $\frac{7}{8} + \frac{1}{3} \div \frac{1}{9} =$

Check your answers on page 215.

Unit 5 Wrap-up

Here are examples of the skills in this unit and the pages to refer to for practice. Read the examples and work the problems. Then check your answers. If you do well here, go on to the unit review. If not, study the pages listed below before you do the unit review.

Read.

1. Write the fraction for the shaded part.   **(Refer to page 118)**

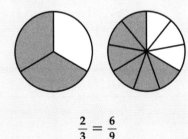

$\frac{2}{5}$

2. Write the location of this point.   **(Refer to page 119)**

$\frac{5}{8}$

3. Write equivalent fractions.   **(Refer to page 120)**

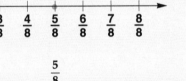

$\frac{2}{3} = \frac{6}{9}$

4. Reduce $\frac{4}{8}$ to lowest terms.   **(Refer to page 121)**

$\frac{4}{8} = \frac{4 \div 4}{8 \div 4} = \frac{1}{2}$

Solve.

1 Write the fraction for the shaded part.

2 Write the location of this point.

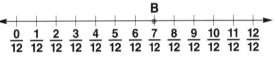

3 Write an equivalent fraction for $\frac{3}{4}$.

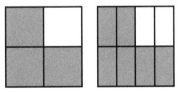

4 Reduce $\frac{12}{18}$ to lowest terms.

Read.

5. Find the lowest common denominator for $\frac{1}{2}$ and $\frac{3}{7}$.

(Refer to page 124)

$\frac{1}{2}$ 2 4 6 8 10 12 **14** 16 18

$\frac{3}{7}$ 7 **14** 21 28

---

6. Change $4\frac{2}{3}$ to an improper fraction.

(Refer to page 125)

$$4\frac{2}{3} = \frac{4 \times 3 + 2}{3} = \frac{14}{3}$$

---

7. Add: $2\frac{1}{2} + 5\frac{3}{5}$

(Refer to page 130)

$$2\frac{1}{2} \;=\; 2\frac{5}{10}$$
$$+\, 5\frac{3}{5} \;=\; 5\frac{6}{10}$$
$$\overline{\qquad\qquad 7\frac{11}{10} = 8\frac{1}{10}}$$

---

8. Subtract: $\frac{4}{5} - \frac{2}{5}$

(Refer to page 131)

$$\frac{4}{5} - \frac{2}{5} = \frac{2}{5}$$

---

9. Multiply: $3\frac{1}{4} \times 1\frac{1}{2}$

(Refer to page 134)

$$3\frac{1}{4} \times 1\frac{1}{2} = \frac{13}{4} \times \frac{3}{2} = \frac{39}{8} = 4\frac{7}{8}$$

---

10. Divide: $5 \div 2\frac{1}{4}$

(Refer to page 136)

$$5 \div 2\frac{1}{4} = \frac{5}{1} \div \frac{9}{4} = \frac{5}{1} \times \frac{4}{9} = \frac{20}{9} = 2\frac{2}{9}$$

Solve.

5 Find the lowest common denominator for the fractions $\frac{3}{4}$ and $\frac{5}{6}$.

6 Change $2\frac{1}{2}$ to an improper fraction.

7 Add: $2\frac{7}{10} + 5\frac{2}{3}$

8 Subtract: $\frac{7}{8} - \frac{3}{8}$

9 Multiply: $2\frac{2}{5} \times 3\frac{3}{4}$

10 Divide: $2\frac{3}{8} \div 2$

Check your answers on page 215.

Write a fraction for each shaded part.

1

2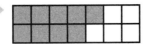

3

_____   _____   _____

Write the location of each point.

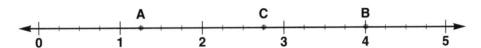

4 Point *A* _____

5 Point *B* _____

6 Point *C* _____

Find the missing number.

7 $\frac{2}{5} = \frac{\square}{15}$

8 $\frac{1}{3} = \frac{\square}{6}$

9 $\frac{4}{7} = \frac{\square}{35}$

10 $\frac{3}{8} = \frac{\square}{32}$

Compare each set of fractions. Write >, <, or =.

11 $\frac{3}{10} \; \square \; \frac{5}{10}$

12 $\frac{1}{2} \; \square \; \frac{2}{7}$

13 $\frac{2}{3} \; \square \; \frac{6}{9}$

14 $\frac{1}{4} \; \square \; \frac{2}{5}$

Change each mixed number to an improper fraction.

15 $2\frac{1}{6} =$

16 $3\frac{7}{8} =$

17 $5\frac{1}{3} =$

18 $1\frac{3}{5} =$

Solve. Change improper fraction answers to mixed numbers. Reduce answers if possible.

19 $\frac{1}{5} + \frac{1}{5} =$

20 $\frac{3}{4} - \frac{1}{3} =$

21 $\frac{7}{8} \times \frac{3}{5} =$

22 $\frac{7}{12} \div \frac{1}{3} =$

Check your answers on page 215.

Unit 5

145

Solve. Reduce answers if possible.

23 $12\frac{4}{5} - 1\frac{2}{3} =$

24 $2\frac{1}{4} \times 4 =$

25 $3\frac{1}{4} \div 2 =$

Solve. Fill in the circle.

26 When rounded to the nearest whole number, $10\frac{1}{2}$ is changed to what number?

Ⓐ $\frac{12}{2}$

Ⓑ $2\frac{1}{2}$

Ⓒ 10

Ⓓ 11

27 When solving the exercise $\frac{1}{3} \times \frac{4}{5} \times \frac{2}{7}$, how many times are fractions inverted?

Ⓐ zero

Ⓑ one

Ⓒ two

Ⓓ three

28 Which of these fractions is equivalent to $\frac{4}{5}$?

Ⓐ $\frac{8}{10}$

Ⓑ $\frac{4}{10}$

Ⓒ $\frac{8}{5}$

Ⓓ $\frac{5}{4}$

29 Kuri walks $1\frac{3}{8}$ miles every morning. How many miles does Kuri walk in one week?

Ⓐ $4\frac{3}{8}$ miles

Ⓑ $5\frac{1}{11}$ miles

Ⓒ $9\frac{5}{8}$ miles

Ⓓ 21 miles

30 To make salad dressing, Sal mixed $\frac{7}{8}$ cup of oil with $\frac{1}{4}$ cup of vinegar. How much salad dressing did Sal make?

Ⓐ $\frac{5}{8}$ cup

Ⓑ $\frac{8}{9}$ cup

Ⓒ 1 cup

Ⓓ $1\frac{1}{8}$ cup

31 For a picnic, Juana made $3\frac{1}{2}$ pounds of potato salad. Eight people each ate the same amount of potato salad. If there was no potato salad left over, how much did each person eat?

Ⓐ $\frac{1}{28}$ pound

Ⓑ $\frac{3}{8}$ pound

Ⓒ $\frac{5}{16}$ pound

Ⓓ $\frac{7}{16}$ pound

Check your answers on page 215.

Compare the numbers. Write >, < , or =.

1 $\frac{7}{12} \square \frac{3}{5}$ **2** 231 $\square$ 213 **3** $1\frac{1}{2} \square \frac{3}{2}$ **4** 0.7 $\square$ 7 **5** 0.4 $\square$ 0.40

Solve. Reduce answers if possible.

6 $\begin{array}{r} 95 \\ -\ 29 \\ \hline \end{array}$ **7** $\frac{5}{6} - \frac{2}{5} =$ **8** $\begin{array}{r} 7\frac{1}{3} \\ +\ 3\frac{1}{2} \\ \hline \end{array}$ **9** $\frac{2}{3} \times \frac{4}{1} \times \frac{5}{5} =$ **10** $\begin{array}{r} 20.4 \\ \times\ 0.5 \\ \hline \end{array}$

11 $4\frac{1}{2} \div 2\frac{1}{4} =$ **12** $26\overline{)390}$ **13** $5.6 + 2.04 =$ **14** $3 \times 4\frac{1}{6} =$

Solve.

15 $\square \times 7 = 42$ **16** $\frac{4}{1} =$ **17** $\frac{37}{7} =$ **18** $\frac{3}{8} \div \frac{1}{3} =$

19 Leah worked for $3\frac{1}{2}$ hours on Saturday and $4\frac{1}{3}$ hours on Sunday. How many hours did Leah work on Saturday and Sunday?

20 Carolina earns $8.50 an hour at work. Last week she worked 37.5 hours. How much money did Carolina earn last week?

Answer _____

Answer _____

Solve. Fill in the circle.

21 Which statement is true?

Ⓐ 1 ten + 9 ones = 109

Ⓑ $\frac{1}{2} = \frac{10}{5}$

Ⓒ 24 > 2.4

Ⓓ $\frac{7}{2}$ is a mixed number.

22 $\frac{5}{4} + \frac{3}{7} =$

Ⓐ $2\frac{11}{12}$

Ⓑ $1\frac{19}{28}$

Ⓒ $\frac{15}{28}$

Ⓓ $\frac{8}{11}$

23 What is 150 rounded to the nearest hundred?

Ⓐ 10

Ⓑ 20

Ⓒ 100

Ⓓ 200

24 Reduce $\frac{48}{60}$ to lowest terms.

Ⓐ $\frac{4}{5}$

Ⓑ $\frac{12}{15}$

Ⓒ $\frac{24}{30}$

Ⓓ $\frac{48}{60}$

25 What number comes next in this pattern? 13, 16, 19, 22, 25, _____

Ⓐ 26

Ⓑ 27

Ⓒ 28

Ⓓ 29

26 Which statement is true?

Ⓐ $\frac{4}{7} + \frac{4}{7} = \frac{8}{7}$

Ⓑ $\frac{4}{7} + \frac{4}{7} = \frac{4}{14}$

Ⓒ $\frac{4}{7} + \frac{4}{7} = \frac{8}{14}$

Ⓓ $\frac{4}{7} + \frac{4}{7} = \frac{16}{49}$

27 The distance from Paula's house to the library is $1\frac{7}{10}$ miles. How far will Paula walk if she goes from her house to the library and then home?

Ⓐ $3\frac{17}{20}$ miles

Ⓑ $1\frac{1}{5}$ miles

Ⓒ $2\frac{2}{5}$ miles

Ⓓ $3\frac{2}{5}$ miles

28 Of the 6 children in the Murray family, $\frac{2}{3}$ have brown eyes. How many children in the Murray family have brown eyes?

Ⓐ 1

Ⓑ 2

Ⓒ 3

Ⓓ 4

Unit 6

RATIO, PROPORTION, AND PERCENT

Percents, like decimals and fractions, show part of a whole. For example, if you have $20 and you spend $10, you have spent $\frac{10}{20}$ or 50% of your money.

Ratios and proportions are used to compare two numbers. Learning ratio and proportion will help you solve percent problems.

List an everyday situation where you've seen percents used.

_____

_____

_____

In this unit you will learn about:

- ◆ reducing ratios to lowest terms
- ◆ solving proportions for missing terms
- ◆ writing percents, fractions, and decimals in equivalent forms
- ◆ solving problems with percents
- ◆ estimating answers to percent problems
- ◆ reading bar and circle graphs

Ratios

A **ratio** is a fraction that shows a relationship between two numbers. For example, if there are 6 men and 15 women, then the ratio of men to women can be shown as the fraction $\frac{6}{15}$.

Always write the first number in the ratio as the numerator and the second number as the denominator. A ratio may be reduced without changing the meaning. It can have a denominator of 1, but it cannot be changed to a mixed number or a whole number.

Write a ratio to show a car traveling 60 miles in 2 hours.

1. Write the first number in the relationship as the numerator of the fraction.

$$\frac{60}{}$$

2. Write the second number as the denominator.

$$\frac{60}{2}$$

3. Reduce.

$$\frac{60 \div 2}{2 \div 2} = \frac{30}{1}$$

Write each ratio as a fraction.

1 2 out of 5 voters

$$\frac{2}{5}$$

2 9 out of 10 adults

3 4 losses in 7 games

4 3 dollars per pound

$$\frac{3}{1}$$

5 56 words per minute

6 28 miles per gallon

Reduce each ratio to lowest terms.

7 $\frac{12}{16}$

$$\frac{12}{16} = \frac{12 \div 4}{16 \div 4} = \frac{3}{4}$$

8 $\frac{3}{9}$

9 $\frac{10}{4}$

10 $\frac{16}{20}$

11 $\frac{25}{5}$

12 $\frac{12}{6}$

13 $\frac{4}{14}$

14 $\frac{8}{50}$

15 $\frac{80}{100}$

16 $\frac{100}{35}$

Write a ratio for each problem. Reduce if possible.

17 Cathy and James invited 72 people to their wedding. Only 64 people attended. Write the ratio of the number of people who attended to the number of people who were invited.

Answer _____

18 Laura delivers 42 newspapers each weekday and 56 newspapers on Sunday. What is the ratio of the number of newspapers she delivers on a Sunday to the number of newspapers she delivers on a weekday?

Answer _____

Check your answers on page 216.

Equal Ratios

Equal ratios are equal fractions. You can change ratios to higher terms by multiplying both the numerator and the denominator by the same number. You can reduce ratios to lower terms by dividing both the numerator and the denominator by the same number.

You can use cross-multiplication to check if two ratios are equal. To cross-multiply, multiply the numbers in the opposite corners. If the ratios are equal, the answers to the cross-multiplication will be equal.

Change $\frac{3}{4}$ to an equal ratio with 8 as the denominator. $\frac{3}{4} = \frac{\square}{8}$

1. Look at the denominators. The 4 is multiplied by 2 to get the 8.

$$\frac{3}{4} = \frac{3}{4 \times 2} = \frac{\square}{8}$$

2. Multiply the numerator by the same number, 2.

$$\frac{3}{4} = \frac{3 \times 2}{4 \times 2} = \frac{6}{8}$$

3. Check by cross-multiplication.

$$\frac{3}{4} \bowtie \frac{6}{8}$$

$$3 \times 8 = 4 \times 6$$

$$24 = 24$$

Complete each pair of equal ratios.

1 $\frac{1}{5} = \frac{\boxed{2}}{10}$

$\frac{1}{5} = \frac{1 \times 2}{5 \times 2} = \frac{2}{10}$

Check: $\frac{1}{5} \bowtie \frac{2}{10}$

$1 \times 10 = 5 \times 2$

$\qquad 10 = 10$

2 $\frac{5}{12} = \frac{\square}{24}$

3 $\frac{1}{4} = \frac{\square}{12}$

4 $\frac{4}{7} = \frac{\square}{35}$

5 $\frac{5}{8} = \frac{20}{\boxed{32}}$

$\frac{5}{8} = \frac{5 \times 4}{8 \times 4} = \frac{20}{32}$

6 $\frac{4}{15} = \frac{8}{\square}$

7 $\frac{1}{3} = \frac{6}{\square}$

8 $\frac{7}{8} = \frac{21}{\square}$

Use cross-multiplication to check if the ratios are equal.

9 $\frac{6}{8}$ and $\frac{12}{20}$

$6 \times 20 = 120$
$8 \times 12 = 96$
120 and 96
not equal

10 $\frac{4}{6}$ and $\frac{20}{30}$

11 $\frac{12}{15}$ and $\frac{4}{5}$

12 $\frac{4}{12}$ and $\frac{1}{4}$

13 $\frac{6}{9}$ and $\frac{2}{3}$

14 $\frac{3}{4}$ and $\frac{9}{12}$

15 $\frac{2}{5}$ and $\frac{8}{10}$

16 $\frac{4}{10}$ and $\frac{3}{6}$

Check your answers on page 217.

Solving Proportions

Two equal ratios are called a **proportion**. Use cross-multiplying to solve a proportion. First cross-multiply the missing number (n) by the number in the opposite corner. Write the answer on the left side of the equal sign.

Solve for n. $\frac{3}{6} = \frac{n}{10}$

1. Cross-multiply. $6n$ means 6 times n.

$$\frac{3}{6} \diagdown \frac{n}{10}$$

$$6 \times n = 3 \times 10$$
$$6n = 30$$

2. Divide the number to the right of the equal sign by the number next to n, 6.

$$6n = 30$$
$$n = 30 \div 6 = 5$$
$$n = 5$$

3. Check by substituting the answer, 5, for n. Cross multiply.

$$\frac{3}{6} = \frac{5}{10}$$

$$6 \times 5 = 3 \times 10$$
$$30 = 30$$

Solve for n. Check by substituting the answer and cross-multiplying.

1 $\frac{9}{n} = \frac{6}{10}$

$$6 \times n = 9 \times 10$$
$$6n = 90$$
$$n = 90 \div 6 = 15$$
$$n = 15$$
Check: $\frac{9}{15} = \frac{6}{10}$
$$15 \times 6 = 9 \times 10$$
$$90 = 90$$

2 $\frac{12}{9} = \frac{8}{n}$

3 $\frac{2}{10} = \frac{n}{15}$

4 $\frac{n}{5} = \frac{12}{2}$

5 $\frac{90}{30} = \frac{60}{n}$

6 $\frac{2}{n} = \frac{3}{12}$

7 $\frac{n}{15} = \frac{8}{10}$

8 $\frac{15}{6} = \frac{n}{4}$

Write a proportion and solve.

9 A postal employee can sort 3 batches of mail in 10 minutes. How much time is needed to sort 15 batches?

10 A grocery store is selling 3 pounds of bananas for $.96. At this price, how much will 2 pounds of bananas cost?

Answer _____

Answer _____

Check your answers on page 217.

Meaning of Percent

Percent means hundredths. When using percents, the whole is divided into 100 equal parts. Twenty-five percent (25%) means 25 hundredths, or 25 out of 100 parts. The sign % is read *percent*.

50%
fifty percent

100%
one hundred percent

125%
one hundred twenty-five percent

Write a percent for each figure.

1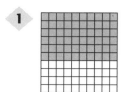

___60%___

2

_____

3

_____

4

_____

5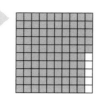

_____

6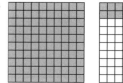

_____

Write each percent using the percent sign.

7 one percent =
1%

8 twenty-five percent =

9 ten percent =

10 forty-five percent =

11 fifty-eight percent =

12 two hundred percent =

13 eighty percent =

14 seventy-five percent =

15 sixteen percent =

16 one hundred fifty percent =

17 eight and one-half percent =

18 fifteen and three-tenths percent =

19 three hundred seventy-five percent =

20 sixty seven and one-third percent =

21 one hundred twelve percent =

Check your answers on page 217.

Percents as Ratios (Fractions)

To change percents to fractions or mixed numbers, write the number over 100 without the percent sign. To change fractions to percents, first change the fraction to a decimal by dividing the numerator by the denominator. Then move the decimal point two places to the right and add a percent sign.

Change 425% to a mixed number.

Write the number over 100 without the percent sign. Change to a mixed number and reduce.

$$425\% = \frac{425}{100} = 4\frac{25}{100} = 4\frac{1}{4}$$

Change $\frac{3}{4}$ to a percent.

First change the fraction to a decimal. Divide the numerator by the denominator. Then move the decimal point two places to the right. Add a percent sign.

$$\frac{3}{4} = 3 \div 4 = 0.75 = 75\%$$

Change each percent to a fraction, mixed number, or whole number. Reduce answers if possible.

1 35% =

$$\frac{35}{100} = \frac{7}{20}$$

2 500% =

3 4% =

4 55% =

5 250% =

6 70% =

7 30% =

8 260% =

Change each fraction to a percent.

9 $\frac{2}{3}$ =

$$\begin{array}{r} .66\frac{2}{3} \\ 3\overline{)2.00} \\ -\,1\,8 \\ \hline 20 \\ -\,18 \\ \hline 2 \end{array}$$

$$.66\frac{2}{3} = 66\frac{2}{3}\%$$

10 $\frac{4}{5}$ =

11 $\frac{9}{20}$ =

12 $\frac{5}{6}$ =

13 A small grocery store lost $\frac{1}{3}$ of its customers when a large supermarket opened nearby. Write the fraction of customers lost as a percent.

Answer _____

14 A building supply store increased its sales by 130% for the year by offering special sale prices. Write the percent of increased sales as a mixed number.

Answer _____

Check your answers on page 217.

Percents as Decimals

You can write any percent as a decimal. Write the number without the percent sign and move the decimal point two places to the left. For percents less than 10%, write a zero in front of the number so you can move the decimal point two places to the left.

To write a decimal as a percent, move the decimal point two places to the right and add a percent sign.

Change 225% to a decimal.

Write the number without the percent sign. Move the decimal point two places to the left.

$$225\% = 225 = 2.25$$

Change 0.4 to a percent.

Add a zero to the right of the decimal. Then move the decimal point two places to the right. Add a percent sign.

$$0.4 = 0.40 = 40\%$$

Change each percent to a decimal.

1 50% = 50. = 0.5   **2** 380% =   **3** 5% = 05. = 0.05   **4** 73.2% =

5 112% =   **6** 18% =   **7** 49.5% =   **8** 130% =

9 74% =   **10** 7.1% =   **11** 345% =   **12** 93.5% =

Change each decimal to a percent.

13 0.045 = 0.045 = 4.5%   **14** 2.3 =   **15** 0.85 =   **16** 0.2 =

17 0.506 =   **18** 0.07 =   **19** 0.55 =   **20** 1.85 =

21 0.318 =   **22** 0.04 =   **23** 3.41 =   **24** .16 =

25 A soccer team scored 15% more goals this season than last season. Write 15% as a decimal.

26 Mark drove his car to work and used 0.08 of the gas in the gas tank. What percent of the gas in the tank did Mark use?

Answer _____

Answer _____

Check your answers on page 218.

Circle Graphs

Circle graphs are often used to show how a whole group is divided up into different percents. The total of all the percents must add up to 100%. The graph below shows the results of a survey. Parents were asked if they thought their town needed another school. Most of them said *yes*.

What does the circle graph show as the result of the survey?

Do We Need Another School?

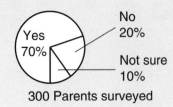

300 Parents surveyed

1. Read all the sections. Check to see they total 100%.

yes — 70%
no — 20%
not sure — + 10%
100%

2. Decide what the graph is telling you. Most (70%) of the parents said they need another school.

Use the circle graphs below to answer the questions.

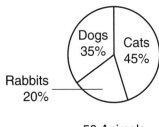

50 Animals

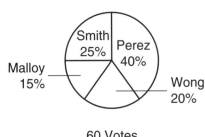

60 Votes

1   a. What percent are cats? ___45%___

    b. What percent are rabbits? _____

    c. What percent are dogs and cats? _____

2   a. What percent voted for Malloy? __

    b. What percent voted for Perez? ___

    c. What percent voted for Smith? ___

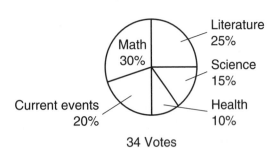

34 Votes

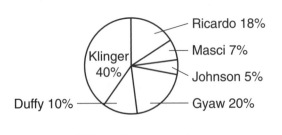

85 People surveyed

3   a. How many total votes? _____

    b. What percent chose Math? _____

    c. What percent chose Literature? _____

4   a. How many were surveyed? _____

    b. What percent chose Ricardo? _____

    c. What percent chose Masci? _____

If a circle graph only gives percents, you can multiply to find the original numbers. First change the percent to a decimal or fraction.

A circle graph shows that 30% of the students plan to take math next year. If 60 students were surveyed, how many plan to take math?

1. Set up the problem.

30% of 60 =

2. Change the percent to a decimal.

30% = 0.30 = 0.3

3. Multiply.

0.3 × 60 = 18

18 students plan to take math.

Use the percents in the circle graphs. Find the number of people who answered *yes*, *no*, or *not sure*.

5 Do We Need More Street Lights?
40 People Surveyed

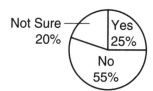

a. Yes: _____10_____

b. No: _____

c. Not Sure: _____

6 Does Your Building Have Smoke Detectors?
60 People Surveyed

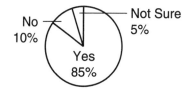

a. Yes: _____

b. No: _____

c. Not Sure: _____

Use the percents in the circle graphs. Find the number of dollars in each part of each budget.

7 Monthly Budget
Monthly Income: $800

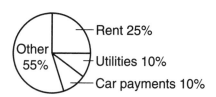

a. Rent: _____

b. Utilities: _____

c. Car payments: _____

d. Other: _____

8 Don's Mini-Market
Weekly Budget: $600

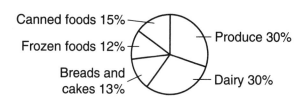

a. Produce: _____

b. Frozen foods: _____

c. Canned foods: _____

d. Dairy: _____

e. Breads and cakes: _____

Check your answers on page 218.

Unit 6

Finding the Part: Percent of a Number

There are three pieces to a percent problem: *the part, the whole,* and *the percent.* Sometimes in a percent problem, one of the three pieces is missing. To solve for the part (percent of a number), you must multiply the whole by the percent (part = whole × percent). Change the percent to a decimal. Then multiply.

1. Write the part, the whole, and the percent in: 30% of 200 is 60.	**2.** What is 30% of 200?

1.
whole = 200
percent = 30%
part = 60

2. Write the pieces.
whole = 200
percent = 30%
part = 200 × 30%

Change the percent to a decimal.
30% = 030. = 0.3

Multiply 200 by .3 to find the part.
200 × 0.3 = 60

Write the whole, the percent, and the part.

1 20% of 40 is 8

whole = 40
percent = 20%
part = 8

2 75% of 48 is 36

3 30% of 150 is 45

4 60% of 25 is 15

5 25% of 200 is 50

6 150% of 80 is 120

Find the percent of each number.

7 What is 10% of 50?

whole = 50
percent = 10% = 0.1
part = 50 × 0.1 = 5

8 What is 80% of 400?

9 What is 120% of 150?

10 30% of 140 is what?

11 15% of 280 is what?

12 110% of 600 is what?

Solve each problem.

13 Lucia saves 15% of her income. She earns $1,600 each month. How much does Lucia save each month?

14 At the Davisville Auto Mart, 30% of the cars are blue. If there are 120 cars on the lot, how many are blue?

Answer _____

Answer _____

Check your answers on pages 218–219.

Finding the Percent

In a percent problem, the missing piece may be the percent.
To solve for the percent, first divide the part by the whole
(percent = part ÷ whole). Then change your answer to a percent.

What percent of 50 is 10?	**10 is what percent of 40?**
part = 10	part = 10
whole = 50	whole = 40
percent = 10 ÷ 50 = 0.2	percent = 10 ÷ 40 = 0.25
Change 0.2 to a percent.	Change 0.25 to a percent.
0.2 = 0.20 = 20%	0.25 = 0.25 = 25%
10 is 20% of 50	10 is 25% of 40

Write the part, the whole, and the percent equation.

1 What percent of 20 is 5?

part = 5
whole = 20
percent = 5 ÷ 20

2 What percent of 40 is 15?

3 8 is what percent of 80?

4 4 is what percent of 100?

5 What percent of 28 is 56?

6 270 is what percent of 360?

Find the percent.

7 30 is what percent of 60?

part = 30
whole = 60
percent = 30 ÷ 60 = 0.50 = 50%

8 What percent of 4 is 7?

9 54 is what percent of 18?

10 What percent of 32 is 8?

11 108 is what percent of 144?

12 What percent of 50 is 30?

Check your answers on page 219.

Finding the Whole

In a percent problem, the missing piece may be the whole.
To solve for the whole, divide the part by the percent
(whole = part ÷ percent).

1. Write the part, the whole, and the percent in: 30 is 25% of 120.

part = 30
percent = 25%
whole = 120

2. 30 is 25% of what number?

Write the pieces.

part = 30
percent = 25%
whole = 30 ÷ 25%

Change the percent to a decimal.

25% = 025. = 0.25

Divide 30 by 25 to find the whole.

30 ÷ 0.25 = 120

Write the part, the percent, and the whole equation.

1 7 is 35% of what number?

part = 7
percent = 35%
whole = 7 ÷ 35%

2 10% of what number is 4?

3 33 is 110% of what number?

Find the whole.

4 20 is 25% of what number?

part = 20
percent = 25%
whole = 20 ÷ 25%
20 ÷ 0.25 = 80

5 15% of what number is 42?

6 225 is 150% of what number?

7 45% of what number is 90?

8 120 is 60% of what number?

9 50% of what number is 70?

Solve each problem.

10 Rick spent $140 on a new bicycle. If he spent 80% of his savings on it, how much did he have before he bought the bicycle?

11 A bookstore spent 60% of its monthly advertising budget on one ad. If $480 was spent on the ad, what is the bookstore's total monthly budget for advertising?

Answer _____

Answer _____

Check your answers on page 219.

Rounding and Estimation

If you practice finding 1% and 10% of a number, then you can use mental math to estimate other percents for tips and taxes. To estimate money amounts, round to the nearest dollar. If the amount has less than $.50, then the dollar amount stays the same. If the amount has $.50 or more, add $1 to the dollar amount.

Estimate: 7% sales tax on $88.56.
Round $89.56 to $90.00
1% = .01   .01 × $90.00 = $0.90
1% of $90.00 is $0.90
7 × $0.90 = $6.30

Estimate: 15% tip on $45.78.
Round $45.78 to $46.00
10% of $46.00 is about $4.60
5% of $46.00 is about $2.30
So 15% of $46.00 is about $6.90

Round to the nearest dollar. Estimate the tips.

1 20% of $74.65

Round $74.65 to $75.00
10% of $75 = $7.50
2 × $7.50 = $15.00

2 15% of $99.54

3 10% of $32.80

4 10% of $7.32

5 20% of $8.40

6 10% of $64.29

Round to the nearest dollar. Estimate the sales tax.

7 8% of $121.32

Round $121.32 to $121.00.
1% of $121.00
is about $1.21.
8 × $1.21 = $9.68

8 6% of $45.20

9 8.5% of $39.90

10 5.5% of $59.78

11 7% of $300.19

12 8% of $698.49

Round to the nearest dollar. Solve each problem.

13 Cesar left a 15% tip on a restaurant bill of $24.58. Estimate the amount of the tip Cesar left.

14 The sales tax where Marsha lives is 6.5%. Estimate the amount of tax Marsha will pay on a coat that costs $99.50.

Answer _____

Answer _____

Check your answers on pages 219–220.

Using a Calculator with Percents

Most calculators have a percent key. It looks like this: %.

You can use this key to find the percent of a number. Always clear your calculator before you begin. Check each number after you enter it.

Solve: 10% of 60 =

Press the key.   **Read the display.**

1. Clear the calculator.   → C   → 0.
2. Enter the second number. → 6 0   → 60.
3. Press the multiply key.   → ×   → 60.
4. Enter the percent.   → 1 0   → 10.
5. Press the percent key.   → %   → 6.
   Read the answer.

If your calculator does not have a percent key, first change the percent to a decimal. Then multiply as you would with decimals.

Use a calculator to solve. Round the answers to the nearest tenth.

1 25% of 74 =
18.5

2 15% of 140 =

3 125% of 65 =

4 45% of 12 =

5 6% of 32 =

6 62% of 175 =

7 240% of 95 =

8 55% of 20 =

9 17.3% of 80 =

10 9.5% of 36 =

11 12% of 87.3 =

12 82% of 2.48 =

13 42% of 16.5 =

14 1.5% of 30 =

15 150% of 60 =

16 11% of 88 =

Solve each problem.

17 A furniture store is having a 15% off sale. How much would you save on a sofa with a regular price of $600?

18 Joann and Bill are buying a house that sells for $55,000. They plan to borrow 85% of the price. How much money do they plan to borrow?

Answer _____

Answer _____

Unit 6

162

Check your answers on page 220.

Check-up on Ratio, Proportion, and Percent

Write each ratio as a fraction. Reduce if possible.

1 8 out of 10 households   **2** 5 wins in 13 games   **3** 350 calories in 8 ounces

Solve for *n*.

4 $\frac{6}{n} = \frac{10}{15}$ **5** $\frac{n}{15} = \frac{8}{20}$ **6** $\frac{16}{4} = \frac{n}{5}$ **7** $\frac{36}{30} = \frac{n}{20}$

Change each percent to a fraction or mixed number. Reduce if possible.

8 40% =   **9** 6% =   **10** 350% =   **11** 85% =

Change each percent to a decimal.

12 3% =   **13** 60% =   **14** 85.1% =   **15** 225% =

Change each fraction or decimal to a percent.

16 $\frac{3}{8}$ =   **17** $\frac{4}{15}$ =   **18** 0.065 =   **19** 0.58 =

Solve.

20 90 is what percent of 120?   **21** What is 15% of 40?

22 60 is 75% of what number?   **23** What is 80% of 260?

24 96 is 150% of what number?   **25** 48 is what percent of 32?

Check your answers on page 220.

Problem Solving

A bar graph is a way to show information in pictures. It includes bars of different lengths that stand for certain numbers. The bars in a bar graph can be drawn across or up and down.

These bar graphs show the amount of sales tax that is charged on purchases in various states.

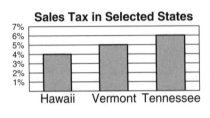

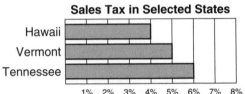

❖STRATEGY: **Think about what is being compared.**

1. Study the titles and labels.

2. Write the information you need.

3. Decide on the operations you need to use. Set up a number problem.

4. Solve the problem.

Example: **Use the bar graphs above to solve the problem.**

How much sales tax will be charged for a $150 purchase in the state of Hawaii?

Step 1   Sales tax in Hawaii is 4%.

Step 2   4% sales tax $150 purchase

Step 3   Change 4% to a decimal. Multiply.

4% = 0.04 $150 × 0.04

Step 4 $150
           ×   .04
             $6.00

Exercises: **Use the graphs on the next page to solve the problems.**

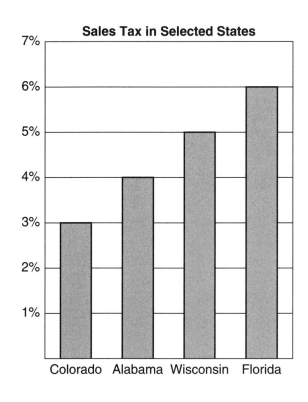

Sales Tax in Selected States

Colorado — 3%
Alabama — 4%
Wisconsin — 5%
Florida — 6%

1 Which state shown on the graph charges the most sales tax?

Answer _____

2 Which state shown on the graph charges the least sales tax?

Answer _____

3 In Alabama, how much sales tax will be charged for a $500 purchase?

Answer _____

---

4 Which states shown on the graph charge the same amount of sales tax?

Answer _____

5 How much sales tax will be charged for a $125 purchase in Connecticut?

Answer _____

6 In Georgia, how much sales tax will be charged for a $36.99 purchase?

Answer _____

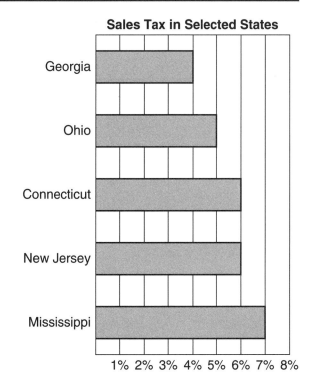

Sales Tax in Selected States

Georgia
Ohio
Connecticut
New Jersey
Mississippi

1% 2% 3% 4% 5% 6% 7% 8%

Using Two or More Steps

You often need to do more than one step to solve a percent problem.

Find the total cost of a rug marked $119.95 if sales tax is 6.5%.

1. Multiply the marked price by the sales tax. Change 6.5% to a decimal.

   6.5% of $119.95 =
0.065 × $119.95 = $7.79675

   $7.79675 rounds to $7.80

2. Add the marked price, $119.95, and the sales tax, $7.80.

$$\begin{array}{r} \$119.95 \text{ marked price} \\ +\quad 7.80 \text{ sales tax} \\ \hline \$127.75 \text{ total cost} \end{array}$$

Find the amount of tax and the total cost.

1 Marked price: $89.67
Sales tax: 6%

0.06 × $89.67 = $5.3802
$5.3802 rounds to
$5.38

Amount of tax: _$5.38_

$$\begin{array}{r} \$89.67 \\ +\quad 5.38 \\ \hline \$95.05 \end{array}$$

Total cost: _$95.05_

2 Marked price: $7.99
Sales tax: 7%

Amount of tax: _____

Total cost: _____

3 Marked price: $201.19
Sales tax: 5.5%

Amount of tax: _____

Total cost: _____

4 Marked price: $49.69
Sales tax: 8%

Amount of tax: _____

Total cost: _____

5 Marked price: $16.49
Sales tax: 3.5%

Amount of tax: _____

Total cost: _____

6 Marked price: $65.69
Sales tax: 7%

Amount of tax: _____

Total cost: _____

7 Pete bought a sewing machine for $124.50. The sales tax rate was 6%. How much did Pete pay in all for the sewing machine?

Answer _____

8 Kim deposited her $200 tax refund into a savings account that earns 5.5% interest per year. What will Kim's account be worth at the end of one year?

Answer _____

Check your answers on page 221.

Percent of Increase and Decrease

Another type of multi-step problem asks for the percent of increase or decrease. You will always subtract one number from another because you are looking for the amount of change.

Lana's monthly salary increased from $675 to $710.
Find the percent of increase to the nearest tenth of a percent.

1. Subtract Lana's starting salary from her new salary to find the amount of increase.

$710 new salary
$\underline{-\ 675}$ starting salary
$35 amount of increase

2. Divide the amount of increase by the starting salary. Divide to 4 places.

$\frac{\$35}{\$675} = 35 \div 675$

$35 \div 675 = 0.0518$

3. Round 0.0518 to 3 places. Change to a percent.

0.0518 rounds to 0.052

0.052 = 5.2%

Lana's raise was 5.2%.

Find the amount and the percent of increase or decrease.
Round your answers to the nearest tenth of a percent.

1 Original price: $445
Sale price: $375

$445
$\underline{-\ 375}$
$70

Amount
of decrease: __$70__

$70 ÷ $445 = 0.1573
0.157 = 15.7%

Percent
of decrease: __15.7%__

2 Last year's price: $125
This year's price: $142

Amount
of increase: _____

Percent
of increase: _____

3 Last month's sales: $65
This month's sales: $83

Amount
of increase: _____

Percent
of increase: _____

4 Contestants in last year's race: 246
Contestants in this year's race: 328

Percent
of increase: _____

5 Starting weight: 178 lb
After dieting: 156 lb

Percent
of decrease: _____

6 Yesterday's attendance: 358
Today's attendance: 316

Percent
of decrease: _____

Check your answers on page 221.

Unit 6 Wrap-up

Below are examples of the skills in this unit and the pages to refer to for practice. Read the examples and work the problems. Then check your answers. If you do well here, go on to the unit review. If not, study the pages listed below before you do the unit review.

Read.

1. Write the ratio $\frac{24}{18}$ in lowest terms.   **(Refer to page 150)**

$$\frac{24}{18} = \frac{24 \div 6}{18 \div 6} = \frac{4}{3} \qquad \text{Check:} \qquad \frac{24}{18} \diagdown \frac{4}{3}$$

$$24 \times 3 = 18 \times 4$$
$$72 = 72$$

2. Solve for n. $\dfrac{24}{n} = \dfrac{36}{6}$ **(Refer to page 152)**

$$36 \times n = 24 \times 6$$
$$36n = 144$$
$$n = 144 \div 36 = 4$$
$$n = 4$$

3. Change 60% to a fraction and to a decimal.   **(Refer to pages 154–155)**

$$60\% = \frac{60}{100} = \frac{3}{5} \qquad 60\% = 0.60 = 0.6$$

4. Change $\frac{5}{6}$ to a percent.   **(Refer to page 154)**

$$\frac{5}{6} = 5 \div 6 = 0.83\frac{1}{3} = 83\frac{1}{3}\%$$

5. Change 0.7 to a percent.   **(Refer to page 155)**

$$0.7 = 0.70 = 70\%$$

6. Find 45% of 250.   **(Refer to page 158)**

whole = 250
percent = 45% $250 \times 0.45 = 112.5$
part = $250 \times 45\%$
$45\% = 45. = 0.45$

Solve.

1 Write the ratio $\frac{55}{90}$ in lowest terms.

2 Solve for n. $\dfrac{15}{20} = \dfrac{n}{16}$

3 Change 8% to a fraction and to a decimal.

4 Change $\frac{1}{4}$ to a percent.

5 Change 0.043 to a percent.

6 Find 120% of 36.

Check your answers on page 221.

Reduce each ratio to lowest terms.

1 $\dfrac{9}{6}$ **2** $\dfrac{10}{15}$ **3** $\dfrac{40}{20}$ **4** $\dfrac{3}{12}$ **5** $\dfrac{4}{10}$ **6** $\dfrac{75}{25}$

Solve for *n*.

7 $\dfrac{4}{n} = \dfrac{20}{55}$ **8** $\dfrac{n}{20} = \dfrac{5}{25}$ **9** $\dfrac{9}{6} = \dfrac{n}{8}$ **10** $\dfrac{32}{12} = \dfrac{24}{n}$

Solve each problem. Round percents to the nearest tenth of a percent.

11 Change 20% to a fraction.

12 Change 105% to a mixed number.

13 Change $\dfrac{11}{20}$ to a percent.

14 45% of 650 =

15 3% of 65 =

16 230% of 90 =

17 40.1% of 200 =

18 15 is what percent of 70?

19 48 is what percent of 16?

20 87 is what percent of 310?

21 78 is 50% of what number?

22 135 is 60% of what number?

23 45 is 110% of what number?

24 A survey asked 800 people if they have or plan to get cable TV. The circle graph shows the survey results. Find the number of people in each category.

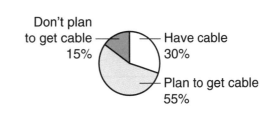

Don't plan to get cable 15%

Have cable 30%

Plan to get cable 55%

Have cable now: _____   Plan to get cable: _____   Don't plan to get cable: _____

Check your answers on page 221.

Solve. Fill in the circle.

25 75 out of 100 people equals the ratio

    (A) $\frac{4}{3}$

    (B) $\frac{3}{4}$

    (C) $\frac{3}{7}$

    (D) $\frac{100}{75}$

26 In $\frac{25}{20} = \frac{n}{16}$, $n =$

    (A) 12.8

    (B) 20

    (C) 31.25

    (D) 400

27 $\frac{7}{12} =$

    (A) 5.8%

    (B) 58%

    (C) $58\frac{1}{3}\%$

    (D) $171\frac{3}{7}\%$

28 1.4 =

    (A) 1.4%

    (B) 14%

    (C) 140%

    (D) 144%

29 32% of 20 =

    (A) 6.4

    (B) 62.5

    (C) 64

    (D) 640

30 12 is what percent of 60?

    (A) 2%

    (B) 5%

    (C) 20%

    (D) 500%

31 Reggie's printer can print 10 pages in 3 minutes. How long will it take to print a report with 150 pages?

    (A) 0.2 minutes

    (B) 4.5 minutes

    (C) 45 minutes

    (D) 500 minutes

32 What is the amount of tax on a $458 purchase if the sales tax rate is 8%?

    (A) $3.67

    (B) $36.64

    (C) $366.40

    (D) $494.64

33 The bar graph shows the results of an election survey. Which candidate is predicted to come in second?

    (A) Pappas

    (B) Schwartz

    (C) Ellerbush

    (D) Finnegan

Check your answers on pages 221–222.

Add, subtract, multiply, or divide.

1 $74 + 392 =$ **2** $591 - 60 =$ **3** $3,049 - 872 =$ **4** $302 + 74 + 1,203 =$

5 $65 \times 4 =$ **6** $41 \times 301 =$ **7** $472 \div 8 =$ **8** $1,482 \div 26 =$

Add, subtract, multiply, or divide.

9 $4.05 + 0.71 =$ **10** $12.3 - 0.62 =$ **11** $1.02 \times 0.6 =$ **12** $4.228 \div 1.4 =$

13 $\frac{2}{5} + 1\frac{1}{3} =$ **14** $1\frac{3}{4} - \frac{1}{6} =$ **15** $\frac{4}{9} \times \frac{7}{12} =$ **16** $2\frac{1}{8} \div \frac{1}{4} =$

Solve each problem. Round answers to the nearest tenth.

17 $\frac{3}{5} = \frac{81}{n}$ **18** $\frac{18}{15} = \frac{n}{20}$ **19** 55% of $84 =$ **20** 3% of $134 =$

21 15 is what percent of 90?   **22** 100 is what percent of 40?

23 Elena bought $3\frac{1}{2}$ pounds of salad at $2.50 per pound. How much change did she get from $10.00?

24 Tim bicycled 13 miles on Saturday and 7.6 miles on Sunday. How many miles did he bicycle all together?

Answer _____   Answer _____

Solve. Fill in the circle.

25 Which digit is in the hundredths place in the number 456.219?

Ⓐ 5

Ⓑ 9

Ⓒ 6

Ⓓ 1

26 What is 0.235 rounded to the nearest tenth?

Ⓐ 0.2

Ⓑ 0.3

Ⓒ 0.23

Ⓓ 0.24

27 Which statement is false?

Ⓐ $456 + 2{,}017 = 2{,}473$

Ⓑ $8{,}109 - 1{,}346 = 6{,}863$

Ⓒ $6 \times 508 = 3{,}048$

Ⓓ $2{,}050 \div 82 = 25$

28 Which statement is false?

Ⓐ $0.08 + 2.1 + 0.3 = 2.48$

Ⓑ $3.09 - 1.6 = 1.49$

Ⓒ $3.2 \times 0.09 = 0.278$

Ⓓ $0.98 \div 1.4 = 0.7$

29 Which statement is false?

Ⓐ $1\frac{1}{2} + \frac{5}{6} = 2\frac{1}{3}$

Ⓑ $3\frac{2}{5} - \frac{1}{10} = 3\frac{1}{10}$

Ⓒ $\frac{1}{8} \times 3\frac{1}{4} = \frac{13}{32}$

Ⓓ $2\frac{1}{10} \div \frac{3}{5} = 3\frac{1}{2}$

30 Which percent equals 0.082?

Ⓐ 8%

Ⓑ 8.2%

Ⓒ 82%

Ⓓ 820%

31 71% of 350 =

Ⓐ 24.85

Ⓑ 248.5

Ⓒ 492.96

Ⓓ 2,485

32 16 is what percent of 80?

Ⓐ 2%

Ⓑ 5%

Ⓒ 20%

Ⓓ 200%

33 At a restaurant, Jules and his brother split an $8.86 pizza. Each ordered iced tea for $1.25. What was each person's share of the bill before tax?

Ⓐ $4.43

Ⓑ $5.68

Ⓒ $6.93

Ⓓ $11.36

34 Julia pays for medical insurance every 3 months. Her quarterly payment increased from $780 to $830. What was the percent of increase rounded to the nearest tenth of a percent?

Ⓐ $50

Ⓑ 6.0%

Ⓒ 6.4%

Ⓓ 94%

Check your answers on pages 222–223.

Place Value

Write the place value of each underlined digit.

1 7̲3,129 _____

2 86̲5 _____

3 4,02̲1 _____

Write each of these numbers.

4 9 tens _____

5 7 hundreds 4 ones _____

6 4 thousands 3 hundreds 8 tens 6 ones _____

Compare each set of numbers. Write > for *greater than* or < for *less than*.

7 62 ☐ 65

8 604 ☐ 488

9 7 ☐ 4

Round each number to the nearest ten.

10 9,234 _____

11 86 _____

12 3,515 _____

Solve.

13 On Sunday afternoon, 10,461 fans attended a basketball game. Rounded to the lead digit, how many fans attended the game?

14 Last year an accounting firm prepared 1,319 business tax returns and 1,561 personal tax returns. Did the firm prepare more business or more personal tax returns?

Answer _____

Answer _____

Adding and Subtracting Whole Numbers

Solve.

15 $\square - 4 = 4$

16 $2 + \square = 8$

17 $11 - 6 = \square$

Write an equation to solve each problem.

18 Seven and what number is equal to seven? _____

19 Nine minus what number is equal to two? _____

Solve.

20
$\begin{array}{r} \$32 \\ + \ 65 \\ \hline \end{array}$

21
$\begin{array}{r} 51 \\ - 17 \\ \hline \end{array}$

22
$\begin{array}{r} \$843 \\ - \ 395 \\ \hline \end{array}$

23
$\begin{array}{r} 570 \\ + 652 \\ \hline \end{array}$

24 $\$115 + \$95 + \$650 =$

25 $9{,}403 - 46 - 312 =$

Round each number to the lead digit. Then add or subtract.

26
$\begin{array}{r} 485 \\ + 196 \\ \hline \end{array}$

27
$\begin{array}{r} \$72 \\ - \ 41 \\ \hline \end{array}$

28
$\begin{array}{r} \$179 \\ + \ 423 \\ \hline \end{array}$

Solve.

29 At the beginning of the year, a volunteer group had 13 members. By the end of the year, 11 more members had joined. How many members were in the group at the end of the year?

30 Ellen earned $1,520 last month. During the month, she made a car payment of $270 and a rent payment of $425. How much money did Ellen have left after making those payments?

Answer _____

Answer _____

Multiplying and Dividing Whole Numbers

Multiply.

31 $\begin{array}{r} \$213 \\ \times \quad 2 \\ \hline \end{array}$

32 $705 \times 16 =$

33 $\begin{array}{r} 2,052 \\ \times \quad 54 \\ \hline \end{array}$

Divide. Use multiplication to check your answers.

34 $5\overline{)255}$

35 $75 \div 6 =$

36 $8\overline{)806}$

Round each number to the lead digit. Then multiply or divide.

37 $\$675 \times 33 =$

38 $592 \div 58 =$

39 $93 \times 41 =$

Solve.

40 ABC Company mailed 5 packages that each weighed 14 pounds. What was the total weight of the packages?

41 While vacationing, Rachel paid $95 to rent a car for 5 days. If the car cost the same amount each day, what was the cost of the car per day?

Answer _____

Answer _____

Decimals

Write each number as a decimal.

42 seven and three tenths _____

43 one dollar and fifteen cents _____

Write each decimal in words.

44 $12.49 _____

45 3.45 _____

Solve.

46　　6.7
　　　+ 3.2

47　　0.12
　　　×　　32

48　　3.6
　　　− 1.5

49 $1.2\overline{)37.2}$

50 $9 − $5.75 =

51 2.5 ÷ 10 =

52 1.06 × 3.2 =

53 8.4 + 13.19 − 4 =

Round both numbers and estimate each answer.

54 $48.7\overline{)505.6}$ =

55 $19.89 + $6.95 =

56 814.50 − 498.2 =

57 39.2 × 20.62 =

58 Sue was baking cookies for her son's party at school. She had 1.5 pounds of flour and bought 5 pounds more. How many pounds of flour did she have all together?

59 Each week, Dora deposits $26.50 from her paycheck into a savings account. At that rate, how much will Dora save in a year (52 weeks)?

Answer _____

Answer _____

Fractions

Compare each set of fractions. Write >, <, or =.

60 $\dfrac{3}{4}$ ☐ $\dfrac{2}{3}$

61 $\dfrac{5}{8}$ ☐ $\dfrac{10}{16}$

62 $\dfrac{5}{9}$ ☐ $\dfrac{1}{2}$

63 $\dfrac{7}{12}$ ☐ $\dfrac{5}{7}$

Solve. Change improper fractions to mixed numbers. Reduce if possible.

64
$$\begin{array}{r} \frac{1}{4} \\ + \frac{3}{4} \\ \hline \end{array}$$

65
$$\begin{array}{r} 14\frac{2}{3} \\ - 10\frac{1}{2} \\ \hline \end{array}$$

66
$$\begin{array}{r} \frac{5}{8} \\ - \frac{1}{5} \\ \hline \end{array}$$

67
$$\begin{array}{r} 2\frac{4}{9} \\ + 6\frac{2}{5} \\ \hline \end{array}$$

68 $\dfrac{3}{4} \times \dfrac{4}{9} =$

69 $4 \div 3\dfrac{1}{3} =$

70 $1\dfrac{5}{8} \times \dfrac{1}{5} =$

71 $2\dfrac{4}{9} \div 6\dfrac{2}{5} =$

Use the number line to round each mixed number to the nearest whole number. Then estimate each answer.

72 $4\dfrac{3}{10} \div 2\dfrac{1}{10} =$

73 $8\dfrac{2}{10} - 6\dfrac{6}{10} =$

74 $3\dfrac{5}{10} + 5\dfrac{4}{10} =$

75 $1\dfrac{7}{10} \times 7\dfrac{9}{10} =$

Solve.

76 Two years ago, Harvey's son Jamal grew $1\dfrac{1}{4}$ inches. Last year he grew $2\dfrac{1}{2}$ inches. How many inches did he grow during those years?

77 Last week, $3\dfrac{7}{10}$ inches of rain fell. If $1\dfrac{2}{10}$ inches of rain fell during the week, how many inches fell during the weekend?

Answer _____

Answer _____

Ratio, Proportion, and Percent

Solve each proportion for _n_.

78 $\dfrac{2}{n} = \dfrac{10}{20}$ **79** $\dfrac{7}{11} = \dfrac{21}{n}$ **80** $\dfrac{5}{8} = \dfrac{n}{32}$ **81** $\dfrac{n}{5} = \dfrac{30}{25}$

Change each percent to a fraction, mixed number, or whole number.

82 10% =   **83** 300% =   **84** 2% =   **85** 120% =

Change each fraction or decimal to a percent.

86 $\dfrac{3}{8}$ =   **87** 3.6 =   **88** $\dfrac{4}{5}$ =   **89** 0.7 =

Solve.

90 30% of 80 is what number?

91 What percent of 4 is 10?

92 20 is what percent of 50?

93 Leon's salary is $1,850 per month. Beginning next month, Leon will get a 3% raise. What will his new salary be?

94 James can pack 12 bottles of shampoo into boxes each minute at work. At that rate, how many bottles can he pack each hour?

Answer _____

Answer _____

When you finish _Check What You've Learned_, check your answers on pages 223–224. Then complete the chart on page 179.

The chart shows you which mathematics skills you should go back and review. Reread each problem you missed. Then look at the appropriate pages of the book for help in figuring out the right answers.

Skills Review Chart

Math Skills	Questions			Pages
The test, like this book, focuses on the skills below.	Check (√) the questions you missed.			Review what you learned in this book.
Whole Number Place Value	___ 1 ___ 2 ___ 3 ___ 4	___ 5 ___ 6 ___ 7	___ 8 ___ 9 ___ 14	Pages 13–28
Whole Number Equations	___ 15 ___ 16	___ 17 ___ 18	___ 19	Pages 31, 43, 61, 71
Addition	___ 20 ___ 23	___ 24	___ 29	Pages 30–41, 52–58
Subtraction	___ 21 ___ 22	___ 25	___ 30	Pages 42–58
Multiplication	___ 31 ___ 32	___ 33	___ 40	Pages 60–69, 81–88
Division	___ 34 ___ 35	___ 36	___ 41	Pages 70–88
Rounding and Estimation	___ 10 ___ 11 ___ 12 ___ 13 ___ 26 ___ 27	___ 28 ___ 37 ___ 38 ___ 39 ___ 54 ___ 55	___ 56 ___ 57 ___ 72 ___ 73 ___ 74 ___ 75	Pages 23, 37, 49, 67, 78, 106, 126, 137
Decimals: Addition, Subtraction, Multiplication, Division	___ 42 ___ 43 ___ 44 ___ 45 ___ 46	___ 47 ___ 48 ___ 49 ___ 50 ___ 51	___ 52 ___ 53 ___ 58 ___ 59	Pages 89–116
Fractions: Addition, Subtraction, Multiplication, Division, Comparing	___ 60 ___ 61 ___ 62 ___ 63 ___ 64	___ 65 ___ 66 ___ 67 ___ 68 ___ 69	___ 70 ___ 71 ___ 76 ___ 77	Pages 117–148
Solving Ratios, Proportions, and Percents	___ 78 ___ 79 ___ 80 ___ 81 ___ 82 ___ 83	___ 84 ___ 85 ___ 86 ___ 87 ___ 88 ___ 89	___ 90 ___ 91 ___ 92 ___ 93 ___ 94	Pages 149–172

Glossary

addends The numbers you add in an addition problem. *page 31*

common denominator A number that two or more denominators divide into evenly. *page 123*

decimal A number that shows an amount less than 1. *page 90*

denominator The bottom number in a fraction; tells how many equal parts are in the whole. *page 118*

digit One of ten symbols—0, 1, 2, 3, 4, 5, 6, 7, 8, 9—used to write numbers. *page 14*

dividend The number that is being divided; in a fraction, the dividend is the numerator. *page 70*

divisor The number that is used to divide another number; in a fraction, the divisor is the denominator. *page 70*

equal ratios Equal fractions. *page 151*

equation A number sentence in which a letter such as n or x stands for a missing number. *page 31*

equivalent fractions Different fractions such as $\frac{1}{2}$ and $\frac{2}{4}$ that represent the same amount. *page 120*

estimate To find an answer by rounding the numbers in a problem. *page 37*

fraction bar The line that separates the numerator and denominator. *page 118*

improper fraction A fraction with a numerator that is equal to or larger than the denominator. *page 125*

invert To turn a fraction upside down. *page 135*

lead digit The first digit on the left in a number with two or more digits. *page 37*

lowest common denominator (LCD) The smallest number that two or more denominators can divide into evenly. *page 124*

mixed number A number made up of a whole number and a fraction part. *page 125*

numerator The top number in a fraction; tells how many parts of the whole or group are being considered. *page 118*

operations The processes you use to solve a math problem. Addition, subtraction, multiplication, and division are the basic mathematical operations. *page 81*

partial product The total you get when multiplying a number by one digit of another number. *page 63*

percent Hundredths; when using percents, the whole is divided into 100 equal parts. *page 153*

place value The value of a digit based on its position in a number. *page 14*

product The answer to a multiplication problem. *page 64*

proper fraction A fraction with a numerator that is smaller than the denominator. *page 125*

proportion Two equal ratios. *page 152*

quotient The answer to a division problem. *page 70*

ratio A fraction that shows a relationship between two numbers. *page 150*

reducing Reducing a fraction to lowest terms means dividing both the numerator and denominator by the same number. *page 121*

remainder The amount left over in a division problem. *page 73*

rename Regrouping numbers using different place values. *page 18*

round An approximation to the nearest number when an exact number is not necessary. Rounding is expressing a number to the nearest ten, hundred, or thousand. *page 23*

sum Total; the answer to an addition problem. *page 31*

Answers and Explanations

Check What You Know

1. 4 thousands
2. 6 hundreds
3. 2 hundred thousands
4. 54
5. 318
6. 2,709
7. >
8. <
9. >
10. 660
11. 340
12. 110
13. Elizabeth
14. 590 people

Page 7

15. 3
16. 5
17. 5
18. $3 + n = 5$
19. $15 - n = 9$
20. $69
21. 30
22. $227
23. 508
24. $698
25. 3,143
26. 110
27. 100
28. 1,400
29. 71 people
30. 238 people

Page 8

31. $369
32. 6,500
33. 64,538
34. 39
35. 41
36. 51
37. 2,400
38. 400
39. 20,000
40. $4
41. 168 hours

Page 9

42. 14.33
43. $.68
44. two and five tenths
45. seventy dollars and twenty-five cents
46. 5.9
47. 123.5
48. 1.5
49. 20.3
50. $26.43
51. 6.01
52. 13.984
53. $2.69
54. 20
55. $320
56. 40
57. 32
58. 78.74 inches
59. $.12

Page 10

60. <
61. >
62. >
63. =
64. $\frac{1}{2}$
65. $3\frac{13}{28}$
66. $\frac{13}{30}$
67. $5\frac{19}{24}$
68. $\frac{1}{12}$
69. $\frac{22}{27}$
70. 11
71. 3
72. 3
73. 5
74. 13
75. 20
76. $7\frac{3}{4}$ inches
77. $17\frac{1}{2}$ miles

Page 11

78. $n = 7$
79. $n = 9$
80. $n = 5$

81. $n = 3$

82. $\frac{9}{20}$

83. 2

84. $\frac{2}{25}$

85. $1\frac{3}{5}$

86. 25%

87. 240%

88. 80%

89. 90%

90. 12

91. 175%

92. 250%

93. $1.20 sales tax

94. $58.50 per week

Unit 1

Page 14

1. 6 tens = 60
4 ones = 4

2. 7 hundreds = 700
3 tens = 30
9 ones = 9

3. 8, 80; 7, 7

4. 4, 400; 0, 0; 6, 6

1.		6	4
2.	7	3	9
3.		8	7
4.	4	0	6

5. tens
6. hundreds
7. tens
8. hundreds
9. ones
10. tens
11. tens
12. ones
13. ones
14. hundreds
15. ones
16. ones
17. ones
18. tens
19. hundreds
20. ones
21. tens
22. ones

Page 15

1. 2 hundreds

2. 5 ones; the model shows
5 groups of ones, or 5 ones.

3. 4 tens

4. 2 tens

5. 7 ones; the 7 is in the ones place
and has a value of 7.

6. 2 hundreds
7. 9 ones
8. 9 hundreds
9. 4 tens
10. 0 tens
11. 1 hundred
12. 7 ones
13. 6 tens
14. 0 ones
15. 5 hundreds
16. 3 ones
17. 4 tens
18. 0 tens
19. 9 ones
20. 7 hundreds
21. 1 ten

Page 16

1. 31

2. 204; 2 hundreds 4 ones = 200 + 4

3. 9
4. 48
5. 773
6. 50
7. 94
8. 686
9. 70
10. 62
11. 111
12. 20

13. 8 tens
5 ones
14. 3 hundreds
2 tens
1 ones

15. 8 hundreds
0 tens
3 ones
16. 2 tens
0 ones

17. 1 hundred
1 ten
6 ones
18. 2 hundreds
0 tens
0 ones

Page 17

1. 121

2. 4 tens + 8 ones = 48

3. 105

4. 20

5. yes
3 hundreds 4 tens 6 ones = 346

6. 735 stamps
7 hundreds 3 tens 5 ones = 735

Page 18

1. 30

2. 4; You can rename 40 ones as 4 tens.

3. 100
4. 1
5. 1
6. 10
7. 24
8. 3; 9
9. 146
10. 21
11. 300
12. 4; 4
13. 20
14. 13

15. 340 sheets
3 hundreds 4 tens = 340

16. 240 paper clips
2 hundreds 4 tens = 240

Page 19

1. >
2. <
47 is less than 463 because 47 has
0 hundreds.

3. <   **4.** >   **5.** <
6. >   **7.** >   **8.** <
9. <   **10.** <   **11.** >
12. <   **13.** <   **14.** <
15. >   **16.** >   **17.** >
18. >   **19.** >   **20.** >
21. <   **22.** >   **23.** <
24. <   **25.** <   **26.** <
27. >   **28.** >   **29.** >
30. <   **31.** <   **32.** >

Page 20

1. 43 > 34   **2.** 15
3. 131   **4.** 72, 75

Page 21

5. 125
6. 27, 30
7. 95, 96, 99, 102, 103
8. 20, 24, 28
9. 210
10. 70, 80
11. Jack
12. 12, 15, 18; 18 minutes

Page 22

1. 4 400,000   **2.** 2 200,000
5 50,000   0 0
9 9,000   6 6,000
3 300   1 100
2 20   7 70
8 8   9 9

3. 4 40,000
7 7,000
0 0
0 0
6 6

1.	4	5	9,	3	2	8
2.	2	0	6,	1	7	9
3.		4	7,	0	0	6

4. 400   **5.** 60,000
6. 7,000   **7.** 0
8. 0   **9.** 80,000

Page 23

1. 30
2. 50
because 45 is exactly halfway between
40 and 50, round up.

3. 60   **4.** 40
5. 30   **6.** 50
7. 40   **8.** 60
9. 640   **10.** 870
11. 750   **12.** 690
13. 780   **14.** 650
15. 830   **16.** 890

17. (B) How many people live in the city
where you live?
Choice (A) has a known, exact answer.

18. (B) How many hours do you sleep
each week?
Choice (A) has a known, exact answer.

Page 24

1. 13   **2.** 5   **3.** 35
4. 3   **5.** 10   **6.** 60
7. 3   **8.** 53   **9.** 2
10. 85   **11.** 42   **12.** 600

13. 279 tickets
18 + 95 + 166 = 279

14. 8 miles
$$\begin{array}{r} 703 \\ -\ 695 \\ \hline 8 \end{array}$$

Page 25

1. 9 hundreds = 900
0 tens = 0
2 ones = 2
2. 4 ones
3. 6 hundreds
5 tens
8 ones
4. 572
5. 37 < 73
6. 7,000
7. 130

Pages 26–27

1. 8 tens   **2.** 3 hundreds
3. 41   **4.** 920

5. 765　　　　　6. 5
7. 3 tens　　　8. 100
9. 2 hundreds　　10. 5 tens
11. <　　　　　12. >
13. >　　　　　14. >
15. <　　　　　16. >
17. >　　　　　18. <
19. 80　　　　　20. 70
21. 80　　　　　22. 70
23. 320　　　　　24. 360
25. 310　　　　　26. 330
27. Sharise　　　28. 30 hours
29. (C) 14 Choices (A), (B), and (D) are incorrect because the models show 1 ten 4 ones, or 10 + 4.
30. (B) 120 Choices (A), (C), and (D) are incorrect because the models show 1 hundred 2 tens, or 100 + 20.
31. (A) 107 Choices (B), (C), and (D) are incorrect because the models show 1 hundred 7 ones, or 100 + 7.
32. (C) 231 Choices (A), (B), and (D) are incorrect because the models show 2 hundreds 3 tens 1 one, or 200 + 30 + 1.
33. (A) 4 ones Choices (B), (C), and (D) are incorrect because the underlined digit is in the ones place and it has a value of 4.
34. (B) 50 ones Choices (A), (C), and (D) are incorrect because 5 tens is the same as 10 + 10 + 10 + 10 + 10 = 50, the same value as 50 ones.
35. 2 tens 5 ones
36. 70 dimes

Page 28
1. 4 hundreds　　2. 0 ones
3. 7 thousands　　4. <
5. >　　　　　6. >
7. 120　　　　　8. 200
9. 160　　　　　10. 37
11. 119　　　　　12. 20 strips
13. There are many ways to answer the question. Here is an example. If you are 32 years old, your age rounded to the nearest ten is 30.
14. afternoon
15. Mark; 835 < 860 or 860 > 835

Unit 2

Page 30

+	0	1	2	3	4	5	6	7	8	9
0	0	1	2	3	4	5	6	7	8	9
1	1	2	3	4	5	6	7	8	9	10
2	2	3	4	5	6	7	8	9	10	11
3	3	4	5	6	7	8	9	10	11	12
4	4	5	6	7	8	9	10	11	12	13
5	5	6	7	8	9	10	11	12	13	14
6	6	7	8	9	10	11	12	13	14	15
7	7	8	9	10	11	12	13	14	15	16
8	8	9	10	11	12	13	14	15	16	17
9	9	10	11	12	13	14	15	16	17	18

1. 10
2. 9

$$\begin{array}{r} 7 \\ +\ 2 \\ \hline 9 \end{array}$$

3. 10　　　4. 5　　　5. 11
6. 13　　　7. 9　　　8. 16
9. 4　　　10. 14　　11. 18
12. 12　　13. 17　　14. 13
15. 12　　16. 14　　17. 11
18. 2　　　19. 12　　20. 12
21. 10　　22. 9　　　23. 15
24. 11

$$\begin{array}{r} 7 \\ +\ 4 \\ \hline 11 \end{array}$$

25. 10　　　　26. 7
27. 7　　　　28. 10

Page 31
1. 3
2. 5
   3 + 2 = 5
3. 6　　　　4. 6
5. 8　　　　6. 6
7. 5　　　　8. 0
9. 8　　　　10. 3
11. 5　　　　12. 4
13. $n = 2$
14. $x = 6$
   3 + 6 = 9

15. $n = 6$ **16.** $n = 8$
17. $n = 15$ **18.** $x = 3$
19. $x = 7$ **20.** $n = 13$
21. $x = 3$ **22.** $n = 8$
23. $x = 7$ **24.** $n = 9$
25. $n = 8$ **26.** $x = 6$
27. $x = 11$ **28.** $n = 1$
29. $6 + n = 8$
30. $n = 1 + 9$

Use *n* or *x* to stand for *what number*.

31. $n + 4 = 8$ **32.** $5 + n = 12$
33. $7 + n = 7$ **34.** $n + 4 = 5$

Page 32

1. 98
2. 99

Add the digits in the ones column.
$2 + 7 = 9$. Then add the digits in the tens column. $9 + 0 = 9$.

```
   92
 +  7
 ────
   99
```

3. 66   **4.** 55
5. 57   **6.** 88
7. 369   **8.** 599
9. 978   **10.** 367
11. 866   **12.** 535
13. 756   **14.** 488
15. 843   **16.** 685
17. 1,876   **18.** 4,878
19. 7,766   **20.** 8,757
21. 4,053   **22.** 5,550
23. 5,088   **24.** 8,189
25. 558   **26.** 1,599
27. 2,673   **28.** 978

Page 33

1. 77
2. 79

First put the digits in a column. Add the ones digits. $4 + 5 = 9$. Then add the tens digits. $2 + 5 = 7$.

```
   24
 + 55
 ────
   79
```

3. 48   **4.** 84
5. 349   **6.** 589
7. 678   **8.** 385
9. 2,939   **10.** 4,800

11. 9,337   **12.** 6,893
13. 4,884   **14.** 887
15. 5,666
16. 56 miles   **17.** $186
```
       32              $165
     + 24            +    21
     ────            ──────
       56              $186
```

Page 34

1. 151
2. 74

Add the ones. $8 + 6 = 14$. Carry 1 ten.
Add the tens. $1 + 6 = 7$.

```
    1
   68
 +  6
 ────
   74
```

3. 61   **4.** 80
5. 127   **6.** 181
7. 100   **8.** 23
9. 80   **10.** 110
11. 51   **12.** 73
13. 614   **14.** 724
15. 1,031   **16.** 1,163
17. 717   **18.** 280
19. 808   **20.** 909
21. 921   **22.** 490
23. 2,098   **24.** 8,105
25. 4,700   **26.** 11,520

Page 35

1. 372
2. 125

First put the digits in a column. Add the ones. $7 + 8 = 15$. Carry 1 ten. Add the tens. $1 + 3 + 8 = 12$.

```
    1
   37
 + 88
 ────
  125
```

3. 81   **4.** 54
5. 408   **6.** 773
7. 785   **8.** 1,008
9. 1,480   **10.** 4,060
11. 4,072   **12.** 14,018
13. 309   **14.** 90
15. 463   **16.** 4,104
17. 2,137   **18.** 3,014
19. 911   **20.** 5,231

21. $153

$$\begin{array}{r} {\scriptstyle 1} \\ \$125 \\ +\quad 28 \\ \hline \$153 \end{array}$$

22. $203

$$\begin{array}{r} {\scriptstyle 11} \\ \$135 \\ +\quad 68 \\ \hline \$203 \end{array}$$

Page 36

1. 50

2. 13

Add the first two digits. $5 + 2 = 7$.
Then add the last digit to the 7.
$7 + 6 = 13$.

$$\begin{array}{r} 5 \\ 2 \\ +\ 6 \\ \hline 13 \end{array}$$

3. 111 **4.** 597

5. 353 **6.** 812

7. 895 **8.** 788

9. 587 **10.** 832

11. 1,120 **12.** 133

13. 936 **14.** 251

15. 180 gallons **16.** 318 tickets

$$\begin{array}{r} {\scriptstyle 1\,2} \\ 38 \\ 75 \\ +\,67 \\ \hline 180 \end{array}\qquad \begin{array}{r} {\scriptstyle 2\,1} \\ 192 \\ 67 \\ +\,59 \\ \hline 318 \end{array}$$

Page 37

1. 450

2. 150

Round 63 to 60. Round 89 to 90. Then
add the rounded numbers.

$$\begin{array}{r} 60 \\ +\,90 \\ \hline 150 \end{array}$$

3. 900 **4.** 2,500

5. 170 **6.** 740

7. 6,500 **8.** 910

9. 890 **10.** 760

11. 290 **12.** 4,500

13. 5,250

14. $160

$$\begin{array}{r} \$\ 20 \\ 40 \\ +\ \ 100 \\ \hline \$160 \end{array}$$

15. 370 people

$$\begin{array}{r} {\scriptstyle 1} \\ 50 \\ 80 \\ 40 \\ +\,200 \\ \hline 370 \end{array}$$

Page 38

1. 104

2. 303

Clear the calculator. Enter 237. Press
the + key. Enter 66. Press the = key.
Read the display.

3. 5,125 **4.** 7,612

5. 121 **6.** 819

7. 5,312 **8.** 332

9. 5,214 **10.** 5,045

11. 7,877 **12.** 1,514

13. 977 **14.** 4,513

15. 6,064

16. $392

$$\begin{array}{r} {\scriptstyle 2} \\ \$\ 47 \\ 128 \\ +\ 217 \\ \hline \$392 \end{array}$$

17. 6,500 sheets

$$\begin{array}{r} 5,000 \\ 1,000 \\ +\quad 500 \\ \hline 6,500 \end{array}$$

Page 39

1. 11 **2.** 9

3. 119 **4.** 579

5. 1,138 **6.** 1,679

7. 9 **8.** 47

9. 497 **10.** 4,885

11. 70 **12.** 604

13. 1,109 **14.** 2,164

15. 10,820 **16.** 65

17. 416 **18.** 1,234

19. 3,507 **20.** 22

21. 705 **22.** 3,105

23. 589 **24.** 1,984

25. 74 **26.** 996

27. 2,333 **28.** 1,061

29. 9,513 **30.** 18,506

31. 397 **32.** 22,460

33. 560 miles

$$\begin{array}{r} 310 \\ +250 \\ \hline 560 \end{array}$$

34. 1,032 votes

$$
\begin{array}{r}
^{11} \\
251 \\
732 \\
+\ \ 49 \\
\hline
1,032
\end{array}
$$

Page 41

1. Step 1
94 calls in the morning
101 calls in the afternoon
Step 2 Since you need to find out how many calls *in all*, add.
Step 3

$$
\begin{array}{rcr}
 & & \text{Estimate} \\
94 & \rightarrow & 90 \\
+\ 101 & \rightarrow & +\ 100 \\
\hline
 & & \text{about } 190
\end{array}
$$

Step 4

$$
\begin{array}{r}
94 \\
+\ 101 \\
\hline
195
\end{array}
$$

Step 5 Stella received 195 calls.

2. Step 1
197 large gifts
42 small gifts
Step 2 Since you need to find out how many gifts in all, add.
Step 3

$$
\begin{array}{rcr}
 & & \text{Estimate} \\
197 & \rightarrow & 200 \\
+\ 42 & \rightarrow & +\ 40 \\
\hline
 & & \text{about } 240
\end{array}
$$

Step 4

$$
\begin{array}{r}
^{1} \\
197 \\
+\ 42 \\
\hline
239
\end{array}
$$

Step 5 Kara wrapped 239 gifts.

3. Step 1
1 sheet of one hundred stamps
1 strip of ten stamps
6 loose stamps
Step 2 Since you need to find out how many stamps, rename.

Step 3
1 hundred 1 ten 6 ones = _____
Step 4
1 hundred 1 ten 6 ones =
100 + 10 + 6 = 116
Step 5 Eric had 116 stamps.

4. Step 1
$103
$98
$89
$111
Step 2 Since you need to find out how much all together, add.
Step 3

$$
\begin{array}{rcr}
 & & \text{Estimate} \\
\$103 & \rightarrow & \$100 \\
98 & \rightarrow & 100 \\
89 & \rightarrow & 90 \\
+\ \ 111 & \rightarrow & +\ \ 100 \\
\hline
 & & \text{about } \$390
\end{array}
$$

Step 4

$$
\begin{array}{r}
\$103 \\
98 \\
89 \\
+\ \ 111 \\
\hline
\$401
\end{array}
$$

Step 5 Glenn spent $401 on groceries.

5. Step 1
48 customers for breakfast
67 customers for lunch
104 customers for dinner
Step 2 Since you need to find out how many customers were served, add.
Step 3

$$
\begin{array}{rcr}
 & & \text{Estimate} \\
 & & ^{1} \\
48 & \rightarrow & 50 \\
67 & \rightarrow & 70 \\
+\ 104 & \rightarrow & +\ 100 \\
\hline
 & & \text{about } 220
\end{array}
$$

Step 4

$$
\begin{array}{r}
^{1} \\
48 \\
67 \\
+\ 104 \\
\hline
219
\end{array}
$$

Step 5 The restaurant served 219 customers.

6. **Step 1**
$2,165 after withdrawal
$940 withdrawal
Step 2 Since you need to find out how much money Gina had before she withdrew $940, add.
Step 3

              Estimate
    $2,165 → $2,000
  +   940 → + 1,000
              about $3,000

Step 4

    1 1
  $2,165
+   940
  $3,105

Step 5 Gina had $3,105 in her account before paying for the class.

7. **Step 1**
$150 on brakes
$78 on new tires
$30 for oil change
Step 2
Since we need to find the total bill we need to add.
Step 3

            Estimate
              1
  $150 → $200
    78 →   80
+   30 → + 30
           about $310

Step 4

    1
  $150
    78
+   30
  $258

Step 5 Andrea paid $258 for car repairs.

8. **Step 1**
There were 550 customers on Wednesday and 560 customers on Saturday.

Step 2
Since we need to find the total, add.
Step 3

              Estimate
    550 →   600
  + 560 → + 600
         about 1,200

Step 4

    1
  550
+ 560
 1,110

Step 5
1,110 customers

Page 42
1. 6
2. 4

    6
  − 2
    4

3. 3	4. 8	5. 7
6. 1	7. 5	8. 7
9. 9	10. 0	11. 2
12. 5	13. 9	14. 9
15. 6	16. 7	17. 1
18. 8	19. 3	20. 9
21. 5	22. 2	
23. 4	24. 3	

23.
   10
 − 6
   4

24.
   11
 − 8
   3

25. 4
   9
 − 5
   4

26. 7
  13
 − 6
   7

27. 5
   7
 − 2
   5

28. 6
   9
 − 3
   6

Page 43
1. 6
2. 8
  13 − 5 = 8

3. 9	4. 7
5. 2	6. 1

7. 14   **8.** 7
9. 8   **10.** 1
11. 5   **12.** 8
13. $n = 9$
14. $x = 3$
     $7 - 3 = 4$
15. $n = 9$ **16.** $n = 4$
17. $x = 8$ **18.** $n = 10$
19. $x = 8$ **20.** $n = 9$
21. $n = 0$ **22.** $x = 10$
23. $x = 8$ **24.** $n = 4$
25. $14 - n = 7$
26. $12 - 3 = n$
     Use *n* or *x* to stand for *what number*.
27. $n - 5 = 3$ **28.** $7 = 15 - n$
29. $6 - n = 1$ **30.** $n - 2 = 8$

Page 44
1. 24
2. 37
     Subtract the digits in the ones column. $7 - 0 = 7$. Then subtract the digits in the tens column. $6 - 3 = 3$. Add to check.

$$\begin{array}{r} 67 \\ -\ 30 \\ \hline 37 \end{array} \qquad \begin{array}{r} 37 \\ +\ 30 \\ \hline 67 \end{array}$$

3. 31   **4.** 84
5. 21   **6.** 61
7. 12   **8.** 11
9. 612   **10.** 120
11. 312   **12.** 291
13. 181   **14.** 352
15. 204   **16.** 813
17. 3,147   **18.** 1,123
19. 3,262   **20.** 4,423
21. 1,220   **22.** 4,115
23. 332   **24.** 2,244

Page 45
1. 42
2. 33
     Line up the digits. Subtract the digits in the ones column. $6 - 3 = 3$. Then subtract the digits in the tens column. $5 - 2 = 3$. Add to check.

$$\begin{array}{r} 56 \\ -\ 23 \\ \hline 33 \end{array} \qquad \begin{array}{r} 33 \\ +\ 23 \\ \hline 56 \end{array}$$

3. 51   **4.** $52
5. 202   **6.** 522
7. $49   **8.** 222
9. 8,212   **10.** $4,120
11. 1,114   **12.** 1,212
13. $345

$$\begin{array}{r} \$865 \\ -\ 520 \\ \hline \$345 \end{array}$$

14. 313 miles

$$\begin{array}{r} 638 \\ -\ 325 \\ \hline 313 \end{array}$$

Page 46
1. 18
2. 19
     Since you can't subtract 7 from 6, borrow 1 ten. Rename the borrowed ten as 10 ones and add it to the 6 ones. $16 - 7 = 9$ ones. Then subtract the tens. $3 - 2 = 1$ ten. Add to check.

$$\begin{array}{r} \scriptstyle 3\ 16 \\ 4\!\!\!/6 \\ -\ 27 \\ \hline 19 \end{array} \qquad \begin{array}{r} \scriptstyle 1 \\ 19 \\ +\ 27 \\ \hline 46 \end{array}$$

3. 67   **4.** 28
5. 5   **6.** 25
7. 6   **8.** 86
9. 385   **10.** 107
11. 791   **12.** 206
13. 152   **14.** 486
15. 196   **16.** 68
17. 1,182   **18.** 1,557
19. 4,398   **20.** 5,341

Page 47
1. 135
2. 664
     Borrow 1 ten and rename. You now have 13 ones and 9 tens. Subtract the ones. $13 - 9 = 4$. Borrow 1 hundred and rename. You now have 6 hundreds. $6 - 0 = 6$. Subtract the tens. $9 - 3 = 6$. Add to check.

$$\begin{array}{r} \scriptstyle 6\ 9\ 13 \\ 7\!\!\!/0\!\!\!/3 \\ -\ 39 \\ \hline 664 \end{array} \qquad \begin{array}{r} \scriptstyle 1\ 1 \\ 664 \\ +\ 39 \\ \hline 703 \end{array}$$

3. 503 **4.** 748
5. 367 **6.** 325
7. 582 **8.** 79
9. 42 **10.** 376
11. 98 **12.** 819
13. 5,429 **14.** 1,476
15. 3,363 **16.** 2,086
17. 3,237 **18.** 2,929
19. 645 **20.** 6,544

Page 48

1. 37
2. 26

First put the digits in columns. Since you cannot subtract 9 ones from 5 ones, borrow a ten from the 4 tens. You now have 15 ones and 3 tens. Subtract the ones. $15 - 9 = 6$. Subtract the tens. $3 - 1 = 2$. Add to check.

$$\begin{array}{r} \overset{3\ 15}{4\cancel{5}} \\ -\ 19 \\ \hline 26 \end{array} \qquad \begin{array}{r} \overset{1}{26} \\ +\ 19 \\ \hline 45 \end{array}$$

3. $64 **4.** 26
5. 345 **6.** $643
7. 565 **8.** 568
9. 4,172 **10.** 4,578
11. $386 **12.** 2,378
13. 57 **14.** 17
15. 255 **16.** 850
17. 48 minutes **18.** $80
$55 - 7 = 48$ $115 - 35 = 80

Page 49

1. 300
2. 30

Round 73 to 70. Round 35 to 40. Subtract the rounded numbers.

$$\begin{array}{r} 70 \\ -\ 40 \\ \hline 30 \end{array}$$

3. $200 **4.** 400
5. 510 **6.** $500
7. 5,000 **8.** 5,000
9. 2,000 **10.** 40
11. 400 **12.** $7,200
13. 4,000 **14.** 3,700
15. $30 **16.** 300
17. 2,000

18. $1,100
$2,000 - $900 = $1,100$
19. 6,000 miles
$8,000 - 2,000 = 6,000$

Page 50

1. 45
2. $74
Clear the calculator. Enter 92. Press the − key. Enter 18. Press the = key.
3. 287 **4.** 384
5. 219 **6.** 663
7. $39 **8.** 141
9. 2,838 **10.** 4,346
11. $552 **12.** 2,887
13. 429 **14.** $513
15. 1,399 **16.** 2,953
17. 3,872
18. $65
$225 - 160 = 65
19. 578 employees
$1,051 - 473 = 578$

Page 51

1. 9 **2.** 6
3. 5 **4.** $15
5. 31 **6.** 30
7. $9 **8.** 6
9. 23 **10.** 16
11. 451 **12.** 422
13. 193 **14.** $302
15. 103 **16.** 313
17. 822 **18.** 7,910
19. 5,105 **20.** 29
21. $66 **22.** 574
23. 139 **24.** 3,890
25. 18 **26.** 63
27. $475 **28.** 1,733
29. 609 **30.** 558
31. 4,718 **32.** 2,948
33. $180
$225 - 45 = 180
34. 48 days
$365 - 317 = 48$

Page 52

1. 33
2. 80
Subtract the first two numbers.

$76 - 19 = 57$. Then add the answer to the third number. $57 + 23 = 80$.

```
    6 16                 1
    7̶6̶                  57
  − 19               + 23
  ─────              ─────
    57                 80
```

3. 27   **4.** 44

5. 249   **6.** $425

7. $518   **8.** 97

9. 438   **10.** 937

11. $28   **12.** 81

13. 38   **14.** 325

15. $873   **16.** 982

17. $3

$13 + $4 = $17

$20 − $17 = $3

18. 1,348 empty seats

1,287 + 365 = 1,652

3,000 − 1,652 = $1,348

Page 53

1. 197

2. 169

Subtract the first two numbers. $256 − 73 = 183$. Subtract the third number from the answer. $183 − 14 = 169$.

```
   1 15                7 13
   2̶5̶6               1 8̶ 3̶
  −  73              −  14
  ─────             ─────
    183               169
```

3. 110   **4.** 110

5. 705   **6.** 757

7. 167   **8.** 413

9. 656   **10.** 250

11. 443   **12.** 239

13. $9

$30 − $4 = $26

$26 − $17 = $9

14. $19

$20 − $7 = $13

$13 + $5 + $1 = $19

Page 54

1. 6,035   **2.** 3,921

3. 3,770   **4.** 604

5. 4,125   **6.** 700

Pages 55–56

1. 145   **2.** 82

3. 895   **4.** 4,346

5. 4,636   **6.** 77

7. 171   **8.** 857

9. 2,702   **10.** 52

11. 46   **12.** 847

13. 454   **14.** 3,753

15. 53   **16.** 54

17. 253   **18.** 7,343

19. 290   **20.** 400

21. 7,300   **22.** 3,800

23. 6,100   **24.** 510

25. 690   **26.** 4,000

27. 450

28. 378 reams of white paper

```
   3 14 16
   4̶ 5̶ 6̶
  −    78
  ──────
    3 7 8
```

29. $448

```
       1
    $160
  +  288
  ──────
    $448
```

30. (D) 561 Choices A, B, and C are incorrect because of solving or renaming errors.

31. (B) 5,731 Choices A, C, and D are incorrect because of solving or renaming errors.

32. (A) 811 Choice D is incorrect because the numbers were added rather than subtracted. In Choice C, the numbers were added incorrectly. Choice B is incorrect because of a solving error.

33. (D) 5,735 Choice A is incorrect because the digits were not lined up in the correct columns. Choices B and C are incorrect because of solving or renaming errors.

34. (C) 1,100 Choice A is incorrect because of a place value error. Choices B and D are incorrect because of rounding errors.

35. (C) 3,200 Choices A, B, and D are incorrect because of rounding errors.

36. (A) 138 miles Choice D is incorrect because the numbers were added rather than subtracted. Choices B and C are incorrect because of solving or renaming errors.

37. (D) 235 miles Choice A is incorrect because the numbers were subtracted rather than added. In Choice B, the numbers were subtracted incorrectly. Choice C is incorrect because of solving or renaming errors.

38. (B) 335 tons Choice D is incorrect because the numbers were added rather than subtracted. In Choice C, the numbers were added incorrectly. Choice A is incorrect because of solving or renaming errors.

39. (C) 111 yards Choice B is incorrect because the numbers were subtracted rather than added. In Choice A, the numbers were subtracted incorrectly. Choice D is incorrect because of solving or renaming errors.

Pages 57–58

1. ones	**2.** tens
3. ones	**4.** thousands
5. tens	**6.** hundreds
7. >	**8.** <
9. >	**10.** <
11. >	**12.** 60
13. 20	**14.** 90
15. 300	**16.** 3,000
17. 900	**18.** 49
19. 17	**20.** 968
21. 425	**22.** 123
23. 33	**24.** 65
25. 571	**26.** 1,066
27. 575	**28.** 522
29. 1,328	**30.** 2,200

31. 15 square yards
32. 1,007 miles
33. (A) 17 Choice B is incorrect because 7 tens is greater than 2 tens. Choices C and D are incorrect because each has a digit in the hundreds place.

34. (D) 700 Choice A is incorrect because the number was rounded down rather than up. Choices B and C are incorrect because they show numbers rounded to the nearest ten.

35. (B) 7 Choice A is incorrect because 0 is in the tens place. Choice C is incorrect because 8 is in the ones place. Choice D is incorrect because 100 is not a digit.

36. (D) 403 > 304 Choices A and B are incorrect because each uses the less than symbol. Choice C is incorrect because the two numbers are reversed.

37. (C) 958 Choices A and D are incorrect because the digits were not lined up in the correct columns. Choice B is incorrect because of a solving error.

38. (B) 924 Choice A is incorrect because the digits were not lined up in the correct columns. Choice C is incorrect because of a solving error. Choice D is incorrect because the numbers were added rather than subtracted.

39. (C) 382 Choices A and D are incorrect because the digits were not lined up in the correct columns. Choice B is incorrect because of a renaming error.

40. (A) 4,539 Choice B is incorrect because of a renaming error. Choice C is incorrect because the digits were not lined up in the correct columns. Choice D is incorrect because the numbers were added rather than subtracted.

41. (B) 340 boxes Choices A, C, and D are incorrect because the wrong numbers were added.

42. (B) $552 Choice C is incorrect because the numbers were added rather than subtracted. In Choice D, the numbers were added incorrectly. Choice A is incorrect because of a solving error.

Unit 3

×	0	1	2	3	4	5	6	7	8	9
0	0	0	0	0	0	0	0	0	0	0
1	0	1	2	3	4	5	6	7	8	9
2	0	2	4	6	8	10	12	14	16	18
3	0	3	6	9	12	15	18	21	24	27
4	0	4	8	12	16	20	24	28	32	36
5	0	5	10	15	20	25	30	35	40	45
6	0	6	12	18	24	30	36	42	48	54
7	0	7	14	21	28	35	42	49	56	63
8	0	8	16	24	32	40	48	56	64	72
9	0	9	18	27	36	45	54	63	72	81

1. 20
2. 42

Find the row that begins with 6 and the column that begins with 7. The answer, 42, is in the box where the row and column meet.

3. 0   4. 12   5. 35
6. 12   7. 28   8. 21
9. 0   10. 45   11. 16
12. 1   13. 48   14. 9
15. 14   16. 64   17. 6
18. 72   19. 56   20. 0
21. 32   22. 27   23. 7
24. 18   25. 56
26. 2

Find the row that begins with 2 and the column that begins with 1. The answer, 2, is in the box where the row and column meet.

27. 54   28. 32   29. 9
30. 48   31. 30   32. 21
33. 14   34. 36   35. 24
36. 0   37. 24   38. 5
39. 12

1. 9
2. 3

Think, "What number times 8 equals 24?" The answer is 3 because $3 \times 8 = 24$.

3. 45   4. 7

5. 45   6. 3
7. 9   8. 8
9. 5   10. 6
11. 8   12. 6
13. $n = 6$
14. $n = 4$

Think, "What number times 3 equals 12?" The answer is 4 because $4 \times 3 = 12$.

15. $n = 49$ 16. $n = 18$
17. $n = 6$ 18. $n = 6$
19. $n = 9$ 20. $n = 2$
21. $n = 16$ 22. $n = 56$
23. $n = 5$ 24. $n = 0$
25. $n = 3$ 26. $n = 9$
27. $n = 32$ 28. $n = 9$
29. $3 \times n = 6$
30. $8 \times 4 = n$

An n or other letter such as x can be used to stand for the expression *what number*.

31. $n \times 8 = 0$ 32. $6 \times 6 = n$
33. $n \times 2 = 2$ 34. $5 \times n = 10$
35. $8 \times 9 = n$ 36. $n \times 7 = 7$

1. $96
2. $20

Multiply the ones. $2 \times 0 = 0$. Write 0 in the ones place. Multiply the tens. $2 \times 1 = 2$. Write 2 in the tens place. Write a dollar sign in front of the answer.

3. 84   4. 13
5. 153   6. 864
7. 606   8. $936
9. $3,699   10. 4,648
11. 6,244   12. 5,896
13. $86
14. 3,633

Multiply the ones. $3 \times 1 = 3$ ones. Write 3 in the ones place. Multiply the tens. $3 \times 1 = 3$ tens. Write 3 in the tens place. Multiply the hundreds. $3 \times 2 = 6$ hundreds. Write 6 in the hundreds place. Multiply the thousands. $3 \times 1 = 3$ thousands. Write 3 in the thousands place.

15. $68   16. 484
17. 6,306   18. 48

19. 369
21. 36 baseballs
$$\begin{array}{r} 12 \\ \times\ \ 3 \\ \hline 36 \end{array}$$

20. $6,266
22. 64 children
$$\begin{array}{r} 32 \\ \times\ \ 2 \\ \hline 64 \end{array}$$

Page 63

1. $672
2. $5,076
Multiply 423 by 2 ones. 2 × 423 = 846. Multiply 423 by 1 ten. The second partial product is 4,230. Add the partial products. Write a dollar sign in front of the answer.
3. 169
4. 3,322
5. 750
6. 1,608
7. $299
8. 16,828
9. $516
10. 17,173
11. $132
12. 3,648
Multiply 304 by 2 ones. 2 × 304 = 608. Multiply 304 by 1 ten. The second partial product is 3,040. Add the partial products.
13. $913
14. $3,080
15. $264
$$\begin{array}{r} \$24 \\ \times\ \ 11 \\ \hline 24 \\ +\ \ 24 \\ \hline \$264 \end{array}$$

16. 2,880 customers
$$\begin{array}{r} 120 \\ \times\ \ 24 \\ \hline 480 \\ +\ 240 \\ \hline 2,880 \end{array}$$

Page 64

1. 712
2. 98
Multiply the ones. 7 × 4 = 28. Write 8 in the ones place and carry the 2 tens. Multiply the tens. 7 × 1 = 7. Add the carried 2. 7 + 2 = 9 tens. Write 9 in the tens place.
3. 6,420
4. $748
5. 728
6. $6,860
7. 8,145
8. 166
9. 3,682
10. 7,890
11. 60
12. 12,024
13. $4,140
14. 14,910

15. 650 cartons of milk
$$\begin{array}{r} 1\ \ \ \ \\ 130 \\ \times\ \ 5 \\ \hline 650 \end{array}$$

16. 870 pounds
$$\begin{array}{r} 2\ 3\ \ \\ 145 \\ \times\ \ 6 \\ \hline 870 \end{array}$$

Page 65

1. 1,081
2. 66,822
Multiply 1,806 by 7 ones. The first partial product is 12,642. Multiply 1,806 by 3 tens. The second partial product is 54,180. Add the partial products.
3. $23,576
4. 110,736
5. $32,310
6. $1,464
7. 231,768
8. $3,610
9. $12,642
10. 418,965
Multiply 8,215 by 1 one. 8,215 × 1 = 8,215. Multiply 8,215 by 5 tens. 8,215 × 5 = 41,075. Add the partial products.
11. 2,240
12. 21,750 tickets
$$\begin{array}{r} 1,450 \\ \times\ \ \ \ 15 \\ \hline 7250 \\ +\ 1450 \\ \hline 21,750 \end{array}$$

13. 30,000 cans
$$\begin{array}{r} 2,500 \\ \times\ \ \ \ 12 \\ \hline 5000 \\ +\ 2500 \\ \hline 30,000 \end{array}$$

Page 66

1. 2,440
2. 423,100
Write two zeros in the answer. Multiply 1 times 4,231. 1 × 4,231 = 4231. Write these digits to the left of the two zeros.
3. $10,480
4. $73,500
5. 126,840
6. $168,400
7. 540
8. $63,900
9. 249,240
10. $380,800
11. 15,550

12. $112,700

Write two zeros in the answer.
Multiply 7 times 161. $7 \times 161 = 1127$.
Write these digits to the left of the two
zeros.

13. 9,270   **14.** $500
15. 2,010   **16.** 252,000
17. 165,300   **18.** 166,600
19. 75,000 sheets **20.** 960 bottles

$$
\begin{array}{r}
150 \\
\times\ 500 \\
\hline
75,000
\end{array}
\qquad
\begin{array}{r}
12 \\
\times\ 80 \\
\hline
960
\end{array}
$$

Page 67

1. $30 \times 20 = 600$
2. $90 \times 40 = 3,600$
 Round 93 to 90. Round 41 to 40.
 Multiply the rounded numbers.
 $90 \times 40 = 3,600$
3. $90 \times 30 = 2,700$
4. $70 \times 50 = 3,500$
5. $70 \times 30 = 2,100$
6. $300 \times 20 = 6,000$
7. $500 \times 40 = 20,000$
8. $800 \times 90 = 72,000$
9. $400 \times 40 = 16,000$
10. $900 \times 40 = 36,000$
11. $6,000 \times 60 = 360,000$
12. $2,000 \times 40 = 80,000$
13. $4,000 \times 60 = 240,000$
14. $3,000 \times 50 = 150,000$
15. $90 \times 90 = 8,100$
16. $300 \times 30 = 9,000$
17. $8,000 \times 60 = 480,000$
18. $100 \times 70 = 7,000$
19. $400 \times 20 = 8,000$
20. $1,000 \times 20 = 20,000$
21. $900 \times 50 = 45,000$
22. $2,000 \times 80 = 160,000$
23. $200 \times 10 = 2,000$
24. $300 \times 40 = 12,000$ cars
 Round 312 to 300. Round 39 to 40.
 Multiply the rounded numbers.
25. $9,000 \times 10 = 90,000$ cards
 Round 8,765 to 9,000. Round 12 to 10.
 Multiply the rounded numbers.

Page 68

1. 3,420
2. 1,518
 Clear the calculator. Enter 23. Press the
 multiply key. Enter 66. Press the
 equals key. Read the answer.
3. 3,404   **4.** 8,244
5. 25,915   **6.** 321,376
7. 148,352   **8.** 600,075
9. 17,172   **10.** 276,597
11. 109,228   **12.** 740,652
13. 1,610
14. 1,416

$$
\begin{array}{r}
59 \\
\times\ 24 \\
\hline
236 \\
+\ 118 \\
\hline
1,416
\end{array}
$$

15. 3,975   **16.** 3,038
17. 6,450   **18.** $40,754
19. 14,326   **20.** 33,594
21. 13,167   **22.** $18,825
23. $13,476   **24.** $40,196

$$
\begin{array}{r}
\$1,123 \\
\times\qquad 12 \\
\hline
2246 \\
+\ 1123 \\
\hline
\$13,476
\end{array}
\qquad
\begin{array}{r}
\$773 \\
\times\qquad 52 \\
\hline
1546 \\
+\ 3865 \\
\hline
\$40,196
\end{array}
$$

Page 69

1. 3   **2.** 8
3. $n = 6$ **4.** $n = 40$
5. 462   **6.** 248
7. 7,500   **8.** 4,092
9. 252   **10.** 792
11. $1,440   **12.** 124,852
13. 140   **14.** 4,207
15. 9,711   **16.** 280
17. 30,500   **18.** 42,500
19. $60 \times 400 = 24,000$; 23,712
20. $2,000 \times 30 = 60,000$; 56,869
21. $800 \times 40 = 32,000$; 31,654
22. 750 miles   **23.** 240 calls

$$
\begin{array}{r}
150 \\
\times\ \ 5 \\
\hline
750
\end{array}
\qquad
\begin{array}{r}
30 \\
\times\ \ 8 \\
\hline
240
\end{array}
$$

Page 70

1. 6
2. 8

Find the row that begins with 9. Read across the row until you find 72. Move up the column to the answer, 8.

3. 3	**4.** 5	**5.** 4
6. 2	**7.** 2	**8.** 2
9. 8	**10.** 9	**11.** 7
12. 8	**13.** 5	**14.** 6
15. 3	**16.** 1	**17.** 8
18. 4	**19.** 5	**20.** 3
21. 9	**22.** 6	**23.** 0
24. 1	**25.** 4	

26. 7

Find the row that begins with 2. Read across the row until you find 14. Move up the column to the answer, 7.

27. 4	**28.** 8	**29.** 6
30. 7	**31.** 9	**32.** 1
33. 5	**34.** 0	**35.** 3
36. 5	**37.** 3	**38.** 6
39. 6	**40.** 4	**41.** 4
42. 8	**43.** 3	**44.** 8

Page 71

1. 4
2. 35

Think, "What number divided by 7 equals 5?" The answer is 35 because $35 \div 7 = 5$.

3. 5	**4.** 8
5. 9	**6.** 7
7. 72	**8.** 6
9. 15	**10.** 2
11. 4	**12.** 8
13. 9	**14.** 9
15. 14	**16.** 42

17. $n = 5$
18. $n = 3$

Think, "$21 \div 7$ equals what number?" The answer is 3 because $21 \div 7 = 3$.

19. $n = 6$	**20.** $n = 1$
21. $n = 16$	**22.** $n = 7$
23. $n = 3$	**24.** $n = 6$
25. $n = 3$	**26.** $n = 12$
27. $n = 2$	**28.** $n = 3$
29. $n = 8$	**30.** $n = 16$
31. $n = 45$	**32.** $n = 6$

33. $n = 21$	**34.** $n = 3$
35. $n = 2$	**36.** $n = 10$

37. $3 \div n = 1$
38. $28 \div 4 = n$

An n or other letter such as x can be used to stand for the words *what number*.

39. $n \div 4 = 8$	**40.** $12 \div 6 = n$
41. $n \div 5 = 8$	**42.** $40 \div n = 5$

Page 72

1. 74
2. $91

Write a dollar sign in the quotient. Divide 3 into 27. $27 \div 3 = 9$. Write 9 in the tens place in the quotient. Divide 3 into 3. $3 \div 3 = 1$. Write 1 in the ones place in the quotient.

3. 11	**4.** 411	**5.** 111
6. 511	**7.** 81	**8.** $21
9. $411	**10.** 32	**11.** 41
12. 71	**13.** 52	**14.** $71
15. 421	**16.** 93	

17. 11 presents

$$\begin{array}{r} 11 \\ 8\overline{)88} \end{array}$$

18. 64 customers

$$\begin{array}{r} 64 \\ 2\overline{)128} \end{array}$$

Page 73

1. 27 R5
2. 73 R3

You can't divide 4 into 2. Divide 4 into 29. The closest basic fact is $4 \times 7 = 28$. Write 7 in the tens place in the quotient. Multiply and subtract, getting a difference of 1. Bring down the 5. Divide 4 into 15.

$15 \div 4$ is 3 with a remainder of 3. Write 3 in the ones place in the quotient. Write R3 to show the remainder.

3. 45 R2	**4.** 17 R1
5. 23 R2	**6.** 98 R3
7. 28 R5	**8.** 12 R3
9. 46 R3	**10.** 12 R3
11. 16 R2	**12.** 25 R3

Page 74

1. 402 R1
2. 608

    You can't divide 4 into 2. Divide 4 into 24, getting 6. Bring down the 3. You can't divide 4 into 3, so write 0 in the tens place in the quotient. Bring down the 2. Divide 4 into 32 and write the answer, 8, in the ones place in the quotient.

3. 513 R5   4. 207
5. 904   6. $850
7. 118   8. 201
9. 150 packages

$$
\begin{array}{r}
150 \\
4\overline{)600} \\
\underline{-4} \\
20 \\
\underline{-20} \\
0
\end{array}
$$

10. 800 guests

$$
\begin{array}{r}
800 \\
3\overline{)2{,}400} \\
\underline{-24} \\
00 \\
\underline{0} \\
00 \\
\underline{0} \\
0
\end{array}
$$

Page 75

1. 14 R2
2. 32 R3

    Estimate: 2 goes into 7 about 3 times. Try 3 as the first digit of the quotient. 3 × 24 = 72. Subtract 72 from 77, which leaves 5. Bring down the 1. Divide 24 into 51. 2 × 24 = 48. Write 2 in the quotient. Subtract 48 from 51, which leaves 3. Write R3 for the remainder in the quotient.

3. 12 R3   4. 46 R6
5. 21 R9   6. 14 R10
7. $37   8. 27 R12

9. 35 hours

$$
\begin{array}{r}
35 \\
14\overline{)490} \\
\underline{-42} \\
70 \\
\underline{-70} \\
0
\end{array}
$$

10. 15 chapters

$$
\begin{array}{r}
15 \\
22\overline{)330} \\
\underline{-22} \\
110 \\
\underline{-110} \\
0
\end{array}
$$

Pages 76–77

1. twice as many; multiplication
2. difference; subtraction
3. in all; addition
4. split; division
5. subtraction; 30 items
6. multiplication or addition; $3
7. addition; $6
8. subtraction; 9 eggs
9. division; 64 ounces
10. multiplication; about $140
11. subtraction; 700 calories
12. division; 175 calories

Page 78

1. $300 \div 30 = 10$
2. $\$800 \div 40 = \$20$

    Round 42 to 40. Round $785 to $800. Divide the rounded numbers. $800 \div 40 = 20$. Write a dollar sign in front of the answer.

3. $200 \div 10 = 20$
4. $\$600 \div 60 = \$10$
5. $1{,}000 \div 20 = 50$
6. $600 \div 20 = 30$
7. $40 overtime pay

    Round $825 to $800. Round 19 to 20. Divide the rounded numbers.

8. 100 tapes

    Round 950 to 1,000. Round 9 to 10. Divide the rounded numbers.

9. 20 magazines

    Round 198 to 200. Round 8 to 10. Divide the rounded numbers.

10. 20 books

    Round 575 to 600. Round 28 to 30. Divide the rounded numbers.

Page 79

1. 32
2. $18
   Clear the calculator. Enter 576. Press the divide key. Enter 32. Press the equals key. Read the answer and write it using a $ sign.
3. 21
4. 20
5. $50
6. 41
7. 18
8. $90
9. 243
10. 538
11. 6,314
12. 645
13. 1,429
14. 95
15. 20
16. 8,327
17. 78
18. $46
19. $84
20. 60
21. $15
22. $6

$$\begin{array}{r} \$15 \\ 4\overline{)\$60} \\ -\ 4 \\ \hline 20 \\ -\ 20 \\ \hline 0 \end{array}$$

$$\begin{array}{r} \$6 \\ 2\overline{)\$12} \\ -\ 12 \\ \hline 0 \end{array}$$

Page 80

1. 31
2. 30
3. 42 R5
4. 21 R4
5. 28 R2
6. 104
7. $123
8. 64 R49
9. 30; 29
10. 10; 11
11. 30; 29
12. multiplication; 195 fans
13. division; 30 minutes

Page 81

1. $9 \times 2 = 18$
2. $4 + 10 = 14$
   Multiply first. $5 \times 2 = 10$. Add the 10 to the 4. $10 + 4 = 14$.
3. $6 + 2 = 8$
4. $3 + 2 = 5$
5. $10 \div 5 = 2$
6. $20 - 1 = 19$
7. $8 + 1 = 9$
8. $3 - 3 = 0$
9. $6 \times 1 = 6$
10. $12 + 3 = 15$
11. $21 + 3 = 24$
12. $30 - 1 = 29$
13. $2 - 2 = 0$
14. $16 \div 8 = 2$
15. $7 \times 7 = 49$
16. $45 - 5 = 40$
17. $12 \times 2 = 24$
18. $30 + 3 = 33$
19. $14 + 4 = 18$
20. $33 + 4 = 37$

21. $45 \div 9 = 5$
22. $11 + 48 = 59$
23. $65 - 5 = 60$
24. $6 + 12 = 18$

Page 82

1. $12 - 9 = 3$
2. $107 + 112 = 219$
   Multiply first. $14 \times 8 = 112$. Add the 112 to 107. $112 + 107 = 219$
3. $8 - 5 = 3$
4. $318 - 204 = 114$
5. $384 \div 24 = 16$
6. $85 + 2 = 87$
7. $878 - 52 = 826$
8. $288 \div 3 = 96$
9. $45 + 36 = 81$
10. $55 \times 55 = 3,025$
11. $1,428 \div 7 = 204$
12. $278 + 222 = 500$

Pages 83–84

1. $n = 8$
2. 804
3. $504
4. 628
5. 51,600
6. $300 \times 60 = 18,000$; 18,411
7. 2
8. 3
9. 31
10. 27 R1
11. $5 - 1 = 4$

Pages 85–86

1. $n = 7$
2. $n = 7$
3. $n = 3$
4. $n = 9$
5. $n = 16$
6. $n = 8$
7. $n = 4$
8. $n = 63$
9. 288
10. 2,048
11. 832
12. 32,643
13. 416
14. 4,555
15. 3,360
16. 207,120
17. 27
18. 23 R1
19. 671 R1
20. 42 R1
21. 16
22. 44
23. 367 R4
24. 245 R3
25. $2

$$\begin{array}{r} \$2 \\ 8\overline{)\$16} \end{array}$$

26. $2,375

```
     $125
   ×   19
     1125
   +  125
    $2,375
```

27. (C) 1,776 Choices A and D are incorrect because of renaming errors. Choice B is incorrect because of a multiplication error.

28. (C) 5,278 Choices A, B, and D are incorrect because of renaming errors.

29. (C) 11,010 Choices A and D are incorrect because the digits were not lined up correctly. Choice B is incorrect because of a renaming error.

30. (B) 87 R4 Choices A, C, and D are incorrect because of addition, subtraction, and multiplication errors.

31. (A) 508 Choice B is incorrect because a zero was not placed in the quotient before bringing down the 4. Choices C and D are incorrect because of multiplication and subtraction errors.

32. (D) 46 R12 Choices A and C are incorrect because of subtraction errors. Choice B is incorrect because the remainder is greater than the divisor.

33. (D) 40 Choices A, B, and C are incorrect because of multiplication and subtraction errors.

34. (C) $4,208 Choice A is incorrect because the numbers $263 and 16 were added. The numbers should have been multiplied. Choice B is incorrect because of a multiplication error. Choice D is incorrect because of a renaming error.

35. (D) 1,400 Choice A is incorrect because the numbers 50 and 28 were subtracted. Choice B is incorrect because the numbers 50 and 28 were added. Choice C is incorrect because the digits were not lined up correctly while multiplying.

36. (A) 9 Choices B and C are incorrect because 216 should have been divided by 24. Choice D is incorrect because

216 should have been divided by 24, not multiplied by 24.

Pages 87–88

1. <	**2.** >
3. <	**4.** >
5. <	**6.** 100
7. 100	**8.** 500
9. 700	**10.** 1,000
11. 28	**12.** 62
13. $541	**14.** 616
15. 6,233	**16.** $1,854
17. 1,838	**18.** 3,866
19. $211	**20.** 1,198
21. 58	**22.** $25
23. 739	**24.** 809
25. $736	**26.** 7,812
27. 540	**28.** $3,003
29. 8	**30.** 27
31. 405	**32.** 86 R8

33. 745 calories

```
   1,800        1,125
 −   675      −   380
   1,125          745
```

34. 544 campers

```
      136
   ×    4
      544
```

35. (D) 2,943 Choices A and B are incorrect because the digit 4 is in the ones place. Choice C is incorrect because the digit 4 is in both the ones and the hundreds place.

36. (D) 837 < 962 Choice A is incorrect because 837 is not greater than 962. Choice B is incorrect because 962 is not less than 837. Choice C is incorrect because 837 is not greater than 837.

37. (B) 615 Choice A is incorrect because of a renaming error. Choices C and D are incorrect because the digits were not lined up correctly.

38. (B) 2,051 Choice A is incorrect because of a subtraction error. Choices C and D are incorrect because of renaming errors.

39. (C) 1 + (9 ÷ 3) = Choices A, B, and D are incorrect because the order of operations was not followed.

40. (C) 72 Choice A is incorrect because $56 \div 8 = 7$. Choice B is incorrect because $64 \div 8 = 8$. Choice D is incorrect because $81 \div 8 = 10$ R1.

41. (B) 4 Choice A is incorrect because $3 \times 6 = 18$, not 24. Choice C is incorrect because $6 \times 6 = 36$. Choice D is incorrect because $8 \times 6 = 48$.

42. (C) $8 \div 1 =$ Choice A is incorrect because $4 \div 4 = 1$. Choice B is incorrect because $8 \times 0 = 0$. Choice D is incorrect because $4 - 4 = 0$.

43. (A) 14 minutes Choice B is incorrect because of a renaming error. Choice C is incorrect because both addition and subtraction were performed. Choice D is incorrect because addition was performed instead of subtraction.

44. (C) 240 Choice A is incorrect because $6 \times 40 = 240$. Choice B is incorrect because deliveries are made 6 days each week (Monday through Saturday), not 5 days each week (Monday through Friday). Choice D is incorrect because deliveries are made 6 days each week (Monday through Saturday), not 7 days each week (Monday through Sunday).

Unit 4

Page 90

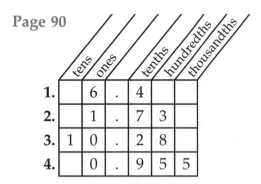

	tens	ones		tenths	hundredths	thousandths
1.		6	.	4		
2.		1	.	7	3	
3.	1	0	.	2	8	
4.		0	.	9	5	5

1. 6 ones 4 tenths

2. 1 one 7 tenths 3 hundredths
The ones place is just to the left of the decimal point, and the digit 1 is in the ones place. The tenths place is just to the right of the decimal point, and the

digit 7 is in the tenths place. The hundredths place is just to the right of the tenths place, and the digit 3 is in the hundredths place.

3. 1 ten 0 ones 2 tenths 8 hundredths

4. 0 ones 9 tenths 5 hundredths 5 thousandths

5. 7

6. 9
The tenths place is just to the right of the decimal point. The digit 9 is in the tenths place.

7. 0	**8.** 3
9. 1	**10.** 4
11. 3	**12.** 6
13. 5	**14.** 1
15. 0	**16.** 7
17. 0	

18. 8
The hundredths place is two places to the right of the decimal point. The digit 8 is in the hundredths place.

19. 1	**20.** 5
21. 4	**22.** 2
23. 0	**24.** 3
25. 1	**26.** 0
27. 6	**28.** 9

Page 91

				•				
1.		1	4	•	5			
2.			8	•	2	2	5	
3.		3	0	•	2			
4.			7	•	0	4		
5.	5	0	8	•	0	1		
6.			0	•	6	3		
7.			4	•	9			
8.		4	0	•	1	0	8	
9.	2	1	0	•	0	5	0	
10.			0	•	0	0	8	6

1. fourteen and five tenths

2. eight and two hundred twenty-five thousandths
The right-hand digit is in the thousandths place. The decimal part of the number is 225 thousandths.

3. thirty and two tenths
4. seven and four hundredths
5. five hundred eight and one hundredth
6. sixty-three hundredths
7. four and nine tenths
8. forty and one hundred eight thousandths
9. two hundred ten and fifty thousandths
10. eighty-six ten-thousandths
11. 70.33
12. 9.052

The digit 9 for nine ones goes to the left of the decimal point. The right-hand digit must go in the thousandths place, so the digits 052 go the right of the decimal point.

13. 0.26
14. 0.409
15. 1.7
16. 10.016

Page 92

1. ≠
2. =

Drop the zeros in $12.00. Both numbers have a place value of one ten and two ones.

3. ≠   4. ≠
5. =   6. =
7. ≠   8. ≠
9. ≠   10. ≠
11. =   12. =
13. is equal to
14. is equal to
60.02 = 60.020
15. is not equal to
16. is equal to

Page 93

1. =
2. ≠

The decimals 2.10 and 1.20 are not equal. The number 2.10 has 2 ones, while the number 1.20 has only 1 one.

3. ≠
4. =
5. ≠
6. =
7. <

8. <
Write 0.9 as 0.90. Then compare.
90 < 91, so 0.9 < 0.91.
9. =   10. <
11. >   12. <
13. >   14. <
15. 7.01 is 1   16. 0.003 is 1
7.1 is 2   0.03 is 2
7.11 is 3   0.3 is 3
17. 0.05 is 1
5.05 is 2
50.5 is 3

Page 94

1. $.51
2. $.07

Seven cents is the same as seven pennies, and seven pennies is the same as seven hundredths.

3. $.15
4. $.30
5. $.63
6. $.04
7. 3 dimes + 9 pennies
8. 1 dime + 5 pennies

The 1 is in tenths place, so there is one dime. The 5 is in hundredths place, so there are 5 pennies.

9. 8 pennies
10. 8 dimes + 8 pennies
11. 2 pennies
12. 6 dimes
13. six cents
14. seventy-three cents

73 = 7 tens + 3 ones, so 73¢ is written as seventy-three cents.

15. seventeen cents
16. ninety cents
17. thirty-three cents
18. two cents
19. sixteen cents
20. forty-nine cents
21. eighty-four cents

Page 95
1. $35.72
2. $8.02
   The digit 8 is in the ones place, so it stands for 8 ones, or 8 dollars. The digit 2 is in the hundredths place, so it stands for 2 hundredths, or 2 pennies.
3. $13.30
4. $75.04
5. $30.86
6. $41.11
7. 12 dollars + 3 dimes + 9 pennies
8. 3 dollars + 9 dimes + 5 pennies
   Write the dollars: 3 dollars. Write the dimes: 9 dimes. Write the cents: 5 cents.
9. 2 dollars + 7 pennies
10. 20 dollars + 5 dimes
11. sixty dollars and fourteen cents
12. three dollars and seven cents
    Write the dollars in words: three dollars. Write the cents in words: seven cents.
13. twenty-eight dollars and eighteen cents
14. sixty-six dollars and fifty cents
15. fifty-five dollars and twenty-three cents
16. seven dollars and thirty-five cents

Page 96
1. 51.5
2. 51.4
   The digit in the hundredths place is 2. Since 2 is less than 5, round down to 4.
3. 51.4
4. 51.5
5. 51.4
6. 51.5
7. 0.4
8. 23.6
   The digit in the hundredths place is 0. Since 0 is less than 5, round down to 6.
9. 3.2
10. 184.0
11. 17.6
12. 8.2

13. 7.0
    In 6.96, since the digit 9 is greater than 5, round up to the next whole number, 7.
14. 289.0
15. 19.2
16. 7.6
17. 341.7
18. 60.1

Page 97
1. 0.09
2. 0.09
   The digit in the thousandths place is 7. Since 7 is greater than 5, round 8 up to 9.
3. 0.08
4. 0.09
5. 0.08
6. 0.09
7. 1.43
8. 0.21
   The digit in the thousandths place is 8. Since 8 is greater than 5, round 0 up to 1.
9. 16.62
10. 30.01
11. 0.40
12. 19.43
13. 22.10
14. 9.27
15. 143.40
16. 50.00
17. 38.37
18. 0.62

Page 98
1. $1.00
2. $1.00
   The digit in the tenths place is 0. Since 0 is less than 5, round down to $1.00.
3. $27.00
4. $10.00
5. $52.00
6. $6.00
7. $1.00
8. $15.00
9. $10.00
10. $41.00
11. $7.00
12. $.40
    The digit in the hundredths, or cents, place is 5. Round up. $.35 rounds to $.40.
13. $.80
14. $7.00
15. $19.30
16. $8.40
17. $60.20
18. $43.00
19. $112.00
20. $.40
21. $.49

22. $12.56

The digit in the thousandths place is 1. Since 1 is less than 5, round down to $12.56.

23. $3.00
24. $29.19
25. $4.31

1. 13.1
2. $8.71

Line up the decimal points. Add. Begin with the digits on the right. 3 + 8 = 11. Write 1 in the hundredths place. Carry 1. 7 + 9 = 16. Add the carried 1. 16 + 1 = 17. Write 7 in the tenths place and carry 1 to the dollars column. 7 + 1 = 8. Write 8 in the dollars column.

```
   1 1
  $7.73
+   .98
  $8.71
```

3. $2.08   **4.** $44.00
5. 60.0   **6.** $1.02
7. $352.25   **8.** 4.65
9. 29.9   **10.** 557.92
11. 6.06
12. $56.50

Write $5 with a decimal point and two right-hand zeros: $5.00. Line up the decimal points. Add, starting with the digits on the right.

```
  $51.50
+   5.00
  $56.50
```

13. 109.4   **14.** 66.53
15. 49.44   **16.** $5.85
17. 615.02
18. $26.25

```
  $25.00
+   1.25
  $26.25
```

19. 78.25 hours

```
    1
  36.75
+ 41.50
  78.25
```

Page 100

1. 3.28
2. $2.07

Line up the decimal points. Subtract. Begin with the digits on the right. Rename. 10 − 3 = 7. 9 − 9 = 0. 4 − 2 = 2. Put a decimal point and a dollar sign in the answer.

```
    4 9 10
  $5.0 0
−   2.9 3
  $2.0 7
```

3. 1.1   **4.** 3.89
5. $9.09   **6.** 1.18
7. 5.25   **8.** 0.04
9. 1.09   **10.** 30.76
11. $4.69
12. 2.4

Write 3 as 3.0. Line up the decimal points. Subtract, starting with the digits on the right. Rename. 10 − 6 = 4. 2 − 0 = 2.

```
  2 10
  3.0
− 0.6
  2.4
```

13. 1.68   **14.** $4.89
15. 2.28   **16.** $5.71
17. 74.51   **18.** 4.25
19. 9.45 miles

```
  1 15 11 10
  2 6.2 0
− 1 6.7 5
  9.4 5 miles
```

20. $10.55

```
  1 9 9 10
  $2 0.0 0
−    9.4 5
  $1 0.5 5
```

Page 101

1. 41.6
2. $26.40

Multiply. Count the number of decimal places in the problem, 2. Put a decimal point in the answer to show two decimal places. Drop right-hand

203

zeros in answers unless the answer shows dollars and cents.

$$\begin{array}{r} \$2.64 \\ \times\ \ 10 \\ \hline \$26.40 \end{array}$$ ← two decimal places / ← no decimal places / ← two decimal places

3. $157.50 **4.** 121.8

5. $16.33 **6.** 102

7. $2,010.40 **8.** $34.58

9. 17.5

10. 0.18

Multiply. Count the number of decimal places in the problem, 2. Put a decimal point in the answer to show two decimal places. Write a 0 to the left of the decimal point.

$$\begin{array}{r} 0.02 \\ \times\ \ \ \ 9 \\ \hline 0.18 \end{array}$$ ← two decimal places / ← no decimal places / ← two decimal places

11. $147.25 **12.** 31.35

13. 21.9 **14.** $423.24

15. 0.48 **16.** 18.15

17. $7.38

$$\begin{array}{r} \$3.69 \\ \times\ \ \ \ 2 \\ \hline \$7.38 \end{array}$$

18. 250 pounds

$$\begin{array}{r} 12.5 \\ \times\ \ \ 20 \\ \hline 250.0 \end{array}$$ pounds = 250 pounds

Page 102

1. 0.0038

2. 0.052

Multiply. Rename. Count the number of decimal places in the problem, 3. Put a decimal point in the answer to show three decimal places.

$$\begin{array}{r} 1 \\ 0.26 \\ \times\ \ 0.2 \\ \hline 0.052 \end{array}$$ ← two decimal places / ← one decimal place / ← three decimal places

3. 0.35 **4.** $.19

5. 0.2355 **6.** $90.00

7. 47.25 **8.** 27.473

9. 1.62

10. 0.522

Multiply. Rename. Count the number of decimal places in the problem, 3.

Put a decimal point in the answer to show three decimal places.

$$\begin{array}{r} 7 \\ 0.58 \\ \times\ 0.9 \\ \hline 0.522 \end{array}$$ ← two decimal places / ← one decimal place / ← three decimal places

11. $24.58

12. 8.892

13. $109.20

$$\begin{array}{r} \$16.80 \\ \times\ \ \ \ \ 6.5 \\ \hline \$109.200 \end{array} = \$109.20$$

14. 2.7 miles

$$\begin{array}{r} 0.75 \\ \times\ \ \ 3.6 \\ \hline 2.700 \end{array}$$ miles = 2.7 miles

Page 103

1. 0.84

2. 0.16

Set up the problem. Put a decimal point in the answer. Divide 15 into 24. $24 \div 15 = 1$ with a remainder. Multiply and subtract. Add an extra zero to the dividend. Bring down this zero. Divide again. $90 \div 15 = 6$.

$$\begin{array}{r} 0.16 \\ 15\overline{)2.40} \\ -15 \\ \hline 90 \\ -90 \\ \hline 0 \end{array}$$

3. $1.50 **4.** 0.0625

5. 0.63 **6.** 0.306

7. 120.3 **8.** 1.87

9. 4.09 **10.** 0.08

11. 7.46 **12.** 0.7

13. 22.82 feet

$$\begin{array}{r} 22.82 \\ 3\overline{)68.46} \end{array}$$

14. $1.59

$$\begin{array}{r} \$1.59 \\ 4\overline{)\$6.36} \end{array}$$

Page 104

1. 4.28

2. 9.4

Set up the problem. Put a decimal point in the answer. Divide to two decimal places. Round 9.43 to one decimal place.

```
        9.43
    5)47.16
    − 45
    ─────
       2 1
     − 2 0
     ──────
         16
       − 15
       ────
          1
```

3. 2.3

4. 3.5

5. 0.07

6. $.05

Set up the problem. Put a dollar sign and decimal point in the answer. Divide to three decimal places. Round $.052 to two decimal places.

```
         $.052
    50)$2.600
     − 2 50
     ──────
        100
      − 100
      ─────
          0
```

7. 0.14

8. $.09

9. $1.99

```
         $1.99
    24)$47.70
```

10. $11.42

```
        $11.42
     3)$34.25
```

Page 105

1. 53

2. $18

Set up the problem. Move the decimal point one place to the right. Put a dollar sign and decimal point in the answer. Divide.

```
                       $18
   0.3)$5.40   →   3)$54
                   − 3
                   ────
                    24
                  − 24
                  ────
                     0
```

3. 0.8

4. 0.4

5. 6.18

6. $5.06

Set up the problem. Move the decimal point one place to the right. Put a dollar sign and decimal point in the answer. Divide to three decimal places. Round to two decimal places.

```
                          $5.061
   1.3)$6.58   →   13)$65.800
                   − 65
                   ────
                      80
                    − 78
                    ────
                      20
                    − 13
                    ────
                       7
```

7. $1.20

8. 1.62

9. $1.80

```
                              $1.80
   2.5)$4.500  =  25)$45.00
```

10. $18.00

```
                            $18
   7.5)$135.0  =  75)$1350
```

Page 106

Answers will vary, depending on how you round the numbers in the problems. Sample answers are given.

1. $6.00 \div 0.03 = 200$

2. $15 \div 3 = 5$ **3.** $8.3 \div 0.9 = 9.2$

4. $1.2 \div 30 = 0.04$ **5.** $0.5 \div 2 = 0.25$

6. $0.02 \div 2 = 0.01$ **7.** $3.6 \div 12 = 0.3$

8. $0.5 \div 60 = 0.008$ **9.** $2.0 \div 4 = 0.5$

10. $0.36 \div 0.9 = 0.4$ **11.** $0.05 \div 2 = 0.025$

12. $3 \div 15 = 0.2$ **13.** $10 \div 30 = 0.3$

14. $3 \div 6 = 0.5$

15. $150 \div 0.05 = 3,000$

16. $0.4 \div 2 = 0.2$

17. $1.20

Round 6.7 to 7. Divide $8.40 by 7. $8.40 \div 7 = 1.20

18. 1 pound per day

Round both 32.5 and 31 to 30. Divide 30 by 30. 30 pounds \div 30 days = 1 pound per day

Page 107

1. 4.15

2. 19.28

Clear the calculator. Enter 12.78. Press the + key. Enter 6.5. Press the = key.

3. $2.89

4. $1.22

5. $2.83

6. $38.78

7. 0.34

8. 9.36

9. 38.22

10. $86.49

11. 1.08

12. $1.0755 = $1.08

13. 0.05

14. $49.14

Clear the calculator. Enter 589.67. Press the ÷ key. Enter 12. Press the = key. Read the answer to three decimal places. $49.139. Round to two decimal places. $49.139 rounds to $49.14.

15. $.30

16. 6.34

17. 27.5 miles per hour

$$\frac{27.5}{1.75\overline{)48.125}}$$

18. $139.65 per week

$$\begin{array}{r} \$19.95 \\ \times 7 \\ \hline \$139.65 \end{array}$$

Pages 108–109

1. 2; 638,432; Washington, DC

2. Tucson

3. Washington, DC

4. Buffalo

5. Washington, DC, Atlanta, Buffalo, and Minneapolis

6. Tucson

7. Washington, DC   638,432
Atlanta   425,022
Minneapolis   370,951
Buffalo   357,870
Tucson   330,537

8. Buffalo   328,123
Minneapolis   368,383
Atlanta   394,017
Tucson   405,390
Washington, DC   606,900

9. Tucson

10. Washington, DC

Page 110

1. 1.53

2. $13.12

3. 10.64

4. 15.39

5. 17.16

6. $13.71

7. 0.15

8. 4.58

9. 7.69

10. 153.0

11. $4.34

12. 0.360

13. 2.052

14. 19.0

15. 123.22

16. $23.10

17. 24.522

18. $7.84

19. 0.02

20. 13.6

21. 0.33

22. 2.26

23. 7.04

24. 685.71

25. 0.51

Page 111

1. 5.3

2. 9.98

First multiply. $4.3 \times 0.6 = 2.58$. Then add 7.4 to the product. $2.58 + 7.4 = 9.98$.

3. 0.23

4. 6.53

5. 3.75

6. 1.24

7. 33.06

8. 12.9

9. 10.4

10. 15.27

11. $2.90

$$\begin{array}{r} \$2.19 \\ \times 3 \\ \hline \$6.57 \end{array} \qquad \begin{array}{r} \$6.57 \\ + .53 \\ \hline \$7.10 \end{array} \qquad \begin{array}{r} \$10.00 \\ - 7.10 \\ \hline \$2.90 \end{array}$$

12. 1,510 pounds

$$\begin{array}{r} 65.5 \\ \times 12 \\ \hline 786.0 \end{array} \qquad \begin{array}{r} 90.5 \\ \times 8 \\ \hline 724.0 \end{array} \qquad \begin{array}{r} 786 \\ + 724 \\ \hline 1,510 \end{array}$$

Page 112

1. $0.071 < 0.17$ or $0.17 > 0.071$

2. 2.1

3. 2.25

4. 11.43

5. 0.544

6. 6.12

Pages 113–114

1. <

2. =

3. >

4. >

5. 2.35

6. 0.07

7. 12.01

8. $1.60

9. $.40

10. $8.10

11. 2.41

12. 4.79

13. 0.12

14. 1.55

15. 14.42

16. 21.6

17. 0.06

18. 80.94

19. 2.28

20. 0.41

21. 0.02

22. 0.31

23. 173.7 pounds

24. 46.3 miles

25. 0.37 minutes

26. **(C) 5** Choice A is incorrect because 1 is in the tenths place. Choice B is incorrect because 2 is in the ones place. Choice D is incorrect because 6 is in the thousandths place.

27. **(A) 0.3 > 0.081** Choice B is incorrect because the second number should be 0.081 and not 0.81. Choices C and D are incorrect because each uses the less than symbol. Choice C also uses 0.03 instead of 0.3.

28. **(B) two and three hundredths** Choices A, C, and D are incorrect because of place value errors.

29. **(B) $78.06** Choices A and C are incorrect because of place value errors. Choice D has the wrong digits.

30. **(D) 7.812** Choice A is incorrect because the digits were not lined up in the correct columns. Choices B and C are incorrect because of solving errors.

31. **(C) 1.24** Choices A and B are incorrect because the digits were not lined up in the correct columns. Choice D is incorrect because of a renaming error.

32. **(B) 0.148** Choice A is incorrect because of a renaming error. Choices C and D are incorrect because the decimal point is in the wrong place.

33. **(D) 42** Choices A, B, and C are incorrect because the decimal point is in the wrong place.

34. **(A) $4.89** Choice B is incorrect because the tax was not included. Choice C is incorrect because 1 pair of jeans and the tax were added but that total should be subtracted from $30. Choice D is incorrect because it is the cost of 1 pair of jeans subtracted from $30 before tax is added.

35. **(C) 2,550 miles** Choice A is incorrect because subtraction was performed instead of addition. Choices B and D have a renaming error.

Pages 115–116

1. tens

2. hundreds

3. hundredths

4. ones

5. thousandths

6. <

7. >

8. =

9. 124

10. 637

11. 4.01

12. 5.21

13. 76.35

14. 7,272

15. 249

16. 7.31

17. 7.58

18. 136

19. 645

20. 3.30

21. 8.43

22. 12.79

23. 5,768

24. 34.08

25. 28.64

26. 45.82

27. $411.42

28. 11.75 feet

29. **(D) 6** Choice A is incorrect because 0 is in the hundredths place. Choice B is incorrect because 1 is in the tenths place. Choice C is incorrect because 3 is in the ones place.

30. **(C) 690** Choice A is incorrect because the number was rounded down rather than up. Choices B and D are incorrect because the number was rounded to the wrong place.

31. **(D) 7,645 − 1,902 = 5,343** Choices A, B, and C show correct answers. Choice D has a subtraction error; the correct answer for D is 5,743.

32. **(A) 4 × 68 = 242** Choices B, C, and D show correct answers. Choice A has a renaming error. The correct product is 272.

33. **(C) 88.34** Choices A and D are incorrect because the digits were not lined up in the correct columns. Choice B is incorrect because of a renaming error.

34. **(A) 4.26** Choices B and C are incorrect because the digits were not lined up in the correct columns. Choice D is incorrect because the numbers were added rather than subtracted.

35. **(B) 2.22** Choice A is incorrect because of a renaming error. Choice D has the decimal point in the wrong place. Choice C has both a renaming error and a misplaced decimal point.

36. (A) 0.024 Choice C is incorrect because the decimal point is in the wrong place. Choice B is incorrect because of a division error. Choice D has both a division error and a misplaced decimal point.

37. (D) $1,244.35 Choice A is incorrect because only three of the numbers were added. Choices B and C have renaming errors.

38. (B) $1.64 Choice A is incorrect because the answer was rounded down rather than up. Choice C is incorrect because of a multiplication error. Choice D has a misplaced decimal point.

Unit 5

Pages 118–119

1. $\frac{4}{5}$

2. $\frac{2}{3}$
There are 3 equal parts, so the denominator is 3. 2 parts are shaded, so the numerator is 2.

3. $\frac{1}{10}$

4. $\frac{4}{7}$

5. Shade 3 parts of the figure.
6. Shade 5 parts of the figure.
7. Shade 1 of the 2 figures.
8. Shade 3 of the 10 figures.

9. $\frac{3}{12}$

10. $\frac{6}{12}$
The line extends from 0 to the mark for $\frac{6}{12}$.

11. $\frac{10}{12}$ **12.** $\frac{1}{12}$

13. $\frac{3}{8}$ **14.** $\frac{1}{8}$

15. $\frac{5}{8}$ **16.** $\frac{7}{8}$

Page 120

1. $\frac{3}{4} = \frac{6}{8}$

2. $\frac{1}{2} = \frac{3}{6}$

The first figure has 1 out of 2 parts shaded. The second figure has 3 out of 6 parts shaded.

3. $\frac{1}{3} = \frac{5}{15}$ **4.** $\frac{3}{5} = \frac{6}{10}$

5. $\frac{1}{4} = \frac{2}{8}$ **6.** $\frac{1}{2} = \frac{8}{16}$

7. $\frac{2}{4} = \frac{4}{8}$

Page 121

1. $\frac{3}{7}$

2. $\frac{2}{3}$
Dividing both parts of the fraction by 4 will reduce it to lowest terms.
$\frac{8}{12} = \frac{8 \div 4}{12 \div 4} = \frac{2}{3}$

3. $\frac{5}{9}$ **4.** $\frac{2}{5}$

5. $\frac{3}{4}$ **6.** $\frac{1}{3}$

7. $\frac{4}{5}$ **8.** $\frac{5}{7}$

9. 3
10. 7
$\frac{7}{14} = \frac{7 \div 7}{14 \div 7} = \frac{1}{2}$

11. 3   **12.** 6
13. 4   **14.** 9
15. 4   **16.** 5
17. 14

Page 122

1. $\frac{4}{6}$

2. $\frac{6}{10}$
Multiply the numerator by 2. $2 \times 3 = 6$. Multiply the denominator by 2. $2 \times 5 = 10$.
The new fraction is $\frac{6}{10}$.
$\frac{3}{5} = \frac{3 \times 2}{5 \times 2} = \frac{6}{10}$

3. $\frac{8}{14}$ **4.** $\frac{10}{16}$

5. $\frac{8}{10}$ **6.** $\frac{2}{6}$

7. $\frac{10}{24}$ **8.** $\frac{2}{10}$

9. 2
10. 4
$\frac{4}{5} = \frac{4 \times 4}{5 \times 4} = \frac{16}{20}$

11. 3

12. 5
13. 6
14. 6

$$\frac{3}{8} = \frac{3 \times 2}{8 \times 2} = \frac{6}{16}$$

15. 10   **16.** 21
17. 8   **18.** 27
19. 15   **20.** 100

Page 123

1. >
2. <

Multiply the denominators. $7 \times 3 = 21$. Use 21 as the common denominator. Raise each fraction to higher terms, with 21 as the denominator. Compare the numerators.

$12 < 14$, so $\frac{4}{7}$ is less than $\frac{2}{3}$.

$$\frac{4}{7} = \frac{4 \times 3}{7 \times 3} = \frac{12}{21}$$

$$\frac{2}{3} = \frac{2 \times 7}{3 \times 7} = \frac{14}{21}$$

3. =   **4.** >
5. <   **6.** >
7. >   **8.** <
9. =   **10.** <
11. >   **12.** <

13. Enrique; $\frac{2}{3} > \frac{1}{2}$

14. onion; $\frac{3}{8} > \frac{1}{3}$

Page 124

1. <
2. >

List the multiples of each denominator. 15 is the LCD. Raise $\frac{2}{5}$ to higher terms with 15 as the LCD. Compare the numerators.

$\frac{8}{15}$ $\boxed{15}$ 30 45

$\frac{2}{5}$ 5 10 $\boxed{15}$ 20 25

$$\frac{2}{5} = \frac{6}{15}$$

$$\frac{8}{15} > \frac{6}{15} \text{ so } \frac{8}{15} > \frac{2}{5}$$

3. >   **4.** <
5. <   **6.** >
7. >   **8.** <

Page 125

1. M
2. P

The fraction is proper because the numerator is less than the denominator.

3. I
4. W
5. I
6. $2\frac{3}{4}$
7. 3

Divide 30 by 10. $30 \div 10 = 3$. The improper fraction $\frac{30}{10}$ equals the whole number 3.

8. $2\frac{2}{3}$
9. $4\frac{1}{5}$
10. $2\frac{2}{7}$
11. $\frac{11}{2}$
12. $\frac{26}{3}$

$8 \times 3 = 24$
$24 + 2 = 26$

13. $\frac{6}{1}$ **14.** $\frac{51}{4}$
15. $\frac{13}{8}$ **16.** $\frac{18}{5}$
17. $\frac{15}{2}$ **18.** $\frac{64}{7}$
19. $\frac{32}{3}$ **20.** $\frac{35}{6}$

Page 126

1. 3
2. 4

$4\frac{2}{8}$ is less than $4\frac{1}{2}$. So, $4\frac{2}{8}$ is closer to 4 than to 5. $4\frac{2}{8}$ rounds to 4.

3. 6
4. 4
5. 5
6. 1

$1\frac{3}{8}$ is less than $1\frac{1}{2}$. So, $1\frac{3}{8}$ is closer to 1 than to 2. $1\frac{3}{8}$ rounds to 1.

7. 3
8. 2
9. 2
10. 2

11. 2 cups

$2\frac{1}{8}$ is less than $2\frac{1}{2}$. So, $2\frac{1}{8}$ is closer to 2 than to 3. $2\frac{1}{8}$ rounds to 2.

12. 4 inches

$4\frac{3}{8}$ is less than $4\frac{1}{2}$. So, $4\frac{3}{8}$ is closer to 4 than to 5. $4\frac{3}{8}$ rounds to 4.

Page 127

1. 0.5

2. 0.375

Clear the calculator. Enter 3. Press the ÷ key. Enter 8. Press the = key. Read the display.

3. 0.2		**4.** 0.75	
5. 1.5		**6.** 0.8	
7. 0.875		**8.** 2.25	
9. 0.625		**10.** 2.5	
11. 1.2		**12.** 0.6	
13. 1.6		**14.** 0.75	
15. 0.60		**16.** 0.16	
17. 3.6		**18.** 0.375	
19. 0.80		**20.** 3.5	
21. 3.25		**22.** 0.5	
23. 4.0		**24.** 0.4	

25. $.01

$\frac{1}{100}$ written as a decimal is .01. Add a dollar sign.

26. $2.50

The word *and* represents the decimal point. $\frac{1}{2}$ is the same as .50.

2 + .50 = 2.50. Add a dollar sign.

Page 128

1. $\frac{4}{8} = \frac{1}{2}$

2. $\frac{5}{6}$

There are 6 circles. Write 6 as the denominator. 5 circles are shaded. Write 5 as the numerator.

3. $\frac{2}{5}$

4. $\frac{2}{3}$

5. Student shades 3 figures.

6. Student shades 1 part of the figure.

7. Student shades 2 parts of the figure.

8. Student shades 5 figures.

9. $\frac{1}{4}$	**10.** $\frac{3}{5}$
11. $\frac{1}{2}$	**12.** $\frac{4}{7}$
13. <	**14.** >
15. =	**16.** <
17. $1\frac{3}{4}$	**18.** $3\frac{2}{5}$
19. 2	**20.** $4\frac{1}{2}$
21. 3	**22.** $3\frac{1}{2}$
23. $6\frac{4}{7}$	**24.** $8\frac{3}{4}$

Page 129

1. $1\frac{2}{5}$

2. $1\frac{1}{10}$

Add the fraction parts by adding only the numerators. $\frac{6}{10} + \frac{5}{10} = \frac{11}{10}$. Reduce to lowest terms. $\frac{11}{10} = 1\frac{1}{10}$

3. $\frac{2}{3}$	**4.** $2\frac{3}{5}$
5. $3\frac{2}{3}$	**6.** $\frac{5}{6}$
7. $\frac{11}{12}$	**8.** $\frac{5}{6}$
9. $3\frac{1}{2}$	**10.** $10\frac{1}{10}$

11. $5\frac{1}{3}$

Add the fraction parts by adding only the numerators. $\frac{2}{9} + \frac{1}{9} = \frac{3}{9}$. Add the whole numbers. 3 + 2 = 5. Reduce the fraction part to lowest terms. $5\frac{3}{9} = 5\frac{1}{3}$.

12. $25\frac{2}{5}$

13. $8\frac{2}{5}$

14. 10

15. $\frac{4}{5}$ mile

Add $\frac{2}{10} + \frac{6}{10}$.

$\frac{2}{10} + \frac{6}{10} = \frac{8}{10}$.

Reduce $\frac{8}{10}$ to $\frac{4}{5}$.

16. $7\frac{3}{4}$ yards

Add $\frac{1}{8} + \frac{5}{8} = \frac{6}{8}$.

Add the whole numbers. $4 + 3 = 7$.

Reduce $\frac{6}{8}$ to $\frac{3}{4}$.

$7 + \frac{3}{4} = 7\frac{3}{4}$.

Page 130

1. $\frac{1}{2}$

2. $\frac{5}{6}$

    Use 12 as a common denominator.
    Raise $\frac{1}{3}$ to higher terms with 12 as the
    denominator. Add the numerators.
    Reduce.

    $\frac{1}{3} = \frac{4}{12}$

    $\frac{4}{12} + \frac{6}{12} = \frac{10}{12} = \frac{5}{6}$

3. $1\frac{5}{16}$

4. $\frac{15}{28}$

5. $8\frac{11}{20}$

6. $16\frac{13}{15}$

    Use 15 as a common denominator.
    Raise $\frac{2}{3}$ and $\frac{1}{5}$ to higher terms with
    15 as the denominator. Add the
    numerators. Add the whole numbers.

    $9\frac{2}{3} = 9\frac{10}{15}$

    $+ 7\frac{1}{5} = 7\frac{3}{15}$

    $\overline{\phantom{+ 7\frac{1}{5} = } 16\frac{13}{15}}$

7. $9\frac{37}{40}$

8. $11\frac{1}{36}$

9. $7\frac{11}{48}$

10. $3\frac{4}{5}$ miles

    Add $2\frac{1}{2}$ and $1\frac{3}{10}$.

    $2\frac{1}{2} = 2\frac{5}{10}$

    $2\frac{5}{10} + 1\frac{3}{10} = 3\frac{8}{10}$

    $3\frac{8}{10} = 3\frac{4}{5}$

11. $9\frac{3}{4}$ pounds

    Add $6\frac{1}{4}$ and $3\frac{1}{2}$.

$3\frac{1}{2} = 3\frac{2}{4}$

$6\frac{1}{4} + 3\frac{2}{4} = 9\frac{3}{4}$

Page 131

1. $\frac{1}{2}$

2. $\frac{2}{3}$

    Subtract the fraction parts by sub-
    tracting only the numerators.

    $\frac{5}{6} - \frac{1}{6} = \frac{4}{6}$. Reduce the fraction part to
    lowest terms.

    $\frac{4}{6} = \frac{2}{3}$

    $\frac{5}{6} - \frac{1}{6} = \frac{4}{6} = \frac{2}{3}$

3. $\frac{1}{2}$ 　　　　　 4. $\frac{3}{5}$

5. $\frac{1}{3}$ 　　　　　 6. $\frac{3}{7}$

7. $\frac{2}{9}$ 　　　　　 8. $\frac{2}{5}$

9. $\frac{1}{2}$ 　　　　　 10. $1\frac{1}{5}$

11. $2\frac{2}{7}$ 　　　　 12. $5\frac{3}{5}$

13. $\frac{3}{8}$ 　　　　　 14. $9\frac{2}{3}$

15. $1\frac{1}{2}$ cups

    Subtract $2\frac{1}{4}$ from $3\frac{3}{4}$. Then reduce.

    $3\frac{3}{4} - 2\frac{1}{4} = 1\frac{2}{4}$

    $1\frac{2}{4} = 1\frac{1}{2}$

16. $17\frac{1}{4}$ inches

    Subtract $8\frac{5}{8}$ from $25\frac{7}{8}$. Then reduce.

    $25\frac{7}{8} - 8\frac{5}{8} = 17\frac{2}{8}$

    $17\frac{2}{8} = 17\frac{1}{4}$

Page 132

1. $\frac{1}{12}$

2. $\frac{4}{5}$

    Multiply the denominators. $6 \times 5 = 30$.
    Use 30 as a common denominator.
    Raise both fractions to higher terms
    with 30 as the denominator. Subtract

the numerators. Reduce the answer to lowest terms.

$$\frac{6}{6} = \frac{6 \times 5}{6 \times 5} = \frac{30}{30}$$

$$\frac{1}{5} = \frac{1 \times 6}{5 \times 6} = \frac{6}{30}$$

$$\frac{30}{30} - \frac{6}{30} = \frac{24}{30}$$

$$\frac{24}{30} = \frac{24 \div 6}{30 \div 6} = \frac{4}{5}$$

3. $\frac{1}{14}$

4. $\frac{7}{24}$

5. $\frac{13}{36}$

6. $2\frac{7}{40}$

7. $5\frac{4}{9}$

Find the LCD. The LCD of 3 and 9 is 9. Raise $\frac{1}{3}$ to higher terms with 9 as the denominator. Subtract the numerators and subtract the whole numbers.

$$\frac{1}{3} = \frac{1 \times 3}{3 \times 3} = \frac{3}{9}$$

$$8\frac{7}{9} - 3\frac{3}{9} = 5\frac{4}{9}$$

8. $2\frac{1}{40}$

9. $4\frac{1}{16}$

10. $1\frac{19}{60}$

11. $\frac{3}{8}$ pound

Subtract $\frac{1}{8}$ from $\frac{1}{2}$.

$$\frac{1}{2} = \frac{4}{8}$$

$$\frac{4}{8} - \frac{1}{8} = \frac{3}{8}$$

12. $20\frac{3}{8}$ yards

Subtract $12\frac{1}{4}$ from $32\frac{5}{8}$.

$$12\frac{1}{4} = 12\frac{2}{8}$$

$$32\frac{5}{8} - 12\frac{2}{8} = 20\frac{3}{8}$$

Page 133

1. $\frac{1}{4}$

2. $\frac{5}{24}$

Multiply the numerators. $5 \times 1 = 5$.

Multiply the denominators. $8 \times 3 = 24$.

$$\frac{5}{8} \times \frac{1}{3} = \frac{5 \times 1}{8 \times 3} = \frac{5}{24}$$

3. $\frac{3}{8}$

4. $\frac{7}{30}$

5. $\frac{3}{80}$

6. $\frac{7}{12}$

7. $\frac{1}{12}$

8. $\frac{5}{21}$

9. $\frac{9}{100}$

10. $\frac{5}{24}$

11. $\frac{1}{6}$

12. $\frac{3}{16}$

13. $\frac{10}{13}$

14. $\frac{3}{100}$

15. $\frac{1}{9}$

16. $\frac{1}{6}$ pound

To find $\frac{1}{3}$ of $\frac{1}{2}$, multiply. $\frac{1}{3} \times \frac{1}{2} = \frac{1}{6}$

17. $\frac{3}{16}$ of the class is married women

To find $\frac{1}{2}$ of $\frac{3}{8}$, multiply. $\frac{3}{8} \times \frac{1}{2} = \frac{3}{16}$

Page 134

1. $6\frac{1}{2}$

2. $7\frac{1}{2}$

Change $2\frac{1}{2}$ to an improper fraction.

$2\frac{1}{2} = \frac{2 \times 2 + 1}{2} = \frac{5}{2}$. Change 3 to an improper fraction. $3 = \frac{3}{1}$.

Multiply the numerators. $5 \times 3 = 15$. Multiply the denominators. $2 \times 1 = 2$. Change the answer to an improper fraction.

$$2\frac{1}{2} \times 3 = \frac{5}{2} \times \frac{3}{1} = \frac{5 \times 3}{2 \times 1} = \frac{15}{2} = 7\frac{1}{2}$$

3. $5\frac{3}{5}$

4. $4\frac{1}{5}$

5. $14\frac{7}{8}$

6. $3\frac{4}{15}$

7. 8

8. $9\frac{11}{12}$

9. $65\frac{1}{3}$

10. 44

11. $4\frac{1}{3}$

12. $6\frac{13}{20}$

13. $3\frac{1}{2}$ miles

Change 7 to an improper fraction, then multiply $\frac{1}{2}$ by 7.

$$\frac{1}{2} \times 7 = \frac{1}{2} \times \frac{7}{1} = \frac{7}{2} = 3\frac{1}{2}.$$

14. 21 plants

Change $3\frac{1}{2}$ and 6 to improper fractions, then multiply.

$3\frac{1}{2} \times 6 = \frac{7}{2} \times \frac{6}{1} = \frac{42}{2} = 21.$

Page 135

1. $\frac{4}{7}$

2. $\frac{8}{9}$

Invert the fraction to the right of the divide sign and multiply.

$\frac{2}{3} \div \frac{3}{4} = \frac{2}{3} \times \frac{4}{3} = \frac{2 \times 4}{3 \times 3} = \frac{8}{9}$

3. $2\frac{1}{4}$ **4.** $\frac{7}{8}$

5. $\frac{8}{15}$ **6.** $2\frac{1}{12}$

7. $\frac{4}{7}$ **8.** $1\frac{1}{15}$

9. $\frac{12}{13}$ **10.** $1\frac{1}{2}$

11. $\frac{8}{9}$ **12.** $1\frac{5}{21}$

13. $\frac{7}{24}$ **14.** $1\frac{17}{25}$

15. $\frac{15}{16}$ **16.** $\frac{8}{9}$

17. 3 pieces

Divide $\frac{3}{4}$ by $\frac{1}{4}$. Invert the fraction $\frac{1}{4}$ and multiply.

$\frac{3}{4} \div \frac{1}{4} = \frac{3}{4} \times \frac{4}{1} = \frac{12}{4} = 3.$

18. 6 pieces

Divide $\frac{3}{4}$ by $\frac{1}{8}$. Invert the fraction $\frac{1}{8}$ and multiply.

$\frac{3}{4} \div \frac{1}{8} = \frac{3}{4} \times \frac{8}{1} = \frac{24}{4} = 6.$

Page 136

1. 2

2. 2

Change both mixed numbers to improper fractions. Invert the fraction to the right of the divide sign and multiply. Change the answer to a whole number.

$2\frac{2}{3} \div 1\frac{1}{3} = \frac{8}{3} \div \frac{4}{3} =$

$\frac{8}{3} \times \frac{3}{4} = \frac{8 \times 3}{3 \times 4} = \frac{24}{12} = 2$

3. $3\frac{1}{8}$ **4.** 4

5. $1\frac{1}{7}$ **6.** $8\frac{2}{3}$

7. $1\frac{5}{11}$ **8.** $6\frac{2}{3}$

9. $4\frac{2}{7}$ **10.** $2\frac{16}{25}$

11. $2\frac{1}{27}$ **12.** 17

13. 20 packages

Change $2\frac{1}{2}$ to an improper fraction and divide by $\frac{1}{8}$.

$2\frac{1}{2} = \frac{2 \times 2 + 1}{2} = \frac{5}{2}$

$\frac{5}{2} \div \frac{1}{8} = \frac{5}{2} \times \frac{8}{1} = \frac{40}{2} = 20$

14. 50 pieces

Change 25 to an improper fraction and divide by $\frac{1}{2}$.

$25 = \frac{25}{1}$

$\frac{25}{1} \div \frac{1}{2} = \frac{25}{1} \times \frac{2}{1} = \frac{50}{1} = 50$

Page 137

1. 3

2. 2

$6\frac{3}{10}$ rounds to 6. $2\frac{9}{10}$ rounds to 3. Divide the rounded numbers. $6 \div 3 = 2.$

3. 50   **4.** 6

5. 24   **6.** 6

7. 36   **8.** 8

9. 13

10. 3 blankets

$8\frac{7}{10}$ rounds to 9. $2\frac{9}{10}$ rounds to 3. Divide the rounded numbers. $9 \div 3 = 3.$

11. 2 miles

$2\frac{2}{10}$ rounds to 2. $\frac{9}{10}$ rounds to 1. Divide the rounded numbers. $2 \div 1 = 2.$

Page 138

1. 1.5
2. 2

   Change $\frac{2}{5}$ to a decimal and multiply by 5.

   $\frac{2}{5} = 5 \div 2 = 0.4$.

   $0.4 \times 5 = 2.0 = 2$

3. 0.3125
4. 0.3
5. 1.5
6. 0.375
7. 6
8. 4.375
9. 0.02
10. 36
11. 5.6
12. 0.12
13. 9.75
14. 0.05
15. 1.0
16. 8.25
17. 210 students

   Change 240 to an improper fraction and multiply by $\frac{7}{8}$.

   $240 = \frac{240}{1}$

   $\frac{240}{1} \times \frac{7}{8} = \frac{1680}{8} = 210$

18. 15 children

   Change 60 to an improper fraction and multiply by $\frac{1}{4}$.

   $60 = \frac{60}{1}$

   $\frac{60}{1} \times \frac{1}{4} = \frac{60}{4} = 15$

Page 139

1. 1
2. $\frac{2}{7}$
3. $5\frac{1}{2}$
4. $11\frac{11}{12}$
5. $\frac{4}{9}$
6. $5\frac{1}{9}$
7. $1\frac{3}{5}$
8. $\frac{1}{24}$
9. $16\frac{1}{5}$
10. $\frac{1}{8}$
11. 2
12. 17
13. $2\frac{1}{4}$
14. 4
15. $9\frac{3}{4}$
16. $1\frac{19}{20}$
17. 14
18. $22\frac{11}{15}$
19. 16
20. 14
21. $\frac{1}{36}$

22. $\frac{3}{8}$ yards

   Change 3 and $2\frac{5}{8}$ to improper fractions with a denominator of 8. Then subtract.

   $3 = \frac{24}{8}$

   $2\frac{5}{8} = \frac{21}{8}$

   $\frac{24}{8} - \frac{21}{8} = \frac{3}{8}$

23. 4 rooms

   Find $\frac{2}{3}$ of 6 by multiplying 6 by $\frac{2}{3}$.

   $6 \times \frac{2}{3} = \frac{6}{1} \times \frac{2}{3} = \frac{12}{3} = 4$

Pages 140–141

1. $\frac{7}{8}$
2. $5\frac{13}{16}$
3. $2\frac{5}{8}$
4. $1\frac{1}{2}$
5. $4\frac{3}{16}$
6. $\frac{3}{8}$
7. $2\frac{1}{4}$
8. $1\frac{3}{16}$
9. $4\frac{5}{8}$ inches

   $5\frac{13}{16} - 1\frac{3}{16} = 4\frac{10}{16} = 4\frac{5}{8}$

10. $\frac{1}{2}$ inch

   $\frac{7}{8} - \frac{3}{8} = \frac{4}{8} = \frac{1}{2}$

11. $1\frac{1}{8}$ inches

   $2\frac{5}{8} - 1\frac{1}{2} = 2\frac{5}{8} - 1\frac{4}{8} = 1\frac{1}{8}$

12. $1\frac{1}{4}$ inches

   $3\frac{1}{2} - 2\frac{1}{4} = 3\frac{2}{4} - 2\frac{1}{4} = 1\frac{1}{4}$

13. $\frac{9}{16}$ inch

   $4\frac{3}{4} - 4\frac{3}{16} = 4\frac{12}{16} - 4\frac{3}{16} = \frac{9}{16}$

14. $1\frac{7}{16}$ inches

   $2\frac{5}{8} - 1\frac{3}{16} = 2\frac{10}{16} - 1\frac{3}{16} = 1\frac{7}{16}$

15. $4\frac{5}{16}$ inches

   $5\frac{13}{16} - 1\frac{1}{2} = 5\frac{13}{16} - 1\frac{8}{16} = 4\frac{5}{16}$

16. $\frac{3}{8}$ inch

   $2\frac{5}{8} - 2\frac{1}{4} = 2\frac{5}{8} - 2\frac{2}{8} = \frac{3}{8}$

Page 142

1. $1\frac{1}{10}$

2. $\frac{2}{3}$

First multiply $\frac{1}{3}$ by $\frac{3}{4}$.

$\frac{1}{3} \times \frac{3}{4} = \frac{3}{12}$.

Add $\frac{3}{12}$ to $\frac{5}{12}$.

$\frac{3}{12} + \frac{5}{12} = \frac{8}{12}$.

Reduce. $\frac{8}{12} = \frac{2}{3}$.

3. $\frac{2}{5}$ 4. 1

5. $\frac{4}{5}$ 6. $\frac{11}{20}$

7. 1 8. $\frac{2}{3}$

9. $2\frac{2}{3}$ 10. $\frac{7}{8}$

11. $\frac{1}{12}$ 12. $3\frac{7}{8}$

Pages 143–144

1. $\frac{11}{12}$ 2. $\frac{7}{12}$

3. $\frac{6}{8}$ 4. $\frac{2}{3}$

5. 12 6. $\frac{5}{2}$

7. $8\frac{11}{30}$ 8. $\frac{1}{2}$

9. 9 10. $1\frac{3}{16}$

Pages 145–146

1. $\frac{1}{3}$ 2. $\frac{9}{14}$

3. $\frac{3}{7}$ 4. $1\frac{1}{4}$

5. 4 6. $2\frac{3}{4}$

7. 6 8. 2

9. 20 10. 12

11. $<$ 12. $>$

13. $=$ 14. $<$

15. $\frac{13}{6}$ 16. $\frac{31}{8}$

17. $\frac{16}{3}$ 18. $\frac{8}{5}$

19. $\frac{2}{5}$ 20. $\frac{5}{12}$

21. $\frac{21}{40}$ 22. $1\frac{3}{4}$

23. $11\frac{2}{15}$ 24. 9

25. $1\frac{5}{8}$

26. **(D) 11** Choices A and B are not rounded to whole numbers. Choice C is rounded incorrectly.

27. **(A) zero** Choices B, C, and D are incorrect because fractions are not inverted during multiplication.

28. **(A) $\frac{8}{10}$** Choices B, C, and D are incorrect because each is not a higher term of $\frac{4}{5}$.

29. **(C) $9\frac{5}{8}$ miles** Choice A is incorrect because the wrong improper fraction was used. Choice B is incorrect because the fraction $\frac{11}{8}$ was inverted. Choice D is incorrect because of an addition, subtraction, multiplication, or division error.

30. **(D) $1\frac{1}{8}$ cup** Choice A is incorrect because subtraction was performed instead of addition. Choice B is incorrect because the answer was inverted. Choice C is incorrect because it does not include the remainder in the answer.

31. **(D) $\frac{7}{16}$ pound** Choice A is incorrect because the fraction $\frac{7}{2}$ was inverted. Choice B is incorrect because the wrong improper fraction was used. Choice C is incorrect because of a renaming error.

Pages 147–148

1. $<$ 2. $>$

3. $=$ 4. $<$

5. $=$ 6. 66

7. $\frac{13}{30}$ 8. $10\frac{5}{6}$

9. $2\frac{2}{3}$ 10. 10.2

11. 2 12. 15

13. 7.64 14. $12\frac{1}{2}$

15. 6 16. 4

17. $5\frac{2}{7}$ 18. $1\frac{1}{8}$

19. $7\frac{5}{6}$ hours

20. $318.75

21. (C) 24 > 2.4 Choice A is incorrect because 1 ten + 9 ones = 19. Choice B is incorrect because $\frac{1}{2} = \frac{5}{10}$. Choice D is incorrect because $\frac{7}{2}$ is not a mixed number.

22. (B) $1\frac{19}{28}$ Choice A is incorrect because the fraction $\frac{3}{7}$ was inverted, then multiplied. Choice C is incorrect because the numerators and denominators were multiplied. Choice D is incorrect because the numerators and denominators were added.

23. (D) 200 Choices A and B are incorrect because each number is in tens, not hundreds. Choice C is incorrect because 150 is rounded up to 200, not down to 100.

24. (A) $\frac{4}{5}$ Choices B, C, and D are incorrect because each fraction is not in lowest terms.

25. (C) 28 Choices A, B, and D are incorrect because the pattern is increasing by 3 each time.

26. (A) $\frac{4}{7} + \frac{4}{7} = \frac{8}{7}$ Choice B is incorrect because only the numerators should be added when adding fractions. Choice C is incorrect because denominators should not be added when adding fractions. Choice D is incorrect because the operation is addition, not multiplication.

27. (D) $3\frac{2}{5}$ miles Choice A is incorrect because only the numerators should be added together when adding fractions. Choice B is incorrect because the numerators were not added together correctly, and the denominators should not have been added together. Choice C is incorrect because of a renaming error.

28. (D) 4 Choices A, B, and C are incorrect because of addition, subtraction, multiplication, or division errors. To find $\frac{2}{3}$ of 6, multiply $\frac{2}{3}$ by 6.

Unit 6

Page 150

1. $\frac{2}{5}$

2. $\frac{9}{10}$
Write the first number, 9, as the numerator. Write the second number, 10, as the denominator.

3. $\frac{4}{7}$

4. $\frac{3}{1}$

5. $\frac{56}{1}$

6. $\frac{28}{1}$

7. $\frac{3}{4}$

8. $\frac{1}{3}$
Divide both the numerator and the denominator by 3.
$$\frac{3}{9} = \frac{3 \div 3}{9 \div 3} = \frac{1}{3}$$

9. $\frac{5}{2}$ **10.** $\frac{4}{5}$

11. $\frac{5}{1}$ **12.** $\frac{2}{1}$

13. $\frac{2}{7}$ **14.** $\frac{4}{25}$

15. $\frac{4}{5}$ **16.** $\frac{20}{7}$

17. $\frac{8}{9}$
Write 64, the number of people who attended, as the numerator. Write 72, the number of people who were invited, as the denominator. Reduce.
$$\frac{64}{72} = \frac{64 \div 8}{72 \div 8} = \frac{8}{9}$$

18. $\frac{4}{3}$
Write 56, the number of newspapers delivered on Sunday, as the numerator. Write 42, the number of newspapers delivered on weekdays, as the denominator. Reduce.
$$\frac{56}{42} = \frac{56 \div 14}{42 \div 14} = \frac{4}{3}$$

Page 151

1. 2
2. 10

Look at the denominators. 12 has been multiplied by 2 to get 24. Multiply 5 by 2.

$5 \times 2 = 10$

$\frac{5}{12} = \frac{5 \times 2}{12 \times 2} = \frac{10}{24}$

3. 3   4. 20
5. 32   6. 30
7. 18   8. 24
9. not equal
10. equal

$4 \times 30 = 120$

$6 \times 20 = 120$

$4 \times 30 = 6 \times 20$, so the ratios are equal.

11. equal   12. not equal
13. equal   14. equal
15. not equal   16. not equal

Page 152

1. 15
2. 6

$12 \times n = 9 \times 8$

$12n = 72$

$n = 72 \div 12 = 6$

$n = 6$

3. 3   4. 30
5. 20   6. 8
7. 12   8. 10
9. 50 minutes

$\frac{3}{10} = \frac{15}{n}$

$3n = 150$

$n = 150 \div 3 = 50$

$n = 50$ minutes

10. $0.64

$\frac{3}{\$0.96} = \frac{2}{n}$

$3n = \$1.92$

$n = \$1.92 \div 3 = \$0.64$

$n = \$0.64$

Page 153

1. 60%
2. 7%

7 out of 100 squares are shaded.
7 out of 100 equals 7%.

3. 145%

4. 75%
5. 95%
6. 120%
7. 1%
8. 25%

Write twenty-five in numerals and then write a percent sign.

9. 10%   10. 45%
11. 58%   12. 200%
13. 80%   14. 75%
15. 16%   16. 150%
17. $8\frac{1}{2}\%$
18. 15.3% or $15\frac{3}{10}\%$
19. 375%
20. 67.33% or $67\frac{1}{3}\%$
21. 112%

Page 154

1. $\frac{7}{20}$
2. 5

Write 500 over 100. $\frac{500}{100} = \frac{5}{1} = 5$

3. $\frac{1}{25}$ 4. $\frac{11}{20}$
5. $2\frac{1}{2}$ 6. $\frac{7}{10}$
7. $\frac{3}{10}$ 8. $2\frac{3}{5}$
9. $66\frac{2}{3}\%$
10. 80%

Divide 4 by 5. Write the answer with two decimal places. Move the decimal point two places to the right. Add a percent sign.

$4 \div 5 = 0.80$

$0.80 = 80\%$

11. 45%
12. $83\frac{1}{3}\%$
13. $33\frac{1}{3}\%$

$1 \div 3 = 0.33\frac{1}{3}$

$0.33\frac{1}{3} = 33\frac{1}{3}\%$

14. $1\frac{3}{10}$

$130\% = \frac{130}{100}$

$\frac{130}{100} = 1.3$

$1.3 = 1\frac{3}{10}$

Page 155

1. 0.5
2. 3.8
   Write the number without the percent sign. Move the decimal point two places to the right. Drop the zero at the right. 380% = 3.80 = 3.8
3. 0.05
4. 0.732
5. 1.12
6. 0.18
7. 0.495
8. 1.3
9. 0.74
10. 0.071
11. 3.45
12. 0.935
13. 4.5%
14. 230%
   Add a zero at the right so there are two decimal places. Move the decimal point two places to the right. Add a percent sign.
   2.3 = 2.30
   2.30 = 230%
15. 85%
16. 20%
17. 50.6%
18. 7%
19. 55%
20. 185%
21. 31.8%
22. 4%
23. 341%
24. 16%
25. 15% = 0.15
   Move the decimal point two places to the left. Drop the percent sign.
26. 0.08 = 8 = 8%
   Move the decimal point two places to the right. Add a percent sign.

Pages 156–157

1. a. 45%
   b. 20%
      Locate the section of the circle graph labeled *Rabbits*. Write the percent.
   c. 80%
2. a. 15%
   b. 40%
   c. 25%
3. a. 34 votes
   b. 30%
   c. 25%
4. a. 85 people
   b. 18%
   c. 7%

5. a. 10 people
   b. 22 people
      Fifty-five percent of the 40 people surveyed said *no*. Find 55% of 40. Change 55% to a decimal. 55% = 0.55. Multiply by the whole. 0.55 × 40 = 22. 22 people said *no*.
   c. 8 people
6. a. 51 people
   b. 6 people
   c. 3 people
7. a. $200
   b. $80
   c. $80
   d. $440
8. a. $180
   b. $72
   c. $90
   d. $180
   e. $78

Page 158

1. whole = 40
   percent = 20%
   part = 8
2. whole = 48
   percent = 75%
   part = 36
3. whole = 150
   percent = 30%
   part = 45
4. whole = 25
   percent = 60%
   part = 15
5. whole = 200
   percent = 25%
   part = 50
6. whole = 80
   percent = 150%
   part = 120
7. 5
8. 320
   Change 80% to a decimal.
   80% = 0.80 = 0.8
   Multiply 400 by 0.8
   400 × 0.8 = 320.0

Drop the zero to the right of the
decimal point.
80% of 400 =
$0.8 \times 400 = 320.0 = 320$
9. 180
10. 42
11. 42
12. 660
13. $240
15% of $1,600 = n
15% = 0.15
$0.15 \times \$1,600 = \$240$
14. 36 blue cars
30% of 120 = n
30% = 0.30 = 0.3
$0.3 \times 120 = 36$

Page 159
1. part = 5
whole = 20
percent = 5 ÷ 20
2. part = 15
whole = 40
percent = 15 ÷ 40
3. part = 8
whole = 80
percent = 8 ÷ 80
4. part = 4
whole = 100
percent = 4 ÷ 100
5. part = 56
whole = 28
percent = 56 ÷ 28
6. part = 270
whole = 360
percent = 270 ÷ 360
7. 50%
8. 175%
Part is 7. Whole is 4. Divide the part
by the whole. 7 ÷ 4 = 1.75.
Change 1.75 to a percent. 1.75 = 175%
9. 300%
10. 25%
11. 75%
12. 60%

Page 160
1. part = 7
percent = 35%
whole = 7 ÷ 35%
2. part = 4
percent = 10%
whole = 4 ÷ 10%
3. part = 33
percent = 110%
whole = 33 ÷ 110%
4. 80
5. 280
part = 42
percent = 15%
whole = 42 ÷ 15%
Change 15% to a decimal.
15% = 0.15
42 ÷ 0.15 = 280
6. 150
7. 200
8. 200
9. 140
10. $175
Change 80% to a decimal.
80% = 0.80 = 0.8
$140 ÷ 0.8 = $175
11. $800
Change 60% to a decimal.
60% = 0.60 = 0.6
$480 ÷ 0.6 = $800

Page 161
There are many ways to answer the
problems, depending on how the
numbers are rounded. Sample answers
are given.
1. $15
2. $15
Round $99.54 to $100.
Find 10% of $100.
$0.1 \times \$100 = \$10$.
Find 5 % of $100.
$0.05 \times \$100 = \$5$.
Add $10 and $5.
$10 + $5 = $15.
15% of $99.54 is about $15

3. 10% of $32.80 is about $3.30
4. 10% of $7.32 is about $.70
5. 20% of $8.40 is about $1.60
6. 10% of $64.29 is about $6.40
7. $8 \times \$1.21 = \$9.68$
8. $6 \times \$0.45 = \$2.70$
   Round $45.20 to $45.
   Find 1% of $45.
   $0.01 \times \$45 = \$0.45$.
   Multiply $0.45 by 6.
   $6 \times \$0.45 = \$2.70$
9. $3.40
10. $3.30
11. $21
12. $56
13. $3.75
    Round $24.58 to $25.
    10% of $25 = $2.50
    1% of $25 = $0.25
    $0.25 \times 5 = \$1.25$
    $2.50 + $1.25 = $3.75
14. $6.50
    Round $99.50 to $100
    1% of $100 = $1.00
    $1.00 \times 6 = \$6.00$
    0.5% of $100 = $0.50
    $6.00 + $0.50 = $6.50

Page 162

1. 18.5
2. 21
   Clear the calculator. Enter 140. Press the multiplication key. Enter 15. Press the percent key. Read the answer.
3. 81.3
4. 5.4
5. 1.9
6. 108.5
7. 228
8. 11
9. 13.8
10. 3.4
11. 10.5
12. 2.0
13. 6.9
14. 0.5
15. 90
16. 9.7
17. $90
    Clear the calculator. Enter 600. Press the multiplication key. Enter 15. Press the percent key. Place a dollar sign in the answer.
18. $46,750
    Clear the calculator. Enter 55,000. Press the multiplication key. Enter 85. Press

the percent key. Place a dollar sign in the answer.

Page 163

1. $\frac{8}{10} = \frac{4}{5}$
2. $\frac{5}{13}$
3. $\frac{350}{8} = \frac{175}{4}$
4. 9
5. 6
6. 20
7. 24
8. $\frac{2}{5}$
9. $\frac{3}{50}$
10. $3\frac{1}{2}$
11. $\frac{17}{20}$
12. 0.03
13. 0.6
14. 0.851
15. 2.25
16. $37\frac{1}{2}$% or 37.5%
17. $26\frac{2}{3}$%
18. 6.5%
19. 58%
20. 75%
21. 6
22. 80
23. 208
24. 64
25. 150%

Pages 164–165

1. **Step 1** Sales tax in Colorado is 3%, Alabama is 4%, Wisconsin is 5%, Florida is 6%.
   Step 2 3% 4% 5% 6%
   Step 3 Compare to find the largest number.
   Step 4 6% > 5% > 4% > 3%
   Florida
2. **Step 1** Sales tax in Colorado is 3%, Alabama is 4%, Wisconsin is 5%, and Florida is 6%.
   Step 2 3% 4% 5% 6%
   Step 3 Compare to find the smallest number.
   Step 4 3% < 4% < 5% < 6%
   Colorado
3. **Step 1** Sales tax is 4% in Alabama.
   Step 2 Find 4% of $500.
   Step 3 Multiply. 4% × $500
   Step 4 0.04 × $500 = $20.00
   $20.00
4. **Step 1** Sales tax in Georgia is 4%, Ohio is 5%, Connecticut is 6%, New Jersey is 6%, and Mississippi is 7%.

Step 2 4% 5% 6% 6% 7%
Step 3 Compare to find which states charge the same amount.
Step 4 6% = 6%
Connecticut and New Jersey

5. **Step 1** Sales tax is 6% in Connecticut.
   Step 2 Find 6% of $125.
   Step 3 Multiply. 6% × $125
   Step 4 0.06 × $125 = $7.50
   $7.50

6. **Step 1** Sales tax is 4% in Georgia.
   Step 2 4% of $36.99
   Step 3 Multiply. 4% × $36.99
   Step 4 0.04 × $36.99 = $1.48
   $1.48

Page 166

1. $5.3802 = $5.38, $95.05
2. $0.56, $8.55
   Find 7% of $7.99 to get the amount of sales tax.
   7% of $7.99 = 0.07 × $7.99 = $0.5593.
   Round to the nearest cent.
   $0.5593 rounds to $0.56.
   Add the $0.56 tax to the price.
   $7.99 + $0.56 = $8.55.
3. $11.07, $212.26
4. $3.98, $53.67
5. $0.58, $17.07
6. $4.60, $70.29
7. $131.97
   Find 6% of $124.50.
   Change 6% to a decimal and multiply by $124.50.
   0.06 × $124.50 = $7.47
   $124.50 + $7.47 = $131.97
8. $211
   Find 5.5% of $200.
   Change 5.5% to a decimal and multiply by $211.
   0.055 × $200 = $11.
   In one year, the account will be worth $200 plus $11, or $211.

Page 167

1. $70, 15.7%
2. $17, 13.6%
   Subtract to find the amount of increase. $142 − $125 = $17. Divide the

amount of increase by last year's price.
$17 ÷ $125 = 13.6%.

3. $18, 27.7%
4. $33\frac{1}{3}$% or 33.3%
5. 12.4%
   Subtract to find the amount of decrease.
   178 − 156 = 22 pounds.
   Divide the amount of decrease by the starting weight.
   22 ÷ 178 = 0.1235.
   Change the decimal to a percent and round to the nearest tenth.
6. 11.7%

Page 168

1. $\frac{11}{18}$ 2. 12
3. $\frac{2}{25}$, 0.08   4. 25%
5. 4.3%   6. 43.2

Pages 169–170

1. $\frac{3}{2}$ 2. $\frac{2}{3}$
3. $\frac{2}{1}$ 4. $\frac{1}{4}$
5. $\frac{2}{5}$ 6. $\frac{3}{1}$
7. 11   8. 4
9. 12   10. 9
11. $\frac{1}{5}$ 12. $1\frac{1}{20}$
13. 55%   14. 292.5
15. 2.0   16. 207
17. 80.2   18. 21.4%
19. 300%   20. 28.1%
21. 156   22. 225
23. 40.9
24. Have cable now: 240
    Plan to get cable: 440
    Don't plan to get cable: 120
25. **(B)** $\frac{3}{4}$ Choices A and D are incorrect because the terms are switched. Choice C is incorrect because the denominator is wrong.
26. **(B) 20**   Choice A is based on the incorrect cross-multiplication $25n = 20 \times 16$. Choice C is based on the incorrect

cross-multiplication $16n = 20 \times 25$. Choice D is incorrect because it is the product of 25 and 16. The student did not then divide by 20.

27. **(C) $58\frac{1}{3}\%$** Choice A is incorrect because of a misplaced decimal point. Choice B is incorrect because the division was not carried out far enough. Choice D is incorrect because 12 was divided by 7 rather than the reverse.

28. **(C) 140%** Choices A and B are incorrect because of misplaced decimal points. Choice D has the wrong digit in the ones place.

29. **(A) 6.4** Choice B is incorrect because it equals 20 divided by 32%. Choices C and D have misplaced decimal points.

30. **(C) 20%** Choice A is incorrect because of a misplaced decimal point. In Choice B, 60 was divided by 12 rather than the reverse. Choice D has the numbers reversed in the division, and a misplaced decimal point.

31. **(C) 45 minutes** Choice A is based on the incorrect cross-multiplication $150n = 3 \times 10$. Choice D is based on the incorrect cross-multiplication $3n = 10 \times 150$. Choice B has a misplaced decimal point.

32. **(B) $36.64** Choices A and C are incorrect because of misplaced decimal points. Choice D is the total cost rather than just the tax.

33. **(D) Finnegan** Choice B is incorrect because Schwartz is the candidate with the longest bar and thus the candidate predicted to win. Choices A and C are predicted to be the third and fourth place candidates, respectively.

Pages 171–172

1. 466
2. 531
3. 2,177
4. 1,579
5. 260
6. 12,341
7. 59
8. 57
9. 4.76
10. 11.68
11. 0.612
12. 3.02

13. $1\frac{11}{15}$
14. $1\frac{7}{12}$
15. $\frac{7}{27}$
16. $8\frac{1}{2}$
17. 135
18. 24
19. 46.2
20. 4.0
21. 16.7% or $16\frac{2}{3}\%$
22. 250%
23. $1.25
   Multiply $3\frac{1}{2}$ by $2.50.

   Change $3\frac{1}{2}$ to a decimal.
   $3.5 \times 2.50 = \$8.75$.
   Subtract $8.75 from $10.00 to find the answer.
   $\$10.00 - \$8.75 = \$1.25$.
24. 20.6 miles
   Add a decimal point and a zero to the whole number 13.
   $13 = 13.0$
   Line up the decimal points and add 13.0 and 7.6
   $13.0 + 7.6 = 20.6$
25. **(D) 1** Choice A is incorrect because 5 is in the tens place. Choice B is incorrect because 9 is in the thousandths place. Choice C is incorrect because 6 is in the ones place.
26. **(A) 0.2** Choice B is incorrect because the number was rounded up rather than down. Choices C and D are incorrect because the number was rounded to the wrong place.
27. **(B) $8,109 - 1,346 = 6,863$** Choices A, C, and D show correct answers. Choice B has a renaming error. The correct difference is 6,763.
28. **(C) $3.2 \times 0.09 = 0.278$** Choices A, B, and D show correct answers. Choice C has a renaming error. The correct product is 0.288.
29. **(B) $3\frac{2}{5} - \frac{1}{10} = 3\frac{1}{10}$** Choices A, C, and D show correct answers. Choice B has a subtraction error. The correct difference is $3\frac{3}{10}$.
30. **(B) 8.2%** Choice A is incorrect because the tenths digit was dropped.

Choices C and D are incorrect because of misplaced decimal points.

31. (B) 248.5 Choices A and D are incorrect because of misplaced decimal points. Choice C is incorrect because 350 was divided by 0.71.

32. (C) 20% Choices A and D are incorrect because of misplaced decimal points. Choice B is the quotient of $80 \div 16$.

33. (B) $5.68 Choice A is incorrect because it is half the price of the pizza. In Choice C, $2.50 was added to half the pizza. Choice D is the total for both people rather than each person's share.

34. (C) 6.4% Choice A is incorrect because it is the amount of increase rather than the percent. Choice B is the result of dividing $50 by $830. Students should divide $50 by $780. Choice D is the percent equal to $780 \div 830$.

Check What You've Learned

Page 173

1. 7 ten thousands
2. 6 tens
3. 1 one
4. 90
5. 704
6. 4,386
7. $<$
8. $>$
9. $>$
10. 9,230
11. 90
12. 3,520
13. 10,000 fans
14. personal tax returns

Page 174

15. 8
16. 6
17. 5
18. $7 + n = 7$
19. $9 - n = 2$

20. $97
21. 34
22. $448
23. 1,222
24. $860
25. 9,045
26. 700
27. $30
28. $600
29. 24 members
30. $825

Page 175

31. $426
32. 11,280
33. 110,808
34. 51
35. 12 R3
36. 100 R6
37. $21,000
38. 10
39. 3,600
40. 70 pounds
41. $19

Page 176

42. 7.3
43. $1.15
44. twelve dollars and forty-nine cents
45. three and forty-five hundredths
46. 9.9
47. 3.84
48. 2.1
49. 31
50. $3.25
51. 0.25
52. 3.392
53. 17.59
54. 10
55. $27
56. 300
57. 800
58. 6.5 pounds
59. $1,378.00

Page 177

60. $>$
61. $=$
62. $>$

63. <
64. 1
65. $4\frac{1}{6}$
66. $\frac{17}{40}$
67. $8\frac{38}{45}$
68. $\frac{1}{3}$
69. $1\frac{1}{5}$
70. $\frac{13}{40}$
71. $\frac{55}{144}$
72. 2
73. 1
74. 9
75. 16
76. $3\frac{3}{4}$ inches
77. $2\frac{1}{2}$ inches

Page 178
78. $n = 4$
79. $n = 33$
80. $n = 20$
81. $n = 6$
82. $\frac{1}{10}$
83. 3
84. $\frac{1}{50}$
85. $1\frac{1}{5}$
86. 37.5%
87. 360%
88. 80%
89. 70%
90. 24
91. 250%
92. 40%
93. $1,905.50
94. 720 bottles